The Ecological Self

The Ecological Self

Freya Mathews

London

304·2

First published in Great Britain 1991
by Routledge
11 New Fetter Lane, London EC4P 4EE

Reprinted 1993

Paperback edition 1994

© 1991 Freya Mathews

Typeset in Baskerville by Redwood Press Ltd, Wiltshire
Printed and bound in Great Britain by
T J Press (Padstow) Ltd, Padstow, Cornwall

British Library Cataloguing in Publication Data
A catalogue record for this book is available from the British Library

Library of Congress Cataloging in Publication Data
A catalog record for this book is available from the Library of Congress

ISBN 0-415-05252-1 (hbk)   ISBN 0-415-10797-0 (pbk)

2002556

for my son
Rainer

Contents

Acknowledgements

My intellectual debts for this book go back a long way. It was my Philosophy tutor at Bedford College, the late Doreen Tulloch, who first introduced me to the riches of Spinoza, and for that my debt to her is lifelong. I was initiated into relativity theory by a number of people around the University of London in my postgraduate days there, notably the late Sigurd Zienau and Nicholas Maxwell. I had helpful discussions with Paul Davies and was stimulated by the thought of David Bohm. At University College W. D. Hart helped to channel my bursting ideas into a doctoral thesis on a manageably finite topic within the philosophy of logic, in the process helping me to learn how to negotiate wide theoretical horizons in my philosophical voyages.

During the period in which I have been engaged in writing this book I have enjoyed the support and encouragement of my colleagues in the Philosophy Department at the University of Melbourne. Len Goddard and the late Brenda Judge were particularly nurturing of my research project in its early stages, and patient in awaiting its outcome. John Bigelow, Tony Coady, Graeme Marshall and Marion Tapper all read parts or the whole of the manuscript. Thanks too to Damian Byers, for all the discussions, and to Barry Taylor, for directing me to the Environment, Ethics and Ecology Conference at Monash University in 1984 (little realizing where it would all lead!). I also wish to thank Robert Campbell of the Mathematics Department, Latrobe University, for checking the chapter on relativity theory, and Alan Roberts and Frank Fisher of the Monash University Physics Department and Graduate School of Environmental Science respectively, for commenting on the chapter on systems theory. Many thanks too to J. Baird Callicott, Holmes Rolston III, Jeremy Hayward and several anonymous readers for their helpful comments on the entire manuscript. Any mistakes or unsoundness of course remain my own responsibility.

I am grateful to Warwick Fox, Robyn Eckersley, Patsy Hallen, Frank Fisher and John Seed for their 'deep ecological' likemindedness, and guidance in a local intellectual climate in which the importance of ecophilosophy is not yet fully acknowledged. Patsy Hallen has continually recharged my will to persevere during the final stages of the writing process. The students in my environmental ethics course at Latrobe University and members of the Melbourne Deep Ecology discussion group also reinforced my enthusiasm and have helped me to explore the literature of environmental philosophy by pushing ideas to sometimes unexpected limits.

Josie Winther and Kaye Medlyn not only typed successive drafts of the manuscript but provided endless help and sparkling friendship over the years. Wendy Haboldt came in obligingly at the end, and graciously dealt with the innumerable fiddly finishing touches.

I wish gratefully to acknowledge the support of the University of Melbourne which provided me with a two-year postdoctoral research fellowship from 1982–4.

As this is a first book, and as its gestation period has been so protracted, I have debts and thanks of a personal nature that I would like to mention. I would like to thank my dear friends, Jenny Kemp and Helen Clarke, for their loyalty and the irreplaceable dialogue that I share with them; my brother John, for his support; my parents Alwyn and Sheila, for their perennial openness that always left me free to think for myself; and my son, Rainer, for teaching me the most important things.

Finally, my debts are not only to the human but also to the non-human world. Our cat of many years, our ducks, the trees and plants of our own garden and of this beautiful land, have all been friends and mentors to me, and this book has grown out of my gratitude to them and to the rest of Nature.

Freya Mathews
Murdoch University 1989

Introductory remarks

This book began life a long time ago, in the mid-seventies, when, as a graduate student in London, I discovered twentieth-century physics, and was immediately galvanized by its philosophical implications. I remember delivering a paper entitled 'Persons from the viewpoint of a unified field theory' to a rather stunned philosophy seminar at Bedford College. The whole question of a new emerging paradigm and the ideological implications of physical theories was not at that time on the philosophical agenda, and my paper, my first step in what was to prove a long intellectual journey, was greeted with polite incredulity.

This book to a certain extent recapitulates that journey. Central to its entire argument is the thought of Benedict Spinoza, of which I have been a student and by which I have been enriched from my earliest philosophical days. It was Spinoza above all who demonstrated the link between metaphysics and ethics, and for whom the whole point and goal of metaphysics was moral and spiritual edification. The very structure of his masterpiece, the *Ethics*, is illustrative of the view that ethics must be grounded in metaphysics. Such a view is of course deeply alien to contemporary philosophical thought, which sees questions of metaphysics and cosmology as generally belonging to the realm of fact, and thereby quite divorced from questions of value. I was never persuaded of this divorce. It always seemed plain to me, intuitively, that the way we conceived of reality and of our place in the scheme of things was central to questions about the meaning and the ends of life. Cosmology was the basis of our worldview, but our worldview was informed with value. This view, so spurned throughout most of the twentieth century, has, since the early eighties, been beginning to gain ground again. Everybody is now talking about 'the new paradigm', and they don't mean 'paradigm' in the original, restricted Kuhnian sense which applied only to scientific models, but in a sense more connotative of 'world-view' – a way of viewing the world which has a normative as well as a scientific dimension.

Part of what excited me so much about contemporary physics, when I discovered it, was that it provided a far more sympathetic framework for Spinoza's monistic theory of substance than classical physics had done. For it was not only Spinoza's demonstration of the link between metaphysics and ethics that attracted me to his philosophy; it was also his monism, which promised to give content to the notion that 'all is One', that everything is interconnected. This was an intuitive belief in which I already had a strong emotional investment. It seemed to me ethically and aesthetically satisfying and 'right'. I wanted to see it theoretically spelt out, but I eschewed those eastern philosophies and spiritual traditions which were premised on this insight. It seemed to me, as I explain in the text, that if this insight were to be usable by us it would have to have grown out of our own cultural experience.

There was of course no perfect match between the metaphysics of Spinoza and the implications of twentieth-century physics. But there was a demonstrably strong rapport between Spinoza's thought and at least one strand of the latter, namely the cosmology of Einstein. Einstein's cosmology appeared to be implicitly monistic, and it therefore, like Spinoza's theory, seemed to provide a suitable foundation for the kinds of ethical ideas I wanted to develop. But what about quantum mechanics? If I was prepared to look to physics to provide my metaphysical model, how could I ignore quantum mechanics and elementary particle theory? These are the physical theories which have caused the greatest philosophical upheaval in the last fifty years, and in any case, any appeal to physics obviously must take account of them.

My response to this – which, again, I explain in the text – is that while quantum mechanics does offer some promise of providing support for a metaphysic of interconnectedness, I think that the interpretation of quantum mechanics and the 'new physics' in general is still incomplete. The interpretation of Einstein's General Theory of Relativity and its speculative extension, geometrodynamics, is, in contrast, comparatively straightforward: any final picture of the universe will presumably include these well-understood relativistic features. Such a picture will not necessarily, however, include the philosophical ideas of quantum mechanics, since those ideas are still in flux. In my view it is too early to draw any final philosophical conclusions from quantum mechanics and the 'new physics': physicists themselves admit that they are still far from understanding what it all really means.

My project, then, was to find a metaphysical and ethical expression for the intuition of 'oneness' and interconnectedness, and Spinoza and Einstein provided a starting point. My next big step in this endeavour was my discovery of both systems theory and the new thinking in environmental philosophy. Systems theory provided a way of understanding individuality in a context of interconnectedness. Environmental philosophy revealed the significance of the concept of ecology as both a metaphysical and an ethical model, and in ecophilosophy, and particularly in that area of ecophilosophy known as 'Deep Ecology', all the ideas with which I had been working were pulled together, and their normative implications drawn out in some detail. It was thereafter a relief to have a label to attach to my research: when people asked me what I was working on, I could say 'the foundations of Deep Ecology'! However, in Deep Ecology the notions of interconnectedness, and of our identification with other beings and with wider wholes in Nature, tended to be highly schematic, and to be presented as axiomatic. So although my work had found a kind of intuitive and spiritual resting place in Deep Ecology, this new area of thinking had not provided me with a significant articulation and justification of a metaphysic of interconnectedness.

Such articulation and justification as I have been able to provide is presented in this book. I have related this autobiographical background because it throws light on both the structure and the method of the book. The structure, as I have said, basically recapitulates the journey. It starts with an historical and philosophical examination of the ideological implications of that arch-metaphysic of disconnectedness, atomism. It then charts the development of twentieth-century cosmology in order to arrive at a scientifically plausible metaphysic of interconnectedness, which it discovers in the shape of the theory known as geometrodynamics. The affinities between this theory and Spinoza's are tracked, and some *a priori* arguments in favour of a geometrodynamic-style metaphysic are advanced. In the next chapter a criterion of individuation is borrowed from systems theory, and used to develop a notion of individuality, or 'selfhood', which is consistent with interconnectedness. In the final chapter the significance of this context of interconnectedness for our normative attitudes to Nature is explored. Its implications for our conception of the scope of the human self, and for the meaning of self-realization or fulfilment, are also spelt out.

On the matter of method, however, I feel some explanatory remarks are called for. I have not attempted to give a full analytical justification of every idea or hypothesis I have advanced in the text. My methodology is thus only partly analytical. It is also synthetic and holistic. To show this, the method may be broken down into the following steps.

(i) I assume certain hypotheses, X, Y, Z, drawn from widely different disciplines.

(ii) I show that these hypotheses are rationally plausible by providing analytical arguments in support of them. This is the analytical step. I do not claim, however, that these arguments are in every case conclusive.

(iii) I illuminate the connections between X, Y, Z, and show how they all fit together to form a particular picture, P, of reality and of our place within it. Although I call such a picture a 'worldview', P is not intended to be any kind of 'total' metaphysic or world system. I am in fact concerned only with that aspect of reality that I have called its interconnectedness. P can be seen as a study in the logic and ethics of such interconnectedness. This process of fitting ideas together is the synthetic step, and it is important in its own right, even if there were no immediate evidence or justification for the hypotheses X, Y, Z.

(iv) I demonstrate that P dissolves certain problems which were intractable under other models of reality. This provides a form of justification for P analogous to that which attaches to a new Kuhnian paradigm when it solves some of the anomalies of the old paradigm.

(v) I leave it to the reader to decide whether P 'makes sense of things', in the sense of providing a satisfying account of our life-experience. It may be that P is capable of achieving this even though the independent evidence for X, Y, Z, is inconclusive. What it is that makes a metaphysical theory or worldview such as P satisfying may ultimately have to do with aesthetic and even ethical considerations. Rival theories which are equally consistent with the 'appearances', the empirical evidence, may ultimately need to be judged according to the same sorts of principles which mathematicians and physicists invoke, those of beauty and simplicity. And since theories such as P have a normative dimension, even the ethical 'goodness' of the theory may be relevant to its acceptability. In any case it is likely to be in some larger-than-empiricist sense that a theory such as P is felt to 'make sense of things' or not. If it is felt to do so, then P is accepted for its own sake rather than for the sake of the independent plausibility of its components. In this case we can say that the 'whole', P, validates the 'parts', X,Y,Z. This is the holistic step.

Philosophical works in the English-speaking world today tend to be read and judged from an exclusively analytical perspective. This reflects the reductive and 'atomistic' perspective of which, I would say, philosophy is still very much in the grip. But it is becoming apparent that the analytical method will have to be complemented with synthetic and holistic perspectives if the scope of philosophy is to be broadened to include the larger themes which are of such urgent importance to our endangered and endangering culture. In any case the synthetic and holistic methods with which I complement analysis in the present text reflect the anti-atomistic message of the book itself.

A few comments on the relation between physics and metaphysics in the text might also be in order here. To explain the geometro-dynamical theory, even in its qualitative, thoroughly non-technical outlines, it is necessary, in Chapter 2, to trace its origins in the General Theory of Relativity. Geometrodynamics has not been ex-perimentally confirmed, though General Relativity is of course exper-imentally very well established. Indeed, in certain of its mathematical formulations, geometrodynamics has even been falsified. However, it is in its qualitative, nontechnical outlines that I am interested in geometrodynamics, for in this form it provides a metaphysical blueprint or model for a physical theory. As such a blueprint or model, geometrodynamics is still eminently viable: the experimental indications within physics at present are broadly promising for a geometrodynamic-type theory, though not for the specific geometro-dynamic calculi that have hitherto been tested.

This contrast between a theory considered as a metaphysic and the same theory considered as a part of physics may be illustrated by the case of atomism. Atomism as a blueprint or model had of course been articulated almost two thousand years before it became a scientific theory in the hands of Newton and others. And as a blue-print atomism exerts its influence again at new levels of physical theory, for example at the elementary particle level. In other words, as a metaphysic, atomism is not exhausted by any particular mathematico-physical presentation or calculus. It is my intention to use the basic ideas of geometrodynamics in this way in the text, on the one hand as providing a possible blueprint for an indefinite number of physical theories, but on the other hand as having a metaphysical significance and interest of its own. In the latter capacity geometrodynamics may have plausibility independently of whether or not it is supported by current trends in theoretical physics. I argue for its explanatory power at a metaphysical level – it is shown to dissolve the Humean problem of causation and to demonstrate the substantivality of space. And I mount what I consider to be a strong *a priori* argument in support of it – an argument deriving from the Principle of Sufficient Reason. Thus, while the support of current physics is persuasive, the lack of such support would not be fatal to geometrodynamics considered in its metaphysical aspect. There might well be independent grounds for accepting it. So my purpose in this part of the book is not the illegitimate one of constructing physical hypotheses by *a priori* methods: physics has its own methods, and pure *a priori* reasoning has little place amongst them. Of course, if *a priori* arguments can be devised to demonstrate the metaphysical truth of geometrodynamics, then physicists should indeed take note of them. But the metaphysic thereby verified would not become physics until it was established by the methods of physics.

At the very end of his book, *The Return to Cosmology: Postmodern Science and the Theology of Nature*, Stephen Toulmin ponders the following question:

> Just how far, then, can the natural reason alone inform us in detail about what the overall scheme of things – the cosmos, or Creation – really is? Just how far can it tell us how we ought to act toward the other kinds of creatures that have their own proper places in that scheme – toward whooping cranes or smallpox viruses, toward sign-using chimpanzees or the fish of Lake Erie?[1]

In this book I take 'natural reason' – under which Toulmin subsumes *a posteriori* as well as *a priori* forms of reasoning – as far as I can in addressing the sorts of large and small concerns that he enumerates. But the answers that I give will ultimately depend for their acceptability upon the elusive aesthetic, even ethical – but by no means for that reason arbitrary or subjective – 'satisfactoriness' of the overall vision of Nature that I try to express.

Chapter 1

Atomism and its ideological implications

I TWO METAPHYSICAL ARCHETYPES

As I sit writing this I gaze from time to time out of my study window. My study is in the old quarter of the university, and overlooks a pleasant quadrangle. A magnificent African Cussonia tree dominates the scene, its large sprays of leaves massing layer upon layer right up to the eaves of the sandstone buildings. Yet the leaves are individually delineated, if I take the trouble to pay attention to them – thousands and thousands of them clearly outlined one against another. The blocks of sandstone, too, in the walls of the building opposite, are well-defined, as are the slate tiles that make up the roof. Stray petals from a large blossoming prunus tree just out of view float past the window, dusky pink against the sky. At first I think they are butter-flies, but no, they are petals, turning over and over as they find their way to the ground. Through the windows on the opposite side of the quad I can see books standing in line along snatches of shelves, and below, the cracks in the pavement indicating the boundaries of the stone slabs, the individual planks and lengths of metal piping that make up the scaffolding on which a man is standing, chisel in hand. The university is forever engaged in restoration. There are many, many petals lying flattened on the ground.

It is a world of things, objects, individuals – manifold in their forms, variegated in their hues, intricate in their arrangement, yet none the less invariably ultimately individuated. If I look closely enough I can always find the boundaries, the outlines, the petal that has its sep-arate being within the heart of the flower.

Such, at any rate, has been the presupposition of our thinking, of western thought in general, and of our philosophy in particular: that the world is made up of a plurality of discrete individual substances: the world has been viewed, since classical times, as an array of individual objects which are logically mutually independent but bound in a web of causal ties. That this individualistic bias is merely a contingency of our culture is evidenced by the fact that in many human cultures it has been transcended: ideological, or perhaps experiential, factors have inclined these cultures to a flow view of things – the familiar eastern view of the world as a unity in which the appearances of plurality and diversity are no more than ripples on the surface of an oceanic continuum.

The ideological correlates of these two opposing views of the structure of reality will, in this and later chapters, come under scrutiny, and elements of the ideological motivation for the individualism espoused by western culture will be disclosed. It is not within the scope of this book to examine in any detail eastern systems of thought *per se*, and their ideological origins and implications. But it is my basic aim to articulate, in a purely western idiom and frame of reference, certain insights which, while typically associated with eastern metaphysics, are now germinating independently in western soil.

Individualism, or, as I shall call it, substance pluralism, is a metaphysical archetype, an archetypal representation of the basic structure of the world. It portrays the world as a set of discrete, logically and ontologically autonomous substances. Its rival is the archetype which represents the world as a single universal substance – substance monism. Both of these archetypes are founded on the presupposition that the world is substantival, where by 'substantival' I mean that it is 'substantial', concrete, that it is not an abstraction or a phantasm, but an actual, physical (though not necessarily material) reality. The notion of substance which is central to both these archetypes then has a double aspect: to qualify as a substance a thing must be substantival, must exist in the concrete as opposed to the merely abstract mode; furthermore it must be capable of so existing independently of any other thing. A substance is a thing which is ontologically autonomous, capable of 'standing alone', its identity in no way logically interconnected with the identities of other things – all others could fail to exist without this in any way affecting the identity of the substance in question. It is in this sense that a substance is capable of 'standing alone' – it is capable of existing in an otherwise empty possible world. To say what a given substance essentially is, which is to say, to identify it, thus involves no reference to other substances.

Substances may be simple or compounded out of other, constituent substances. A simple substance is one which cannot be divided into parts which themselves qualify as substances. A simple substance is necessarily an ontological unity: it is indivisible. Simple substances may be considered the units of substantival reality.

Individual substances are, clearly, to be distinguished from logical individuals in general. A logical individual is anything that can be picked out as a logical subject of predication: instances would include not only ordinary material objects, but waves, properties, states, styles and abstract entities such as numbers and sets. Since material objects, as ordinarily understood, are logically though not causally mutually independent, they would appear paradigmatically to satisfy the criterion of ontological independence. Provided the logical possibility of a closed material system, for example a particle in inertial motion, is allowed, no additional problem attends the logical possibility of a universe consisting of just that particle. Such a particle qualifies for substance status. Contrast this apparent autonomy of material objects with the ontological status of other logical individuals however: a particular wave crest could not exist independently of the wave, or the field, which subtends it. Particular properties cannot achieve instantiation in isolation, but only in nexes, so properties do not satisfy the criterion of logical autonomy. Nor do states, since the states of systems cannot be actualized independently of systems. And styles could scarcely be realized in a universe from which their exemplifiers were absent. On the face of it then, the candidate most likely to succeed in the substance stakes is the material body.

In accordance with these considerations, the substance-pluralism archetype tends to be read as an ontology of material bodies. The complex substances are the macro-bodies of the sensible realm, the simple substances are the indivisible units of which these bodies are constituted, the tiny parcels of matter known since classical times as 'atoms'. Atoms stand in causal relations to one another, but these relations are logically contingent, imposed from without; the atoms themselves could exist independently of such relations. Relatedness does not, in other words, belong to their essence. Logically speaking, the entire universe could consist of a single atom, and its uniqueness would make no difference to its identity. Relations between the atoms, and their arrangement in space and time, are contingent. Order may be superimposed on the atomistic manifold, but no order is logically implicit in the manifold itself. Not only are the atoms not intrinsically related to one another, they are intrinsically inert: they embody no intrinsic principle of motion, motion being imposed on the atomistic manifold from without.

Atomism, then, is the traditional theoretical elaboration of the substance pluralism which is so entrenched in common sense that it is not generally recognized as a metaphysical presupposition at all. It has served as the unquestioned metaphysical framework both for ordinary thinking and for classical science. Its assumptions so saturate our western way of thinking that they have scarcely been formulated, let alone challenged, by philosophers: philosophy itself has been, and continues to be, carried out largely within a broadly atomistic framework. It is for this reason that I focus my attention, in this book, on traditional atomism, rather than on other logically possible elaborations of pluralism. I shall content myself with seeking to demonstrate some of the metaphysical and ideological inadequacies of this dominant pluralist theory, rather than attempting to refute the possibility of any variant of pluralism whatsoever. The principal aim of this book, however, is to explore the philosophical implications of the alternative – monistic – metaphysical archetype. The implications of monism have been so neglected in our philosophical tradition that I think this exercise would be a worthy one even if there were no independent grounds for accepting monism and rejecting pluralism. As it is, I think there are such grounds, though I do not think they are necessarily conclusive. In this first chapter I try, as I have already indicated, to highlight the metaphysical and ideological inadequacies of at least the dominant version of substance pluralism, and in Chapter 2 I provide both scientific and metaphysical arguments in favour of a particular version of substance monism.

It is to be the thesis of this chapter that the pluralist bias which was already present in the western outlook received its definitive authorization through the atomism of Newtonian science. And it is a further thesis that such atomism has, and has historically been taken to have, certain social and normative implications. We shall look at these implications, both as they have been historically perceived and as I take them actually to be – where these two sets of propositions do not always coincide. But before launching into this investigation of the Newtonian worldview, I would like to consider in general terms the relation between metaphysics, or cosmology, on the one hand, and ideology, or normative thinking, on the other.

II THE ROLE OF COSMOLOGIES IN A CULTURE

What, in the first place, distinguishes cosmology from metaphysics? Cosmologies depict the large-scale structure, origin and evolution of the concrete world. The domain of cosmology is the *actual* world, and then only the actual world *in its outlines*. In so far as an entity is capable of being actual, it may be included in a cosmology. For example, cosmologies may include not only ordinary concrete items such as material objects, but also forces, fields, minds, spirits, even deities, since all these entities are capable of being actual, of constituting an actual world. The domain of metaphysics, in contrast, ranges over not only the actual world, but also any abstract and possible and ideal realms which may exist. A metaphysic tells of the layering of reality, where the actual may be only one of the layers, others being the abstract, possible, perhaps even spiritual layers transcending the realm of the actual. Questions about the relation of universals to particulars, the ontological status of numbers, the status of possible and necessary beings, problems concerning the classification of substances, belong to metaphysics. Questions about the constitution and structure of the actual world belong to cosmology. A metaphysic and a cosmology may overlap, since the identification of the substances that constitute the actual world is part of the programme of a comprehensive metaphysic, and it is this metaphysic of the actual world, this general outline of a cosmology, which is, I think, relevant to culture.

Is there a perennial human need, which cosmology can meet, and which, unmet, may lead to dangerous cultural dislocations? Is cosmology integral to the worldview a culture embodies, where the currency of such a worldview is a prerequisite of social and psychological integrity within that culture?

Cosmologies have in the present century been dismissed by social critics, particularly those in a broadly Marxian tradition, who have lumped them together with religions and mythologies as outmoded instruments for the ideological legitimation of social orders. Cosmology has likewise been rejected on empiricist grounds – as being beyond the scope of verification procedures – by analytical philosophers in the empiricist tradition of Hume, Russell, Carnap, Ayer, *et al.* For both these parties, though for different reasons, the rise of science and of scientific methodology has spelt the extinction of cosmology as a cultural force. This is ironical, because science itself has seen a renaissance of cosmological speculation in the second half of the twentieth century, a renaissance the implications of which social critics and philosophers alike have underrated.

Do cultures in general then *need* to be informed with cosmologies? The anthropological record suggests that cultures do invariably compose stories to account for the origin and nature of the universe. Such cosmologies have typically been cast in animistic form, and so have fallen within the classifications of religion and mythology. The pre-Socratic culture of ancient Greece was the first to depart from this anthropological norm, and to frame its cosmologies in purely materialist, non-animistic idiom. The post-Hellenic epochs of western culture have witnessed the gradual rise to dominance of this materialist view. But materialist or not, the cosmological impulse has been active in our culture as in others. Its apparent universality suggests that it is innate to human culture, and presumably then of evolutionary significance. What could its adaptive function be? Primarily, perhaps, one of orientation – a cosmology serves to orient a community to its world, in the sense that it defines, for the community in question, the place of humankind in the cosmic scheme of things. Such cosmic orientation tells the members of the community, in the broadest possible terms, who they are and where they stand in relation to the rest of creation. Some conception of a cosmic scheme of things is active too in the prescription of a system of norms, or at least in contributing to the normative tone of the community. For its system of norms circumscribes the aspirations of the community, and aspirations are proportional to expectations. Expectations, in turn, depend in part upon information, the conception of the environment. The conception of the local, empirically accessible environment helps to shape expectations in perfectly obvious ways, but since the nature and stability of the local environment depends on more remote, cosmological factors, the shaping of expectations is not independent of cosmological considerations either.

Consider, for instance, a community in the grip of a cosmology which represents the world as hostile to human interests: this world is represented as inhabited, say, by powerful and malevolent spirits which are nourished on the energies of their human playthings. The degraded status of human beings within such a scheme of things could not fail to influence the normative thinking of its unfortunate denizens: they could be expected to be pessimistic characters, with low individual and collective self-esteem, low expectations of successful interaction with the environment, and low standards of happiness, excellence and self-realization. Appeasement and placation strategies would be likely to dominate their normative thinking. Now compare such a cosmologically discouraged community with one to whom the world is represented as hospitable to human interests. Perhaps it even incorporates a positive design for the human race. At any rate, humanity is shown as standing at, or close to, the apex of creation. Such a community undoubtedly has a headstart over the other in developing enviable morale and an optimistic, expansive spirit. Its expectations of successful interaction with the environment and its standards of happiness, excellence and self-realization will likewise be high. In its canons of morality, qualities such as strength, courage and high-mindedness are likely to be emphasized, and set above more ingratiating characteristics.

Cosmologies are not of course pulled out of the air to suit the convenience of the communities to which they are attached. They are conditioned by many and various historical, environmental, techno-logical, psychological and social factors. A flourishing community is likely to evolve a bright, self-affirming cosmology, and a languishing community is likely to see the world in darker shades. But my point here is that cosmology is not a cultural epiphenomenon; once it has taken hold of the communal imagination, it can on the one hand serve the community, tiding it through periods of material adversity, or on the other hand disserve it, undermining its morale even when ma-terial conditions improve and permit expansion. A good cosmology, in other words, is good for its adherents, and a bad cosmology predictably has the reverse effect. This is not to say however that even a bad cosmology may not be preferable to no cosmology at all. In the face of a world believed to be antagonistic, one can at least plan strategies and develop a defensive persona; one knows where one stands, and to that extent one has a sense of one's identity in relation to the world. But a culture deprived of any symbolic representation of the universe and of its own relation to it will be a culture of non-plussed, unmotivated individuals, set down inescapably in a world which makes no sense to them, and which accordingly baffles their agency. What are they to do in this world to which they do not belong? No natural directives appoint themselves. Self-interest is the only rational motive. Any other values smack of arbitrariness. Vocation-less, such individuals must sink eventually into apathy and alien-ation, or into the mindless and joyless pursuit of material ends. With no cosmological foundation for their identity, they invent precarious individual self-pictures, self-stories, ego-images, but their sense of who they are is tenuous. Metaphysically adrift, these individuals experience insecurity; unless united by an external power, such a group does not offer the best prospect for stable community.

In the pages which follow I plan to unravel the major normative implications of the conventional atomistic cosmology as it informs modern western consciousness. That it is a 'bad' cosmology – representing Nature not as hostile but as indifferent to our interests – will be my conclusion. But our position is in fact even worse than this, for while atomism flourished into the early twentieth century, and has left us its legacy to the present day, the members of the more informed strata of present western society are now aware that atomism has been scientifically superseded. On the question of successor cosmologies however, science has been tight-lipped, or at best indecipherable. We are accordingly left in the position of a culture which clings to an outworn cosmology for fear of slipping into the even worse condition of cosmological deprivation. That many westerners have already individually slipped into this worse condition is poignantly apparent.

Science, like the rest of our thought, has developed within the framework of substance pluralism. By affirming our pluralistic intuitions its theories won an acceptance and credibility that would have been more difficult to attain had they run crossgrain to common sense. With the affirmation of science, those pluralistic intuitions were in turn reinforced, to the point where they became an unchallenged presupposition of thought.

III THE ORIGINS OF NEWTONIAN ATOMISM

The scientific theory in which substance pluralism first came fully to flower was, of course, the prototype of all classical scientific theories, Newtonian physics. In Newtonian physics, atomism was mathematically and conceptually articulated. The scope of the theory was cosmological: its application extended to the universe as a whole. Its significance was metaphysical in that it purported to identify the ultimate units of physical reality – the simple substances – where, as has already been observed, to do so is to delineate the metaphysical structure of the physical world.

Atomism did not of course spring freshly formed from Newton's brow: in Newtonian physics a philosophical tradition of long descent and several strands is realized. It is Gassendi who is credited in the official histories with reviving the atomism of the ancients, Democritus and Lucretius, but atomism was primarily developed, at this time, in the context of mechanism. Kepler is credited with establishing measurement and mathematics as the method for investigating Nature, and thereby breaking with the Aristotelian method, which characterized Nature in terms of forms, functions, essences: a thing was known and individuated by its qualities. For Kepler, matter, understood purely quantitatively, served as the principle of individuation. 'To me differentiation in created things seems to come nowhere else than from matter or on the occasion of matter. But where there is matter, there is geometry.'[1] He is most firmly persuaded, he says, 'that the causes of natural things are constituted by mathematics, . . . because God the creator had mathematics as the archetype with him from eternity in most simple and divine abstraction from quantities materially considered'.[2]

Using this quantitative method, Galileo was able to lay the foundations for the science of mechanics. But it has been suggested, notably by Pierre Duhem and his successors, that mechanistic physics did not originate even with Galileo and Kepler, but was in fact anticipated by the schoolmen of Paris in the fourteenth century.

> The science of mechanics, inaugurated by Galileo, by his rivals, by his disciples, is not a creation. The modern mind did not produce it at once and altogether as soon as the reading of Archimedes had revealed to it the art of applying geometry to natural effects. The mathematical skill acquired by acquaintance with the geometers of antiquity was used by Galileo and his contemporaries to develop and make exact a science of mechanics whose principles had been laid down and whose most essential propositions had been formulated by the Christian Middle Ages. This mechanics was taught by the physicists at the University of Paris in the fourteenth century.[3]

It is a point of controversy within the history of science to what extent the mechanistic view was really thus anticipated by the Schoolmen – whether of Paris, or of the Oxford of the early fourteenth century. The evidence does demonstrate that mechanistic ideas were in the air before they were articulated by Galileo, but it was with Galileo that they emerged as a clearly defined rival to the Aristotelian view.

The components of the mechanistic view included the mathematical methodology developed by Kepler and the atomism of the ancients, Democritus and Lucretius – where this entailed the view that there is a distinction to be made between properties which really inhere in objects, such as figure, size, motion, and properties which only appear to observers to do so, being the product of perception, or more accurately, of the action of objects on the perceptual organs. Of these Galileo remarks, 'tastes, odours and colours and so on are no more than mere names so far as the object in which we place them is concerned, and ... they reside only in the consciousness'.[4] The specifically mechanistic component of the new view consisted in the theses that all phenomena were explicable, in the sense of being governed by laws, and that those laws were mechanistic: they fell under the twin principles of matter and motion. According to this view, then, the universe would be regarded as a cosmic piece of clockwork – it and all its constituents were no more than complicated machines.

Such a view was plainly reductive, in that it reduced the variegated world of appearances to a uniform one of matter in motion. This clockwork model of the universe contradicted the medieval model, which was a blend of ideas from various different traditions. Lewis Beck gives the following account of the workaday universe of the Middle Ages:

> The universe consisted of concentric spheres of material substance, with the earth at the centre. The moon rotated about the earth on the nearest sphere, and all the gross matter in the universe was in the sublunar region, the realm of the corruptible and the changeable. Above that sphere were eight others, one for each of the known planets, for the sun, for the fixed stars, and for the *primum mobile* which, like Aristotle's God, imparted motion to the inscribed spheres. Above that sphere was the immovable Empyrean, or Paradise. Below the sphere of the moon was Purgatory and the earthly paradise; on the underside of the world was hell. Each of the spheres rotated about the earth each day ... [s]uperimposed on the geometrical order was a value hierarchy. It was ... a thoroughly teleological order both in its original design and in its day-by-day operation. This universe, an amalgam of Aristotelian, Arabian, neo-Platonic and Christian elements, was the universe of the theologian who read Aquinas and of the layman who read Dante.[5]

It was in Descartes' thought that mechanism was raised to the status of a philosophy, a worldview encompassing all that is real. As Randall puts it, Descartes

> set forth the idea of an exclusively mechanistic world .... Gone was the Neoplatonic hierarchy of forms; gone were all natural teleology, all final causes, all functional structure, all forms and

species. Gone were 'spirits' and action at a distance. In changing natural explanation from the 'souls' of the Renaissance to the 'force' of the seventeenth century, men gained a corporeal and mechanical conception of nature in place of a 'spiritual' one. All causation is efficient, or mechanical, all is capable of geometrical formulation.... The world is no longer to be seen as a living organism, it has become a clockwork. This Cartesian revolution left a single purpose in the universe, the will of God, whose decrees must be learned by patient investigation.... And one alien substance was left in the universe, the human mind.[6]

In Descartes the reductivism of mechanistic philosophy was elevated to a principle of method, the method of reductive analysis, according to which the whole could be explained exhaustively in terms of the behaviour of its separate parts – where this contrasted with the Aristotelian method of functional analysis, according to which the parts were to be explained in terms of their relation to the whole.

The crux of mechanism is its view of the origin of motion, where it is to the motion of the particles that all material form and process is due. A particle is set in motion solely under the action of an external force and its motion may be altered only in the same fashion. The only 'force' allowed within the mechanistic framework is that of kinetic energy – the energy of motion by contact – all other purported forces, including action at a distance, being regarded as occult. Forces and particles are logically mutually independent, in the sense that the particles are not self-moving, and are not *necessarily* subject to motion. An atomistic ontology is not, we ought to note, necessarily mechanistic: it would be logically permissible to postulate particles which embody a principle of dynamism, which are self-starters and self-movers, from whose own intrinsic nature motion springs. It is also logically possible that particles should exist outside the governance of laws at all – whose motion, if it occurs, is purely random, undetermined. But the modern formulations and implementations of atomism have been emphatically mechanistic, and it is to this conventional mechanistic conception of atomism that the present critique is addressed.

The insistence on mechanism, along with the emphasis on the primary/secondary quality distinction in the Cartesian philosophy, produces a consistent effect in the portrayal of matter: matter is seen as 'dead' – as inert, passive, homogeneous stuff endowed with no inner principle of action. This version of matter receives its definitive expression in Descartes' famous mind/body dualism, a doctrine whose ramifications saturate every aspect of our western culture.[7] As Descartes sees it, mind and matter are distinct substances, logically mutually independent: mind can exist in the absence of matter, and matter in the absence of mind. Each depends for its existence only on a transcendent creator. Mind is the theatre of reason and telos, the screen or sensorium on which colours, scents, sounds, tastes have their ghostly being. Human bodies are the machines which serve as transport for these spirit minds, the only machines in fact which do so, the bodies of animals not being similarly honoured. (Descartes declared all non-human animals to be non-sentient robots.) The tie between body and mind in the human individual is contingent and distinctly tenuous. The locus of agency, of the power of the mind to move the body, is anatomically specific – the pineal gland. But the mechanism whereby the interaction between two distinct logical categories of being is effected is not detailed with any precision. Throughout the Cartesian philosophy there is an adamant identification of the self with the mind or spirit as opposed to the body; their association seems to be viewed by Descartes as an unfortunate contingency, the burden of the human condition.

The recognition of matter as a substance in its own right, devoid of any principle of activity – a recognition which had begun with Kepler's quantitative conception of matter – is given final expression in the mind/body dualism of Descartes. Form, function, quality, agency, are the province of mind, inertia and mechanical motion that of matter.

It was in this Cartesian climate, which was already informed with the thought of Galileo and his predecessors, that the Newtonian worldview was forged. Newton affirmed the Cartesian vision of a universal mathematics, and certain of the seminal tenets of Descartes' view of matter. This is not to say that there were not major discrepancies between their respective accounts of matter. According to Descartes, the essence of matter was extension, whereas Newton declared it to be mass. The Cartesian definition fails to distinguish matter from space, nor does it entail corpuscularianism, though Descartes did postulate, in somewhat ad hoc fashion, that matter was composed of particles of variable extension. Newton's view, in contrast, is essentially atomistic, and it is in terms of mass rather than extension that the 'atoms' or particles are characterized. This recognition of mass as integral to the nature of matter – where mass was a property unknown to Descartes – served definitively to distinguish matter from space, where the essence of space was agreed to be extension.

The Cartesian *physics* is entirely different from the physics of Newton, and was explicity repudiated by him. Cartesian physics was a vortex theory: space was considered a plenum, in which the only possible form of motion was circular – vortices or 'tourbillons'. The universe was set in motion by a First Cause, and the arrangement of matter therein was due to the effect of the vortices – the particles of matter being swept into vortices, where the larger, heavier particles were pushed to the centre, the smaller, subtler ones pushing in on them from the outer edges. In this way dense bodies such as the earth and the heavenly bodies were formed. Newton eliminated the plenum, the vortices, and the particles of variable diameter. Nevertheless the basic conceptual features of the Cartesian view of matter were retained by him: mechanism, reductivism and the insistence on the mathematical method (which Descartes himself had failed to implement in the development of his physics).[8]

Moreover, as I have already remarked, although in mathematical terms the Newtonian particles were unextended, the general interpretation of Newtonian physics – and that in which Newton himself concurred most of the time – was corpuscularian: the atoms were thought *really* to be tiny, solid particles possessed of certain primary properties and aggregatively responsible for the rest. As Newton himself put it, in a by now much quoted passage,

> it seems probable to me that God in the beginning formed matter in solid, massy, hard, impenetrable, moveable particles, of such sizes and figures, and with such other properties, and in such proportion to space, as most conduced to the end for which he formed them; and that these primitive particles, being solids, are incomparably harder than any porous bodies compounded of them; even so very hard as never to wear or break in pieces: no ordinary power being able to divide what God himself made one in the first creation.[9]

The corpuscularianism of Newtonian physics proved fruitful for other sciences, suggesting a kinetic theory of gases and making a truly quantitative chemistry finally feasible. In due course, this corpuscular atomism became the paradigm for science as a whole, and it was in this form, infused with mechanism and the degraded dualist conception of matter, that it infiltrated our culture as 'Newtonian atomism'.

In Newtonian atomism then, the world of matter was presented as a world possessing mathematical characteristics fundamentally. It was composed ultimately of absolutely hard, indestructible particles, equipped with the same characteristics which had now become familiar under the head of primary qualities.... All changes in nature are to be regarded as separations, associations and motions of these permanent atoms.[10]

The spectacular success of the Newtonian physics, its immense authority, and the vast currency which it gained, as well as the simplicity of its first principles, have ensured it an historical dominance which has resulted in the firm entrenchment of this atomistic metaphysic in 'common sense'. The Newtonian worldview has filtered into the culture at large in a fashion which has not been repeated. It is worth taking a look at the ways in which this infiltration was achieved.

IV THE CULTURAL ASSIMILATION OF NEWTONIANISM

How then did atomism make the transition from the difficult technical realm of the exact sciences to that of the popular imagination? The first factor to point to in answer to this question is the educational climate of Europe in the late seventeenth and early eighteenth centuries. It was a climate characterized by its catholicism in learning, its lack of specialization and professionalization. An educated person of the day would typically have interests ranging from the sciences through philosophy to the humanities, arts and theology. To the extent that the educated elite shaped popular consciousness – through literature, entertainment, the arts, journalism and the pulpit – its understanding of the basic tenets of the Newtonian metaphysic flowed into the general culture.

It was not only the amateur status of science, and its fascination for the reading public, that fostered the process of assimilation. Randall tells us that by 1789 not only had eighteen editions of the *Principia* been published, but so also had a flood of popularizations of the Newtonian philosophy – forty in English, seventeen in French, eleven in Latin, three in German, and one each in Italian and in Portuguese. And the most popular of all, he remarks, was Count Alogrotti's *Newtonianism for Ladies*.[11]

Philosophy too was crucial as a bridge from the technical treatises of the new science to the humanistic and literary culture – just as it was crucial in bringing the new science itself to realization. We have seen how Descartes had elaborated and expounded a mechanistic philosophy, tempered by a separate principle of mind to account for human agency. Hobbes was concerned with drawing out the moral and political implications of an even stricter mechanistic materialism, derived by generalizing from Galilean mechanics:

> the universe, that is, the whole mass of all things that are ... is corporeal, that is to say, body; and hath the dimensions of magnitude, namely length, breadth and depth: also, every part of body, is likewise body ... and that which is not body is no part of the universe: and because the universe is all, that which is no part of it, is nothing ....[12]

But it was Locke, later in the seventeenth century, who was preeminent in establishing the new corpuscularian viewpoint as the basis for philosophical reflection. Locke refined the analysis of the primary/secondary quality distinction, and demonstrated its relevance to the problems of perception and epistemology. He did this by showing how this distinction, in a corpuscularian context, together with a mechanistic principle of causation, could ground epistemology, by furnishing a *mechanism* for the production of ideas which represent external objects. The atomism of the seventeenth century is in this way, in Buchdahl's phrase, 'built into the very bones of Locke's theory of knowledge'.[13] Locke also makes full use of the corpuscularian model in demystifying and rationalizing – 'demetaphysicalizing' – some of the central mysteries of scholastic thought, for example the notions of substance, cause, and real and nominal essence.

An indefinite amount could of course be written on the influence of Newtonianism on the philosophy of the eighteenth and nineteenth, and even twentieth, centuries. Suffice it to say here that it was partly through the spontaneous agency of the philosophers that the Newtonian world-picture came to be assimilated by the literate populations of Europe. But the dissemination of Newtonianism was not achieved solely through such spontaneous means; conscious propaganda was also involved. The purveyors of the propaganda, in England, were a group of thinkers – known as the latitudinarians – who represented an ascendant power group within the Church of England. In 1691 the Boyle lectureship was established in England with the express intention of 'proving the Christian religion, against notorious Infidels', as Boyle himself expressed it in his will. The idea was to popularize the Newtonian worldview as the foundation for a new 'natural religion', as this was understood by the latitudinarian apologists. The thinking behind the attempt to develop such a 'natural religion' was that, after the political and religious upheavals of the seventeenth century – the English Revolution, the Commonwealth, the restitution of the monarchy – the Church needed to re-establish its authority by appeal to some broad principles on which all 'reasonable and sober' men could agree, regardless of their sectarian affiliations. It was hoped that Newtonianism could provide these principles.

The thinking of these apologists was explicitly political: the intention was to use the Newtonian philosophy to provide a fresh legitimation for a particular political institution *viz.* the Church, and, more generally, for the new emerging socio-economic order embodied in the commerce of the middle class. This, at any rate, is the thesis persuasively argued by Margaret Jacob in her book, *The Newtonians and the English Revolution 1689-1720.* In the Boyle lectures, she writes,

> the Newtonian natural philosophy received its first and highly simplified explanation aimed at a non-specialist audience, most if not all of whom, like the lecturer, could never have followed the mathematical reasoning inherent in Newton's *Principia.*[14]

She further remarks

> Without their lectures, the new Newtonian philosophy would not have existed by the 18th century as a coherent system to be understood by anyone outside the rather small circle of Newton's scientifically trained followers.[15]

For a decade or so after the establishment of the lectureship, a generation of latitudinarian churchmen – including Richard Bentley, Samuel Clarke, John Harris and William Derham – managed, by way of their widely read lectures, to infuse English culture with the elements of mechano-atomistic thinking. Their strategy was to *pre-empt* the threat of materialism – embodied, to their mind, most notably and shockingly in Hobbes – by appropriating the ideas of the new science for their cause. In this they enjoyed the huge advantage of having the allegiance of Newton himself. Nevertheless, with historical hindsight, it is possible to see that, in the long term, the attempt largely misfired. Their efforts to reconcile mechanistic atomism with theological orthodoxy provided a temporary confidence in the new vision of Nature, but in the long run it served to demonstrate the difficulty of bringing off such a reconciliation. In the process of the attempted legitimation, however, their audiences were being diligently instructed in the tenets of materialism, and they were, ultimately, to draw their own, less optimistic, conclusions. It does seem, in retrospect, that the attempt profited the cause of atheism more than it did their own.

In these various ways, then, Newtonianism filtered into and transformed popular consciousness.[16] But this transformation was equivocal in nature. The official Newtonian philosophies were optimistic and reassuring, but, I would contend, popular consciousness was shaping itself to the natural implications of the mechanistic worldview, and these were far from optimistic and reassuring.

The first demonstrably ideological interpretation of Newtonianism was, as I have just explained, that offered by the latitudinarian Boyle lecturers. How exactly did they construe the new science as underpinning the ideology of free enterprise and middle-class commerce? According to Jacob, their arguments hinged on a Newtonian interpretation of providence, or of a providential deity. Since from within the Newtonian system matter in itself is regarded as inert and passive, motion has to be conferred on it by means of an external, extra-material source.

> The Vis inertiae is a passive Principle by which Bodies persist in their Motion or Rest, receive Motion in proportion to the Force impressing it, and resist as much as they are resisted. By this Principle alone there never could have been any Motion in the World.[17]

The extra-material source of motion is, of course, supposed to be God. Moreover, the gravitational force between particles creates an order which is the manifestation of a divine providential design: the law of universal attraction is the expression of God's will. God is therefore responsible both for the origin and maintenance of order in the world.[18] That He is a providential God is evidenced by the fact that the order manifested in the world is admirable:

> what a noble Contrivance this [Gravity] is of keeping the several Globes of the Universe from shattering to Pieces, as they evidently must do in a little Time by their swift Rotation round their own Axes.[19]

What is true of the material order, the Newtonians argued, is likewise true of the social order. Or rather, the material order provides an ideal model which it is our duty to seek to bring to realization in the social system. In the social context, God had delegated his creative power – his power to move passive matter – to us; we inherit the power to shape the social system in accordance with the materially manifested natural order.

How is this natural order to be imitated in the social sphere? As long as each individual pursues his or her own path, and obeys his or her own 'law', *viz.* the law of self-interest, subject to certain outer social and legal constraints, then, the Newtonians attest, 'order' will spontaneously establish itself at the collective level. This is the promise that animates the faith in providence: it is God's providence, manifested in the material order, that guarantees that the system whereby each individual looks to his own concerns will emanate in an ultimate, optimal social order. In this way, the latitudinarians conferred the sanction not only of Newton, but of God Himself, on the idea of a free market economy in which individuals would pursue their own material interests subject only to minimal legal constraints.

To the extent that the arguments of the Boyle lecturers serve to *legitimate* the emerging individualistic and competitive commercial order, they depend upon the soundness of the argument that the order of Nature is manifestly of *providential* design. The argument that gravitation was the expression of the will of God was incidental to the main thesis of the providentiality manifest in the natural order. But the notion of providence is in this connection ambiguous: is the duty of a providential deity to create the best possible universe with the happiest of denizens, or is it to provide the conditions for the creation and maintenance of ourselves, however imperfect these conditions, and however defective we ourselves, may be. If the latter purely anthropocentric notion of providence is assumed, then any laws which guarantee the world as it is are expressions of divine providence, since they guarantee the conditions for our own existence. But this would be so no matter how inferior the world in which we found ourselves happened to be. So this is hardly a theologically respectable notion of providence. Taking the more objective point of view however, it is by no means clear that a different world order, one which was non-mechanistic, perhaps non-atomistic and in which the principle of gravitation was different, would not be superior to the actual one, and supportive of more perfect life-forms.

That the design exhibited in the material order is reflected in the 'world politick' in the form of an individualistic and competitive economic system, however, is a conclusion with which, for reasons I shall detail shortly, we can agree. But the conclusion that this is a *desirable* state of affairs – the conclusion which motivated the arguments of the latitudinarians and the later generations of the Enlightenment – did not follow from Newtonian premises.

The philosopher whose spectre most threatened the latitudinarian cause at this time was Hobbes. The latitudinarians had simply assumed that the physical universe, whose materiality they were otherwise prepared to concede, could not include the human mind or spirit amongst its material contents: if 'man' were made up exclusively of atoms, they asserted, it would be impossible to imagine that he could 'invent arts and sciences, . . . institute society and government, . . . make leagues and confederacies, . . . devise methods of peace and stratagems of war'.[20] Hobbes, however, had already presented a consistent picture of both the physical and social worlds in purely materialist terms. The human being that Hobbes presents to us in the opening chapters of *The Leviathan* is a machine. It is a machine of a very special sort, in that it is self-moving and self-directed, but it is entirely explainable in machine-terms none the less. Built into the human machine, according to Hobbes, are certain kinds of apparatus by which it alters its motion in response on the one hand to differences in material input, and on the other hand to the impact of external matter on it. The machine is even, by way of this apparatus, able to anticipate such impact, and deflect its own motion to avoid it. It seeks to persevere in its motion, moving towards those things which it registers as being conducive to its continued motion, and away from those things which appear to it as not so conducive. It is, as we would say today, *programmed* to seek whatever furthers its self-preservation, and to avoid whatever would obstruct that end. It is a machine for self-preservation.

Hobbes calls the movement toward whatever furthers the machine's existence desire, and the movement away from whatever obstructs it aversion. The human machine is thus driven by desire and aversion in its quest for self-preservation. This makes for a purely self-interested, or egoistic, psychology, and hence for a purely prudential morality. For when all motivation is reducible to an interest in self-preservation, then the only reasons for acting in the interests of others will be prudential ones: it will only be rational to serve the interests of others when one stands to increase one's own chances of survival by doing so. Hobbes is, then, as we would expect, a subjectivist about ethics: a thing is to be judged good or bad, or an action right or wrong, just to the extent that it benefits or harms the person making the judgement. There is no objective standard of moral goodness, but only the conflicting judgements born of different individuals' desires and passions. There is no common conception of 'the good' or 'the good life' that could unite people in a social order the purpose of which was the realization of such a 'good'. Human nature then is to be understood ultimately in terms of the material interests of self-maintaining machines.

Hobbes captures this highly reductive picture of human nature in his famous image of the 'state of nature'. The state of nature, according to Hobbes, is the state in which men would live if they were not subject to the constraints of civilization. In such a state men, helplessly driven by their appetites and desires, and at the mercy of their entirely self-interested machine natures, would compete ruthlessly with one another for the goods that would benefit them. (Hobbes includes property amongst these goods.) They would in fact be in a perpetual state of war – a war of every man against every other man. In such a condition, Hobbes says,

> there is no place for industry; because the fruit thereof is uncertain: and consequently no culture of the earth; no navigation, nor use of the commodities that may be imported by sea: no commodious building; no instruments of moving, and removing, such things as require much force; no knowledge of the face of the earth; no account of time; no arts; no letters; no society; and, which is worst of all, continual fear, and danger of violent death; and the life of man, solitary, poor, nasty, brutish, and short.[21]

It is Hobbes who arrives at the central insight that, in the state of nature, all men are equal. They are equal in their capacity to kill one another (as he points out, even the strongest have to sleep). They are equal in wisdom, since wisdom is a function of experience, and experience is common to all men. And they are equal in their desire to preserve their own lives, since this impulse is, as we have seen, the essence of the human machine. It is precisely this natural equality, however, which leads in the state of nature to the war of all against all.

This then is the picture of social life that results from Hobbes' attempt both to derive a theory of human nature from a mechanistic metaphysic, and to apply the mechanistic principle of analysis to society. Since, as we have noted, this mechanistic principle of analysis always yields indivisible units of analysis, its application to social reality has the same effect. 'Whereas in natural philosophy', writes historian Collins, this leads usually to some form of physical atomism, in civil philosophy it leads Hobbes to a form of *social atomism*. The bedrock of social analysis is the isolated, solitary, self-enclosed *individual man*. The main problem is to discover how a number of such atomic units can be led to form a commonwealth. Hobbes denies that man is by nature a political animal, even though he needs some meeting ground with others of his kind. The individual never ceases to concentrate upon seeking his own good and satisfying his own irreducible, unassimilable endeavour . . . . His *fellow men* constitute his fate, his ill condition.[22]

Hobbes of course recommends that we try to transcend our 'natural estate', but he does not try to justify his recipe for 'commonwealth' by appeal to its naturalness.

That social atomism is an implication of Newtonianism was acknowledged by apologists and pessimists alike. But whereas in Hobbes the individualism implicit in social atomism is perceived as a grim and inescapable fact, in later thinkers it is transformed into a value which is to be proclaimed and celebrated. In the political philosophy of Locke, for instance, the state of nature is conceived as one in which 'men' live as equal and separate units. 'The figure of the Individual – seated on his desert pillar – this, in brief, is the symbol with which we are left, alike by the *Essay* and the *Two Treatises*.'[23] The body politic is, for Locke, 'an aggregate of consenting individuals'. Social atomism has become, for him, a presupposition of political thought, but the isolation of the individual is not regretted by him. On the contrary, the individual has become invested with a supreme social value, an almost hallowed status expressed in the doctrine of the sacred and inalienable rights of the individual (where these include the right of property). These rights, possessed by all men, mutually limit the freedom of each man to impinge on the person and property of others. (The continual use of 'man' for 'humankind', and 'men' for 'people' or 'human beings' here merely reflects the original statement of these doctrines which arguably apply only to male human beings in any case, and therefore cannot accurately be reformulated in gender-neutral terms.[24]) The unpalatable aspects of mechanistic social atomism, so apparent in Hobbes, are thereby mitigated in Locke. But Locke's softening, indeed celebration, of individualism depends on a vision of the natural or intrinsic value of the individual, a vision which does not sit comfortably with mechano-atomistic principles. Locke was ameliorating the more strictly mechanistic vision of Hobbes with a particular kind of sentiment; he had in him, as Barker puts it,

> the great Puritan sense of the supreme importance of the individual soul; the Puritan feeling for the soul's right to determine its own relations to God, and to enjoy, at the least, toleration from the State and from all authority in doing so.[25]

This veritable institutionalization of the individual, premised on a belief in the supreme importance of the individual soul, was of course consistent with the outlook of Cartesian dualism, according to which matter was the arena of inert, concrete existence and spirit the repository of value. This essentially Cartesian view of the individual – atomistic and dualistic – blossomed into the liberal tradition, notably exemplified in Mill, a tradition which served as the ideology for an economics of *laissez-faire* and free enterprise. In the light of this, we can understand Randall's remark that

> the Enlightenment really meant the rapid spread of the aims and ideals of business enterprise and of the intellectual tests and method and model of Newtonian mechanics .... It meant that a definite and intellectually imposing expression was given to middle class ideals, which gained all the prestige accruing from the success of mathematical physics.[26]

In such ways then was the metaphysic underlying the new science used to *legitimate* the new, emerging, socio-economic order. In the case of the Boyle lecturers, the legitimating intention was conscious; in the case of the later liberal political thinkers, it is doubtful that it was so. Legitimation must be understood in the present connection in two senses: the apologists sought to show that an atomistic social order was *natural* and that it was *good*, in the sense of being beneficial to its members. Of any given social order, it may be possible to show that it is natural without showing that it is good. (Hobbes showed that the 'state of nature', understood in accordance with strictly mechanistic principles, was far from good.) On the other hand, it may be possible to show that a given social order is good, in the sense that it serves the interests of its members, without being able to show that it is natural. But there is nevertheless a powerful incentive for political apologists to show that their favoured political systems are natural, for if they are natural, then people are likely to accept them and not protest against them. If it can be shown that a certain social system is natural, then people are less likely to blame their rulers for it, no matter how onerous they find it. If, on the other hand, a system demonstrably benefits its members, but can be shown to be out of phase with the general scheme of things, then people will tend to lack faith in it, will expect it to collapse. For this reason a thoroughgoing legitimation will seek to demonstrate not only that the system in question is good, but that it is natural.

I have no quarrel, in principle, with the ideological implementation of cosmology or metaphysics. On the contrary, as I indicated at the beginning of the chapter, I think that cosmology furnishes the indispensable context for the formulation of social and ethical norms, and a culture deprived of a cosmology will fail fully to engage with its world. However I do have a quarrel with those ideologues who sought to show that the atomistic social order implicit in Newtonianism was not only natural, but good, that is of overall benefit to its members. I shall, in the remainder of this chapter, offer an analytical – as opposed to historical – account of the social and ethical impli- cations of Newtonianism. Such implications, as I see them, are a lot closer to those drawn by Hobbes than to those drawn by Locke and the latitudinarians. And it is the unsugarcoated implications that our culture has in fact absorbed and built into its normative structure. If Newtonianism did indeed reflect the world as it really is, then a Newtonian social system would indeed be natural, and to that extent legitimate. We would have to lump it, or struggle against the meta- physical grain in order to improve our estate. But it is clear now that Newtonianism does not reflect the world as it really is, so that we have for several centuries been labouring under a social system which is neither natural, nor, I shall contend, good.

V THE SOCIAL IMPLICATIONS OF NEWTONIANISM

Switching then from an historical to an analytical perspective, let us try to identify those features of the Newtonian metaphysic that are truly seminal for social and environmental thought. The first thing to note is that the Boyle lecturers had focused their attention on the gravitational aspects of the Newtonian order, but that in so far as this order is first and foremost a mechano-atomistic order, gravitation is contingent to it. It is the atoms which have logical priority, in any account of the Newtonian metaphysic, because the atoms are the *sine qua non* of the entire system. Without the atoms there would be nothing upon which introduced forces, such as gravitation, could act.

The world could, in other words, consist of atoms minus gravitation, but not gravitation minus atoms. It is in this sense that gravitation is contingent to the Newtonian world order. The fundamental feature of mechano-atomism, logically and metaphysically speaking, then, is that it is an ontology of discrete material substances – atoms – which are in themselves inert, that is they embody no principle of agency: their motion is imparted to them via the agency of external forces, and in no way represents an 'unfolding' of their own inner nature. Their own inner nature is strictly passive, and is determined independently of the presence or absence of external motion. Such a basic mechanistic metaphysic may be causally embroidered in all kinds of ways, by the addition of law-governed forces and agencies. It is by way of such contingent causal elaborations that a fully-fledged physics may be constructed out of the metaphysical ground plan. But such contingent causal addenda hardly rank as seminal features of the metaphysic proper to be reflected in its social corollaries or applications.

It is worth noting, in passing, that Newton himself was well aware of the contingency of gravitation to a mechanistic order. He admitted as much in the second edition of his *Opticks*:

> To show that I do not take gravity for an essential property of bodies, I have added one question concerning its cause, choosing to propose it by way of a question, because I am not yet satisfied about it for want of experiments. (*Opticks*, Advertisement II)[27]

In fact, although the traditional role assigned to Newton is that of the father of mechanistic science (and it is in this traditional sense that I have here used the tag, 'Newtonianism'), it has now become clear that Newton himself, despite the place assigned to him by history, was far from satisfied with mechanism as an exhaustive model of the world order. Historian Carolyn Merchant quotes Newton from draft documents in the Cambridge University Library as follows:

> Matter is a passive principle and cannot move itself. It continues in its state of moving or resting unless disturbed. It receives motion proportional to the force impressing it. And resists as much as it is resisted. These are passive laws, and to affirm that there are no other is to speak against experience for we find in ourselves a power of moving our bodies by our thought. Life and will are active principles by which we move our bodies and thence arise other laws of motion unknown to us.[28]

Newton himself, then, recognized the contingency of gravitation to the mechano-atomistic world order (the order that has historically come to bear his name). Despite received historical interpretation, Newton himself did not consider this a point against gravitation, but rather a point against mechanism. He went so far as to postulate a further non-mechanistic principle, *viz.* that of fermentation, to explain the apparent dynamism of life processes. To return to our argument however, and to the historical use of the tag 'Newtonianism' to refer to the mechanistic view, we can see that, stripped to its logical and metaphysical bones, the Newtonian vision is one of a world of atoms whirling along predetermined trajectories in an absolute void. The original source of motion may be transcendent, but by no means necessarily divine. Newton himself of course represented God as essential to his system, but we, again, are not logically bound by his intentions: from a logical point of view the introduction of God as a Prime Mover is contingent. This is so for two reasons. First, as we have already seen, motion itself is contingent in this system – the whole atomistic aggregate which constitutes the cosmos can exist in its entirety unmoved. Second, there is no reason why a hypothetical First Cause, the external Force which sets the whole system in motion, should be identified with God. Such a Force may have been a purely physical agency, or, if it was in some sense transcendent, it may have lacked any of the other attributes traditionally ascribed to God. In any case, the need for a source of motion in the first place may be obviated by appeal to an infinite regress: each particular motion may simply be referred to an earlier one. Everything perceived by us, then, can be explained as nothing but the aggregation of blind particles. What are the implications of this view for our attitude to (i) Nature, (ii) the self, and (iii) others?

(i) The implications of mechanism for our attitude to Nature, or to the environment, have been recently explored in a number of works.[29] The blindness and deadness, the 'bruteness' of matter in the mechanistic scheme of things, robs us of our respect for Nature. In pre-scientific thought, Nature had been richly informed with telos, and with principles of spirit and agency. Human beings existed in an intricate web of spiritual and teleological relations with the natural world. From the mechanistic point of view however, Nature consists of matter, and matter is insensate, dead, drab, unvarying, devoid of interests and purposes. This draining-off of spirit from matter was naturally expressed in mind–matter dualism : the human mind had to become the repository of spirit since Nature had become the arena of blind matter in motion. Dualism gave expression to the mechanistic idea that matter was essentially utterly unlike ourselves: we are essentially identified with spirit, and matter was conceived as in every respect antithetical to spirit. As such – as the insensate, brute and blind, the inert and formless, the non-self, the Other, the External – matter of course ceased to be an object of moral concern or interest. This categorical division between Self/spirit and World/matter was reinforced by the discretist aspect of atomism: *qua* aggregate of atoms, I am discrete from all other aggregates, and hence from Nature as a whole. Both qualitatively and quantitatively speaking then, I am divorced from Nature, my identity in no way a function of the identity of Nature. My self-interest, accordingly, does not extend to it, and in this respect too it is beyond the purview of moral concern. As Brian Easlea concludes,

> a nature of mere matter in motion has no rights. It is not a nature that rational men, after liberating themselves from its domination, will seek to communicate with, ... will seek to love through ever greater understanding of its ways. It is a nature there for men to use as they will.[30]

Descartes had enthusiastically affirmed the exploitative implications of mechanism for our relations with Nature: the aim of philosophy/science was to make 'men' the 'masters and possessors' of Nature. Bacon, the ideological father of science, was notoriously explicit on the need for men to 'subdue' Nature, the enemy. Bacon's imagery was militaristic – he called on men to 'unite forces against the Nature of Things, to storm and occupy her castles and strongholds, and extend the bounds of the human empire'.[31] (The overtones of sexual aggression in the scientific attitude to Nature have been pointed out by many recent feminist writers. Bacon describes himself as 'leading to you Nature with all her children, to bind her to your service and make her your slave'.[32] To explore the significance of the feminine personification of Nature is however beyond the scope of the present work.[33]) Bacon's ruthlessly exploitative attitude towards Nature would of course be morally indefensible were matter not viewed as inert, devoid of agency and interests. 'The men of the new science,' writes Easlea, 'had provided an image of nature totally appropriate for the emerging society in which nature ... [was] to be exploited for the enhancement of private profit and personal power.'[34]

The deadness of matter from the mechanistic point of view has another implication for our relation to Nature. Nature is, from this perspective, ultimately inexplicable: the fabric of the world has been fragmented, atomized, into discrete units, arbitrarily arranged. Laws of motion were discovered, but these laws were in themselves arbitrary and inexplicable. To appeal to a First Mover in this connection, a Mover which cannot be identified in physical terms, and can, as we have seen, only contingently be identified in theological terms, is simply putting a name to the mystery. It is really no better than the appeal to the dormitive power of opium to explain the fact that it induces sleep. As Whitehead complains, there is, from the Newtonian point of view, no reason to be found in the essence of a material body – in its mass, motion and shape – for the law of gravitation, or for the existence of any forces or stresses between bodies. Newton left

> all the factors of the system – more particularly, mass and stress – in the position of detached facts devoid of any reason for their compresence. He thus illustrated a great philosophic truth, that a dead Nature can give no reasons. All ultimate reasons are in terms of aim at value. A dead Nature aims at nothing.[35]

To view Nature as arbitrary and meaningless, and therefore ultimately inexplicable, is, again, to negate any sense of responsibility for, or identification with, Nature that we must otherwise have borne. In this way, then, too, the natural environment becomes a perfectly legitimate object for our manipulation and control, a means for our ends. But this inexplicability and meaninglessness of Nature also has deep implications for our sense of our own identity and for the status of ethics.

(ii) The second question which we set out to consider in relation to the mechanistic worldview was that of its implications for our attitude to the self.

An immediate prima facie consequence of mechanism is, as Descartes demonstrated, dualism with respect to body and mind. If matter is dead, inert, lifeless and 'blind', and if the human body is material, then it looks as if some extra principle must be present in the body to render it animate and conscious. This extra, non-material principle was identified by Descartes as the principle of spirit or mind. Moreover, since matter is so antithetical in nature to our own experience of ourselves, our identity is based primarily in mind. This is the message of the cogito: the individual self is essentially the mind; the body is contingent to selfhood, and hence to our identity. And given the mechanistic conception of matter, the body is a deadweight that shackles the mind, the cross that the human spirit is, unaccountably, condemned to bear.

How profoundly this Cartesian division of body and mind has reinforced the contemptuous attitude to our own bodies that had already been instilled into us via the Christian tradition is evidenced in the extent of the repression of bodily function and bodily expression in the modern era.[36] (Although this division found its definitive expression in Descartes, we should note that it would be naive to suppose that it was not already a strong current in western culture prior to Descartes and the Scientific Revolution.) Modern western culture is characterized by its revulsive attitudes to the body. As a culture we are devoted to the elimination of the sight and odour, even the mention, of bodily secretions. We are obsessed with 'hygiene', clinical cleanliness, sparkling surfaces and interiors, the 'whiter than white' look which is so inimical to the natural – messy – tendency of the body. The denial of bodily function, and particularly of sexual function, and its relegation to the 'unconscious', was of course the great discovery made by Freud. The significance of the phenomenon of repression, and of the elevation of mental function and repudiation of bodily function, is, again, beyond the scope of this chapter, and indeed this book. I shall confine myself here to a few reflections on the fact that members of modern western cultures identify most intimately and personally with their conscious minds, and harbour irresponsible and sometimes punitive attitudes toward their own bodies.

These attitudes to the body inform the whole structure of values which shape present-day society; they are reflected in the distribution of social value and reward over occupations: the highest rewards, in both material and prestige terms, accrue to the 'white collar' occupations and the professions, the lowest to the 'blue collar' and 'manual' occupations. We have an education system which produces social evaluations of individuals almost exclusively in terms of their intellectual ability – their 'IQ', as this is defined by the system. The contingency of the body to our sense of personal identity is reflected also in our attitudes to health:[37] the body is treated as a Cartesian machine, an instrument for the pursuit of our abstractly conceived ends (ends such as success, money, career, beauty, popularity, fame). We do not regard the body as having a life, and ends, of its own, a life and a set of goals which are our own. We ignore the impulse of our body towards fulfilment and well-being, substituting cognitive ends (ego goals) for bodily ones. This continues to be so, to a large extent, even in the realm of sexuality, in spite of the advent of an era of so-called 'sexual permissiveness'. What sexual permissiveness has meant for many people over the last twenty-five years or so has been less an invitation to relax and enjoy than an exhortation to compete and perform. In other words, sexual achievement can, like fitness, excellence in dance or athletics, and other physical accomplishments, become an ego goal. In such cases, the body remains the instrument of the ego and the mere fact of physical exertion in no way helps to remedy the alienation of the body or ameliorate psychic repression. It has been well documented by psychotherapists, particularly neo-Reichians, that sexual or athletic prowess is in no way equivalent to a true inner freedom of the body, but is rather perfectly compatible with a high degree of chronic internal tension, muscular armouring and a lack of a sense of one's inner physical being.

It should be clear from what I have said that I am not suggesting that contemporary western culture is necessarily characterized by *asceticism*. The dualistic ranking of mind over body, and the attitude to the body that this entails, may, I think, be manifested in sensuous excess just as much as in denial. And the control of the body by the ego can be exercised through a regime of material accumulation and consumerism as much as through one of austerity. These claims reach deep into the realms of psychoanalytic theory, but I shall try to explain very briefly why I make them.

The first claim is not, I think, too tendentious: over-indulgence of 'the flesh' is pretty clearly as much a symptom of 'out-of-touchness' with the body as strenuous over-discipline is. Attunement to the body is not a matter of forcing the body beyond its natural limits but rather of letting it find its own level of gratification. Exaggerated attention to food or sex or whatever is generally a symptom of a neurotic attitude to the body, whether it results in repressive asceticism or compulsive over-indulgence. Indeed, the alternative to dualism is not a matter of giving both the mind and the body their 'due', for to do this is still to treat them as separate dimensions of human existence. The alternative to dualism is rather a matter of integrating the needs and desires of both mind and body. The gratification of the integrated mind-and-body is not definable in terms of sensory pleasure alone, but has emotional, intellectual, aesthetic and perhaps even spiritual, as well as sensory, dimensions. The alternative to the domination of body by mind, then, is not 'la grande bouffe', nor the orgy in the locker room, it is more like the sacred dance in the Balinese temple.

My second claim was that the ethos of material accumulation or consumption, far from being antithetical to dualism, as it might at first sight appear to be, is actually evidence of dualism. My reasons for this claim rest on certain assumptions about the psychological function of dualism. This is an enormous topic, which has been explored extensively from a feminist perspective,[38] but I shall be content to make the following point in connection with it: the 'mind', or more specifically, the ego, seeks to gain control over the body because by doing so it can render the future more predictable and thereby increase its own security. The ego maps out the future for the body – anticipating the body's needs and desires – and tries to provide for them. Material accumulation is one of the optimal strategies of the ego in this regard. To possess all the resources and devices for producing pleasure that the mind can foresee the body needing or wanting, is as far as possible to secure the future against uncertainty and deprivation. The price of this security, however, is spontaneity, particularly physical spontaneity. The ego cannot tolerate any spontaneous eruptions of feeling, need or desire on the part of the body that would disrupt the plan. So mind–body dualism is expressed, in this connection, not in indifference to bodily pleasure but in the predetermination of that pleasure. The consumer is striving to control his or her body just as much as the ascetic is; both mistrust spontaneity as a mode of being.

There is a great deal more to be said in this connection, concerning repression, eros, and the nature of the alternatives to mind–body dualism. My point is only to indicate, in the briefest possible way, why I think it is evident that dualistic attitudes still prevail today. In members of contemporary western cultures the body remains, in my view, very much the instrument of the ego. When, under the pressure of coercive or unsympathetic ego goals the body breaks down, we seek to apply a 'technological fix' – drugs, surgery, radiation/laser/chemotherapies, for instance – to maintain *it* as a means towards *our* ends for as long as possible. Dualism with respect to body and mind then engenders just the same sort of controlling, exploitative and sometimes punitive attitude to the body as it does to Nature as a whole. The fact that most of our present psychotherapies – where psychotherapy is increasingly becoming integral to our western way of life – aim to improve proprioception, to put people back 'in touch' with their bodies, is striking in this connection. The burgeoning repertoire of psychotherapeutic techniques, including relaxation, breathing exercises, massage, postural integration, and eastern practices designed to integrate body and mind, such as yoga, Tai Chi, and various martial arts, demonstrates the extent to which our psychic malaise is still rooted in an ideologically-induced separation of body and mind. Our sense of personal identity, split between the physical and the mental, incorporates an opposition which can only in the long term rend us asunder.

The mechanistic view of Nature influences our sense of identity in another profound respect. It was observed earlier that, from a mechanistic perspective, Nature in itself is devoid of interests and is therefore indifferent, so to speak, to its own fate. Nothing that happens to it matters to it. It is in this sense, in itself, devoid of value. This is tantamount to saying that the fact/value dichotomy is built into the mechanistic worldview. The dichotomy between reason and value, which Hume made explicit, was rooted in this fact/value distinction, and hence in the mechanistic worldview. The dichotomy between reason and value emerged at a time when scientific reason had become identified with reason *per se*. Scientific reason was conceived as the value-neutral tool of an interest-free observer or inquirer, its object being an independently constituted realm of 'fact'. Fact and value were thus implicitly regarded as categorically distinct, and value was therefore no longer the legitimate object – or product – of reason. This irrationalism with respect to values naturally fostered the relativist and subjectivist (not to say sceptical) tendencies which have gained such a stranglehold on later twentieth-century ethical thinking, at least in the sphere of personal morality: if values are not to be determined or judged by reason, then it is natural to consider them to be conditioned by external – material and social – factors, or even invented to suit the purposes of the individual.

In *The Metaphysical Foundations of Modern Science* Burtt describes the Newtonian worldview as being

> that view of the cosmos which saw in man a puny, irrelevant spectator ... of the vast mathematical system whose regular motions according to mechanical principles constituted the world of nature. The gloriously romantic universe of Dante and Milton, that set no bounds to the imagination of man as it played over space and time, had now been swept away.... The world that people had thought themselves living in – a world rich with colour and sound, redolent with fragrance, filled with gladness, love and beauty, speaking everywhere of purposive harmony and creative ideals – was crowded now into minute corners in the brains of scattered, organic beings. The really important world outside was a world hard, cold, colourless, silent and dead; a world of quantity,

a world of mathematically computable motions in mechanical regularity.[39]

What is the natural response to such a cold, hard world? For all of us it is a familiar response, which we may seek to escape by taking a leap of religious faith, or by embracing some occult doctrine, or by way of some other consolation. What do we feel when we gaze into the dark Newtonian abyss, with its mathematical march of inanimate atoms? The illusoriness of human aspirations? The 'blindness' and awesome 'reducibility' of Nature, before which human warmth and worth appear as phantoms, illusions, creatures of the mind-that-cannot-see-into-the-things-in-themselves? The arbitrariness and contingency of history, of biography, of personality? It is a chilling experience, this peering over the brink of appearance into the Newtonian void, yet it is one which is imposed on us virtually from infancy.

In the shadow of this chilling experience our culture, again, splits its realities: we cannot but act as if the world of 'colour and sound, redolent with fragrance' is real, for it is from this world that we extract our values, and our values are integral to our sanity. But our faith in this world is simultaneously negated, nullified, by the cosmology to which we are harnessed. Our Newtonian cosmology makes it plain that values are not objective, not built into Nature. We are thus compelled to acknowledge the hollowness – the 'mind-dependence' – of the values on which our lives are founded. Contemporary ethical relativism and subjectivism then, are to a certain extent corollaries of mechanism, and the perspective they provide deeply moulds our sense of our own identity. We inhabit a meaningless and arbitrary world, and our own lives are accordingly, objectively speaking, mean-ingless and arbitrary, imbued only with the value and significance that we attach to them. It is impossible, in such a context, not to suffer at some level from feelings of isolation, alienation and angst – the well-known psychic malaise of the modern human being. At the core of our identity, where we would expect to find the meaning of our existence, we discover only vacuity. In the light of this a certain cynicism and detachment from the self is inevitable.

(iii) We come now to our third question, that of the implications of the mechanistic worldview for our attitude towards others, and hence for the structure of social relations.

Mechanism is, as we have observed, explicated within a framework of atomism. The Newtonian world is a world of building bricks, an analytical reality – the nature of the whole explicable exhaustively in terms of the nature and arrangement of the elementary units. What does this substance pluralism imply for social theory?

In the first place, it is clear that where an atomistic/analytical mode of explanation is favoured in physics, it has been extended to other areas of discourse.[40] The atomistic model was early adapted to other disciplines within science, the analytical method being equated with scientific method, and analytical, reductive explanation being equated with explanation *per se*. The concept of any other, more holistic form of explanation was neglected, barely if at all understood. It was natural, within this context, that the analytical method was appropriated by social thinkers, as early, as we have seen, as Hobbes and Locke. Viewed from an analytical perspective, societies appear as aggregates of social atoms, the social atoms being, of course, none other than individual human beings. Mechanism, too, is reflected in the image of the social structure in the form of competition between the social units: these social units are, like their material counterparts, competing for each others' space. When 'collision' occurs, the more 'massive' will displace the less. Everyone is on the billiard slate, with nothing but their own mass to hold them in place. What this suggests is nothing less than a socio-economic free-for-all, governed only by the mechanistic 'law' of action and reaction, and the 'right' of the more massive, or mighty, to prevail. No predetermined social niches exist here for individuals as they did in medieval and tribal contexts. The individual 'stands alone', as an independent social agent, buffered by social forces, but not logically informed with them; individual identity is independent of that of greater social wholes or institutions. The individual is a social 'substance' in his or her own right.

It was remarked above that the *first* implication of Newtonian atomism for social thinking was a methodological one: atomism furnished an analytical, reductive methodology which could easily be adapted to the social context, and which, when so adapted, yielded an atomistic picture of the structure of social relations. But in fact the implications of Newtonian atomism for social thinking reach beyond methodology: Newtonianism incorporates not only a methodology, but an ontology, and this ontology cannot fail to find expression at the social level. Since the only principle of individuation available within the framework of Newtonian atomism is the substance principle, the individuation of human beings will be conceptually effected in purely substance terms. A substance is understood to be a discrete ontologically autonomous unity, and from a Cartesian point of view, both minds and bodies qualify as substances.

Earlier, in our discussion of the influence of Newtonianism on the concept of personal identity, I argued that our construction of our *own* identity, within a Cartesian framework, involves a primary identification with our mental substance, and only a grudging, secondary, contingent identification with our bodies. How do we identify and individuate our own minds? We do so *immediately*, simply by including, in our concept of our own mind, everything present to our consciousness. However no general criterion for identifying and individuating mental substances is available within the Cartesian framework. This is why 'the problem of other minds' is one of our Cartesian legacies. But social analysis requires a general criterion for identifying and individuating persons. In the Cartesian framework, the only such criterion available is the spatio-temporal criterion, according to which substances are demarcated in terms of their spatio-temporal boundaries. This criterion is plainly only applicable to things with clearly defined, closed boundaries. Material objects like bricks, and even human bodies, satisfy this condition, and can accordingly qualify as substances. For the purpose of social analysis, then, human beings will be identified with their bodies. This will encourage a crude behaviouristic orientation in social thinking.

Even more important than this behaviouristic bias, however, is the fact that, within the Cartesian framework, human beings are individuated in substantival rather than functional terms, and there is nothing over and above the individual thus individuated, no greater whole, of which he or she can truly be said to be a part. He or she is indeed, ontologically speaking, a unit, an island. I shall argue in Chapter 3 that the substantival conception of human identity misses the point: human unity, and indeed the unity of any organism, can be adequately understood not in substantival but only in functional – systemic – terms.

This concludes my analytical account of the implications of the mechano-atomistic model of reality for our attitudes towards Nature, the self and social relations. The natural – though by no means not-humanly-modifiable – social order, from a Newtonian point of view, is an atomistic one, in which the individual is an isolated unit, whose interactions with others consist in mechanistic collision and displacement, competition for space. Its 'law' is that of the greater displacing the lesser, the survival of the fittest.

It will be clear from the above account of the logical implications of Newtonianism that in my view Hobbes came closer than the later liberal philosophers to recognizing the true ideological message of Newtonianism. The difference between Hobbes' account and the one I have set out here is that where Hobbes bites the bullet and takes on a thoroughgoing materialism, my account accepts dualism as a corollory of mechanism. Otherwise the parallels between the two accounts are evident: both infer social atomism from metaphysical atomism, and both point to the subjectivity of value, and hence of morality, in the mechanistic scheme of things. Hobbes does not shrink from acknowledging the profoundly anti-social implications of individualism, but mobilizes the unlimited power of an absolute sovereign to remedy the potentiality for conflict that such individualism entails. The sovereign is the linchpin of the state, where the state is the compromise to which the purely self-interested parties to the social contract consent in order to secure their own long-term security. The principles of social morality, including that of justice, are artefacts of the state, and therefore rest ultimately on self-interest. Grounding social morality in self-interest in this way sets up a tension at the core of social life: self interest and morality on occasion pull in opposite directions. When self-interest dictates observance of such principles as those of equality and justice, then their observance is rationally justified; when the observance of moral principles is not expedient, however, no justification is available, and only the threat of punishment imposed by the state can enforce them. Ultimately then, in this scheme of things, it is self-interest, and self-interest alone, which remains as the practical guiding light and driving force of social life.

Hobbes' notion of the unredeemed state of nature then lurks behind the political devices and sugar-coated ideological values of the liberal tradition, and in essence matches up with the grim reality of society in the throes of the Industrial Revolution. It is arguable that the liberal rhetoric of freedom, equality and justice acquired a moral momentum of its own, and helped to fuel both certain reform movements, such as the movements for the abolition of slavery and child labour, and the development of the Welfare State. But it is also arguable that these reforms came about only when it suited the capitalist system of production for them to do so. Of course, the history of social and political life in England and Europe over the last four centuries is not reducible to a single formula. But I do think that overall the capitalist era may be characterized as one of ruthless competition and exploitation, which in its broad outlines resembled the Hobbesian scenario

of atoms in collision more than it did the sweetened-up scenario of
equal individuals freely choosing their own good in their own fashion.

When the Romantic reaction to Enlightenment thought arrived, it
delivered a searing perception of the dehumanizing and desocializing
effects of the new scientific worldview. This worldview, with its
reductivism and its invitation to naked self-interest, was considered to
blame for the unprecedented exploitation of humanity and Nature
experienced in the course of the Industrial Revolution and the development of the industrial state. In the inimitable cadences of Blake,
the cry goes up:

> I turn my eyes to the schools and universities of Europe
> And there behold the loom of Locke, whose wool rages dire,
> Wash'd by the water-wheels of Newton: black the cloth
> In heavy wreathes folds over every Nation: cruel works
> Of many wheels I view, wheel without wheel, with cogs tyrannic
> Moving by compulsion each other, not as those in Eden which,
> Wheel within wheel, in freedom revolve in peace and harmony.[41]

The view of Nature as a resource to be exploited and an opponent to
be conquered – a view that had been expressed not only in industrial-
ization but in the formal and utilitarian landscape preferences of the
Enlightenment – started to give way, later in the eighteenth century,
to a view of Nature as a source of moral and aesthetic values. This new
– Romantic – view favoured wild landscapes over pastoral scenes, and
more informal gardening styles over the geometric patterns of the
Enlightenment. According to historian Keith Thomas, there were
many reasons for this change in taste, for the new appreciation of
'untamed' Nature; these reasons included

> an aesthetic reaction against the regularity and uniformity of
> English agriculture; a dislike of the artificialities of the gardening
> movement: a feeling that wilderness, by its very contrast with
> cultivation, was necessary to give meaning and definition to the
> human enterprise; a preoccupation with the freedom of open
> spaces as a symbol of human freedom ... and an element of
> alienation or lack of sympathy for the dominant trends of the age.[42]

It is the latter sentiments that I would emphasize here. Romanticism
was born out of the recognition that there was something lacking
in the utilitarian and disenchanted attitude to Nature fostered by
Newtonianism. It was an expression of the intuitive realization that if
the world itself lacked intrinsic meaning and purpose so, ultimately,

did human life. The Romantic re-evaluation of Nature converged with the emerging doubts about the moral justifiability of treating wild animals as objects of unrestricted recreational hunting, to produce movements for the preservation of wild lands and the protection of wild birds. This new sensibility *vis-à-vis* Nature gave rise to societies dedicated to animal welfare and the prevention of cruelty to animals.[43]

So the acting out of the principles of the Newtonian worldview, with the complete moral indifference to Nature that they entailed, in time bred its own reaction. Prototypal 'counter-cultural' movements for the preservation and protection of non-human Nature sprang into being. These remained strictly minority movements however; the pace of exploitation both of wilderness and of domestic animals only continued to accelerate throughout the nineteenth and twentieth centuries. Western culture was firmly in the grip of the Newtonian vision, and the Romantic revolt did not succeed in overturning its bleak and disenchanting message. Those willing and eager to be motivated by narrow individualism and moral indifference to the non-human world of course flourished under the Newtonian regime. But those with intimations of an alternative scheme of things, who wished for wholeness, interconnectedness, unity, collectivism, harmony with Nature and with humanity in general, saw their impulses invalidated – de-legitimated – by the cosmology to which their science had yoked them.

VI COSMOLOGY AND MYTH

This chapter opened with comments on the cultural role of cosmologies, on the need that peoples and communities have to form some conception of their place 'in the scheme of things entire'. Cosmology furnishes the indispensable context for the social and normative thinking that informs a culture, and even for the individual's own experience of his or her self. Philosophers and social thinkers have become so entangled in epistemology that cosmology is dismissed, by many, as an epistemological anachronism, on a par with mythology. What these thinkers of empiricist, positivist and anti-realist bent have often overlooked is, as I remarked at the outset, the sheer cultural necessity of mythology. Cosmology, in some form, is a part of any mythology. Mythology may be understood as a narrative which tells us what we are, where we came from and where we are going. Joseph Campbell summarizes the fourfold function of myth in a way that brings out its relation to cosmology and its potential relation to science:

> The first [function] is what I have called the mystical function, to waken and maintain in the individual a sense of awe and gratitude in relation to the mystery dimension of the universe, not so that he lives in fear of it, but so that he recognizes that he participates in it, since the mystery of being is the mystery of his own being as well.
>
> *The second function of the living mythology is to offer an image of the universe that will be in accord with the knowledge of the time, the sciences and the fields of action of the folk to whom the mythology is addressed.*
>
> The third function of the living mythology is to validate, support, and imprint the norms of a given specific moral order – that, namely, of the society in which the individual is to live.
>
> And the fourth is to guide him, stage by stage, in health, strength and harmony of spirit, through the whole foreseeable course of a useful life.[44] (my emphasis)

On this account, myth closely resembles what has in the present chapter gone under the name of 'worldview'. The difference is that 'myth' is endowed with a positive connotation by Campbell which I have not extended to 'worldview': I have allowed the possibility that a worldview may undermine, as well as uplift, the morale of a community. But, as I said earlier, even a negative worldview is preferable to none at all, for as many thinkers writing from a psychoanalytic and a psychocultural perspective[45] emphasize, a culture must generate answers to the questions of identity, origin and destiny if its members are to exercise their agency in any kind of sustained and consistent fashion. Myth is a psychological prerequisite for cultural viability.

Mythology has, as I have observed, been dismissed by many philosophers and social thinkers on epistemological grounds. But it has also, to all appearances, disappeared as an explicit force from the wider cultural scene. (That it continues to lead a fractured, lawless and underground life in the popular arts and entertainments is readily apparent.) What is the reason for this apparent fade-out? It cannot be the fact that mythology is beset with epistemological difficulties, for so are science and ordinary empirical knowledge, yet the epistemological obstacles to science and ordinary knowledge are regarded as academic by the community at large, and for practical purposes are set aside. We recognize that ordinary knowledge, and to some extent science, are necessary if we are to live, and epistemological scruples will not persuade us to give them up. So it is not such scruples which have caused the seeming decline of mythology. The real reason for this decline is the popular belief that science has superseded mythology. But what does this mean?

It is clear from Campbell's account of myth and our own deployment of the notion of worldview in the present chapter that cosmology is central to mythology. But there is an ambiguity in the popular conception – and even in Campbell's account – of the logical order of cosmology *vis-à-vis* mythology. Campbell cites as the second function of mythology that it provides an image of the universe which accords with the knowledge of the time. In other words, mythology must provide a cosmology which bears the best epistemological credentials available in the culture in question. When the culture in question is our own, this clearly means that science itself is the source of the cosmology which the mythology embodies. But Campbell goes on to say that a mythology must validate the norms of a given specific moral order, and this requirement may be inconsistent with the previous one. For the scientific method of experiment and observation may well disclose a universe which in no way reflects the social order in which the scientific method originated. This is indeed exactly what happened in the Scientific Revolution: the new science revealed a world order which invalidated the closed, hierarchical and teleological social order of feudal Europe. The second function of myth, in Campbell's account, suggests that mythology does not invent cosmology for its own purposes, but uses the best cosmology available in the culture in question. But Campbell's account of the third function of myth suggests that mythology does invent cosmology to suit its own purposes, and that this purpose is the legitimation of a pre-established social order.

This, I think, reaches the heart of the reason for the popular rejection of mythology: mythology is perceived as a *source* of cosmology. That is, mythology is seen as embodying a *method* for arriving at cosmologies, a method that is projective and anthropomorphic: the cosmos depicted in mythology is merely a projection of psychic realities. This method for arriving at cosmologies has plainly been superseded by the scientific method. So, if mythology is identified with this method – which is to say, if it is perceived as a *source* of cosmology – then it is indeed no longer credible in the scientific age. However, if mythology is understood as the process whereby a normative structure is extracted from a cosmological base, then we can allow science to function as the source of cosmology, while still maintaining that cosmology has a mythological role. Mythology, in modern western culture, is not extinct; it is alive and well, but dressed in scientific guise. In such guise, and for the reasons I have just outlined, it tends to go unrecognized.

Newtonianism, of course, is the case in point. It answers the questions, what are we, whither are we going and from whence do we come, in no uncertain terms: we are aggregates of atoms coming from atoms and bound to return to them. Newtonian cosmology discloses a world which, while not hostile to our concerns, is monolithically indifferent to them. (The opposite of love, the psychologists tell us, is not hate, but indifference; hate is an expression of interest and a form of relating. It is indifference which truly negates our identity, and undermines our agency.) We are mere micro-dots over which this huge engine of a universe rolls unwittingly. We can do what we like, for better or worse, because, from the point of view of the steamroller, nothing, and in particular nothing that micro-dots do, could possibly matter.

A singularly discouraging myth! But it has been the very chorus of this chapter that we must not identify science *per se* with Newtonianism. It is Newtonianism which embodies the fact/value distinction, portraying the world as inert, insensate, devoid of telos, of value, purpose and meaning. There is no reason in principle why scientific method could not reveal a universe that was alive, sentient, and evolving toward some specific ideal. If science can indeed deliver a new cosmology, which can furnish the basis for a new and more inspiring worldview, then all strength to it!

The situation under the Newtonian regime was bad enough. But it is in the present day compounded by the fact, indicated at the beginning of this chapter, that the cosmological basis of our world-view, grim as it is, has in fact in the course of the twentieth century been slipping out from under our feet. There is an uneasy awareness in the community at large that Newtonian physics has been super-seded. Newfangled physics such as quantum mechanics and relativity theory, and the weird world of quarks and quasars, have displaced the old comprehensible mechanism, but as a culture we are still in the dark as to the nature of this strange, new, counterintuitive universe. Unequipped to switch cosmological frameworks, we continue to do our social and normative thinking within the framework of Newtonianism. As Randall remarks,

Men still consider their world in terms of Newtonian science; they are still living, as Whitehead has put it, upon the accumulated capital of ideas laid up by the scientific pioneers of the seventeenth century. They still feel bewildered and afraid when it begins to dawn on them that it is no longer possible to live by the political and economic theory worked out for the businessmen and pro- prietors of the Age of Reason – and free competition. The method and aim of Newtonian science have been transformed by the scientists; that earlier commercial individualism has in fact been rapidly giving way to newer forms of corporate industrial organis- ation and welfare politics. Yet the most widely accepted social theory and ideals, in America rather more than in Europe, still bear the impress of Newtonian science, with its rigid, deductive, and inflexible concepts, and of the private self-interest, the irre- sponsible competition, the rugged individualism of that earlier commercial age.[46]

To this I would add that our culture is progressively becoming *aware* of the invalidity of the cosmological presuppositions of its way of life, and is increasingly manifesting symptoms of cosmological uncer- tainty: anxiety and insecurity, alienation, anomie and a massive confusion over values. Newtonianism cut us adrift into the void. But the void was at least a place, even if an empty one; it was comprehen- sible. We are drifting now into sheer abstraction, a 'universe' which is unimaginable, a higher order mathematical phantasm. As a culture we need, as the psychotherapists say, to get 'grounded', we need to find our way back into a tangible reality. We stand radically in need of cosmological rehabilitation.

Chapter 2

Geometrodynamics: a monistic metaphysic

I SCIENCE AS A SOURCE OF COSMOLOGY

We are, then, a cosmologically dispossessed culture, a culture clinging to a bankrupt worldview which prescribes a cramped materialistic individualism, the consequences of which we are presently reaping. That we need cosmological rehabilitation is drastically apparent. Is the time for a shift to the alternative – monistic – metaphysical archetype which I mentioned in the previous chapter at hand? Such a metaphysic can only serve our culture as a worldview, complete with ideological dimensions, if we have independent grounds for adopting it. Since we have, for the reasons already outlined, accepted science as the source of cosmological discovery, we cannot simply select the cosmology that we find ideologically most appealing. If monism is to become the basis for a new worldview, it needs the sanction of science.

This point deserves a little elaboration. Because scientific method – a method which involves observation, the empirical testing of the predictions yielded by hypotheses – is so widely subsumed under Newtonian mechanism, the response of many people to the felt need for a new, non-Newtonian cosmology has been to adopt extrascientific methods for the search. Thus many groups, movements and individuals who have been complaining, in some cases for decades, that western civilization stands in need of new cultural and spiritual values, and new attitudes both to humankind and to Nature, have been opposed to the influence of science, and have ignored its potential as a wellspring of new values. They have looked instead to eastern philosophies and practices, to occult doctrines, to mystical intuition, and in fact every which way but to science.

There is little doubt however that scientific method, detached from mechanistic assumptions, is a superlative tool for investigating the nature of the physical world. It is also the distinctive discovery of our western culture. We may be discontented or disappointed with its findings, and we may wish to supplement scientific method with other investigative techniques, but if a new worldview is to attain legitimacy and take root in this culture, it must ultimately have the sanction of science. The scope of science, and the values and attitudes to Nature that it presently embodies, may need to be transformed, but science in some form is nevertheless our 'reason to believe'. Divine authority, tradition, mystical revelation or divination may be the 'reasons to believe' that underpin the worldviews of other cultures, but salvation, if it is to come to us, must come from the reservoirs of our own culture. Our new values must be wrought out of our own experience and taught to us in our own idiom if we are truly to understand and assimilate them. And this means that they must be spelt out in scientific terms. It is *not* to say, however, that scientific method is the *ultimate* method of inquiry: the new worldview to which scientific method points may in fact reveal the limitations of that method – it may show us why, in our own terms, other methods of inquiry work. In this respect then, it may serve in the same way as Hume's ladder served – to be kicked aside when the ascent has been accomplished.

We may feel that it is science, and its double-edged technology, which threaten our psychic integrity, but like an individual facing a psychological crisis, the way through is to confront our fears and to use them to develop our strength and wisdom, rather than to avoid and suppress them. A world which rids itself of Frankenstein by simply banishing him or withdrawing its support will not be liberated from his power, for in these circumstances his spirit, repressed, will wax strong, and come to visit the world in many guises, even to dominate. The world which has tried to reject him will be shaken, unsure of itself, living in fear of a spectre it cannot now confront. The way to deal with Frankenstein is to convert him, to enlist his support in creating a new vision. The power of science must be harnessed, not left to its own devices, nor banished to stalk in the dark.

But while we must invoke the findings of science in the construction of our new cosmology, we do not wish to fall into the crude epistemological fallacy of taking scientific lore as the *literal* truth, the last word, as providing an exhaustive map of the terrain of actuality, and an exhaustive preview of possible experience. Without wishing here to enter into a full Heideggerian-style critique of metaphysics, I wish to present the alternative cosmology we are about to explore in a mythological role, as an image of the world which is validated in only a preliminary way by its scientific credentials, but primarily by its potentially integrating effect on our culture. In other words, if a cosmology is to gain currency at all in our culture it must possess scientific credibility. But while this is a necessary condition for its acceptability, it is not a sufficient condition for such a cosmology to function on a mythological level: it must also serve to focus and integrate our experience of reality. It must promote self-realization in those who embrace it. This, after all, is the wider reality test: observation and measurement of quantifiable variables is a narrow test indeed in comparison with this which takes the whole human being as its 'instrument' for exploring reality. But a 'theory' whose validation rests on the flourishing of its human adherents will have more the character of a poetic image than of a literal transcription of a fully renderable reality. It is thus more in a mythopoetic than in a literal spirit that I offer the following cosmology for consideration, as one window on what must always remain an incompletely knowable world.

II THE PRINCIPLES OF QUANTUM MECHANICS

Does science then currently sanction a monistic worldview? What kind of cosmology does contemporary science offer? There is of course no univocal answer to this question. Presently physics consists of a range of theories which explain different aspects, and different levels, of physical reality, but it offers no grand synthesis. In this respect it differs from Newtonianism, which did offer a unified picture of the large-and-small-scale structure of reality. Physics today offers us quantum theories to explain the micro-structure, and relativity theories to explain the cosmos. The principles of quantum theory are regarded as radically non-classical, that is non-Newtonian, while the principles of relativity theory are supposedly less so. Whether or not reality-in-the-round conforms to the former or to the latter is still not known. And yet, interestingly, both theories carry clear intimations of an alternative archetype, the archetype which, in Chapter 1, I characterized as substance monism. Both theories speak of a universe which is one, whole and indivisible, a universe which is not a mere aggregate of discrete individuals, but is itself, as a whole, the 'unit' of reality. Physicist McCusker makes the point explicit for quantum mechanics at the end of his book *Quest for Quarks*, when he says that it is 'anti-atomic'.

> It pictures the universe as one, whole and indivisible. This is not to say that the idea of chemical 'atoms', for instance, is completely false. Such entities as the hydrogen and oxygen 'atoms' exist. But they are *not* fundamental building blocks. They are more like eddies on the surface of a river. The universe is seamless but not featureless.[1]

That other writers make similar claims for relativistic cosmologies we shall see a little later in this chapter.

It is by now clear to everyone that a 'paradigm shift', to use the Kuhnian expression, is currently taking place in physics. Many recent commentators, most notably Fritjof Capra, have seen a new worldview taking shape around the principles of quantum mechanics. Quantum mechanics does not in itself constitute a cosmology, since its domain is restricted to the subatomic. But if the principles which are found to govern that domain are generalized, and taken to characterize the fundamental nature of reality, then there is a sense in which those principles can constitute a blueprint of Nature, even though they fail to reveal the large-scale shape and structure of the cosmos. Capra adumbrates the new view in the following terms:

> In contrast to the mechanistic Cartesian view of the world, the worldview emerging from modern physics can be characterized by words like 'organic', 'holistic', and 'ecological'. It might also be called a systems view, in the sense of general systems theory. The universe is no longer seen as a machine, made up of a multitude of objects, but it has to be pictured as one indivisible, dynamic whole whose parts are essentially interrelated and can be understood only as patterns of a cosmic process.[2]

This is not the place to offer a synopsis of quantum mechanics, since it is not a quantum mechanical worldview or model which is to be presented in this chapter. But it is worth taking a look at the principles in terms of which quantum reality is characterized, and which Capra takes to inform the new view of the world. The two deepest non-classical principles emerging from quantum physics are the principles firstly of the interconnectedness or non-localizability of particles, and secondly of their intrinsic dynamism. Both of these principles bear on the more often cited, but perhaps less radical principle of indeterminism.

Turning to non-localizability first, the principle of localizability, or the separability of physical systems, may be stated as follows:

> If a physical system remains, during a certain time, mechanically (including electromagnetically, etc.) isolated from other systems, then the evolution in time of its properties during this whole time interval cannot be influenced by operations carried out on other systems.[3]

In other words, a system is said to be localizable, or separable, if operations on systems which are spatially and causally separated from it fail to disturb it. This condition is tantamount to the condition of ontological independence – the criterion of substance – which is satisfied by entities whose identity is logically determined by their intrinsic properties alone, that is involves no relation to other entities. Newtonian atoms were clearly localizable/separable in this sense. Quantum systems are not.

An understanding of non-localizability or non-separability cannot be acquired without a certain understanding of the Heisenberg principle of indeterminacy. Heisenberg demonstrated that an exact measurement of one variable of a quantum system, for example its position, will render the value of a complementary variable, for example its momentum, intrinsically indeterminate. As David Bohm explains, Heisenberg showed that

> even if one supposes that the physically significant variables [of a system] actually existed with sharply defined values (as is demanded by classical mechanics), then we could never measure all of them simultaneously, for the interaction between the observing apparatus and what is observed always involves an exchange of one or more indivisible and uncontrollably fluctuating quanta. For example, if one tries to measure the co-ordinate, x, and the associated momentum, p, of a particle, then the particle is disturbed in such a way that the maximum accuracy for the simultaneous determination of both is given by the well-known relation $\Delta \rho \, \Delta \alpha \geqslant h$, [where h is a constant].[4]

In other words, the accuracy of simultaneous measurement of the two properties is in principle limited. The act of measurement itself, then, alters the state of the system. (This raises profound questions concerning the empirical knowability of quantum reality – questions to which we shall return below.) The salient point here is that since an operation which renders the value of one variable determinate simultaneously precludes the possibility of determinacy for the complementary variable, and vice versa, it follows that prior to the measurement the system could not in itself have been fully determinate with respect to either of the variables in question. This then is the *indeterminacy* of quantum reality.

Now a thought experiment devised by Einstein[5] raised the following question: what outcome could be expected if a quantum system which had been measured for a certain property were divided into two separate subsystems, one of which was subsequently measured again for the same property? A simplified account of the type of experiment Einstein proposed is as follows (I shall here follow McCusker's account; numerous other popular accounts could be cited).[6] Suppose we measure a quantum system for angular momentum (spin) and determine its value to be zero. The system then decays into two singular but spatially separate particles, 1 and 2, each with a non-zero spin. Because angular momentum is conserved, the total spin of the final state – the sum of the spin values of the two particles – must also be zero. Suppose, after some time interval, we perform a measurement on particle 1 and discover it to have spin $\frac{1}{2}$. (It is not really quite as simple as this, because spin has to be measured along three axes, x, y, z, and it is not possible within quantum mechanics to measure a system along all three axes simultaneously. However, for the purposes of making the relevant conceptual point the present account of the experiment suffices.) We can now definitely say that particle 2 has spin $-\frac{1}{2}$: we can determine the angular momentum of particle 2 without performing any measurement. However this is either to say that the value of the momentum of particle 2 is determinate prior to measurement, where this violates Heisenberg indeterminacy. Or it is to say that a measurement on particle 1 has an instantaneous effect on particle 2 – where particle 2 may at the time of the measurement be at an indefinitely great distance from particle 1. The latter result violates the principle of causation, at least as this is understood within Relativity Theory, for it is axiomatic in Relativity Theory that all causal signals propagate with finite velocity: causes take time to bring about their effects; there is no such thing as instantaneous action at a distance.

Einstein's intention in proposing the experiment was to cast doubt on the indeterminacy thesis, but the inference that has finally been validated by physics is that a measurement on the one system does induce a change in the other, though this change is not brought about causally or by any form of action at a distance.[7] It is rather a case of the two systems remaining qualitatively connected although spatially separated. It is an inference to non-localizability, or non-separability; there is more to a so-called particle than meets the eye: its true identity cannot be given purely in terms of properties manifested at a given point in space and time, for its identity may take in or reflect the properties of an indefinite number of other particles. Particles are in this sense akin to the 'monads' postulated by Leibniz in the seventeenth century: individuals which were partly if not fully constituted by their relations to other individuals.

The other broad principle which I cited earlier as fundamental to quantum mechanics is that of intrinsic dynamism. This principle too is another aspect of the more oft-noted principle of indeterminacy. For the irreducible lawlessness of individual phenomena in the quantum domain not only constitutes indeterminacy but is, at the same time, an expression of *intrinsic activity*. For this 'lawlessness', manifested in random fluctuations in the energy levels of individual systems, is really an absence of *extrinsic* laws: no external force or cause is required to bring about perturbations or disturbances in the states of the systems. These changes occur spontaneously. Matter at this level is intrinsically 'restless', that is, in motion. When a subatomic particle is confined to a small region of space, it responds, as Capra puts it, by 'jiggling', and the greater the confinement the greater the degree of spontaneous motion it will exhibit. Matter at the micro-level is thus not the inert, stodgy stuff depicted in Newtonianism, but is 'in a continuous dancing and vibrating motion whose rhythmic patterns are determined by the molecular, atomic and nuclear configurations'.[8]

The two above-mentioned, non-classical principles derived from quantum mechanics – non-locality and intrinsic dynamism – properly belong, I think, to any new view of reality which opposes substance-pluralism and in particular its theoretical offshoot, Newtonianism. But Capra conjoins to these, two further principles which I would not wish to include in the new model, for they are only derivable from quantum mechanics under certain – controversial – interpretations thereof. These principles are, firstly, the mind-dependence of physical reality, and, secondly, the primacy of process or system over substance, where this is taken to the point where substance is in effect eliminated from ontology. I shall try to explain why I do not think these principles should be regarded as fundamental to any new model of reality.

It follows from Heisenberg's demonstration of indeterminacy that we cannot measure a physical system in the quantum domain without disturbing it. We can thus never discover what it is like in itself independently of being observed. Or, to put it in another well-worn way, the observer is not distinct from, or outside, the system which is under observation. This fact led one of the founding fathers of the quantum theory, Neils Bohr, to the view that since we cannot in principle come to know reality-as-it-is-in-itself, there is no justification for postulating such a reality. The observer, in other words, is integral to what is observed: the existence of the world is mind-dependent. This positivist view, espoused by the so-called 'Copenhagen school' under the leadership of Bohr, has deeply influenced twentieth-century physicists, who now have idealist and mystical tendencies that would have appalled their nineteenth-century counterparts (and, indeed, their counterparts in the younger, more mechanistic sciences today). This question of the mind-dependence of reality – which is also, as it happens, the launching pad for epistemology and hence for modern philosophy – is too large to enter into in any detail here. But it is worth just looking briefly at the outlines of quantum indeterminacy once again in order to trace its implications for epistemology.

As we have already observed, Heisenberg discovered that it was in principle impossible to measure the exact value of one variable of a system without rendering the value of a complementary variable indeterminate. This fact was connected with the fact that both matter and light could be shown to have dual natures, appearing particle-like under some experimental conditions, and wave-like under others. How reality actually was at a given point in space and time thus appeared to depend, at least partly, on the kind of experiments that were performed on it. As Capra puts it, ask reality a wave question, and you will get a wave answer; ask it a particle question, and you will get a particle answer.[9] If you ask a particle what its momentum is, it gives you a definite answer, that is, it possesses a definite momentum; but it will thereby become indeterminate in respect of position. Yet you know that had you asked for its position, it would have acquired a definite position and become indeterminate in respect of momentum. Had we asked reality no questions at that point, it would not have been definitely wave-like, nor definitely particle-like; it would not have had definite properties describable by us. Capra's inference from these facts is that the crucial feature of quantum theory is that the observer is not only necessary to observe the properties of an atomic phenomenon, but is necessary even to bring about these properties. My conscious decision about how to observe, say, an electron will determine the electron's properties to some extent.... *The electron does not have objective properties independent of my mind.*[10]   (my emphasis)

It does not seem to me that this position, which was that adopted by Bohr in the 1930s, is entailed by the principles of quantum theory. Certainly the theory brings out in a striking way the point that the kind of apparatus we bring to reality partly determines the kind of information that we receive through that apparatus. But this is essentially no different from the basic epistemological insight, entertained by philosophers for centuries, if not millennia, that our mental representation of Nature is partly shaped by the structure of our mind – by our transcendental psychology, in the Kantian sense – and by the structure of our senses. Apply your eyes to a given portion of reality, and you will receive visual information; apply your ears, and you will receive sound information; apply your particle- or wave-measuring apparatus, and you will receive particle or wave information. True, looking at an object does not discernibly alter its state, rendering it inaudible, for instance. In this respect, classical observer-dependence does differ from quantum observer-dependence. But this is a contingency of the conditions of macro-level observation. We can readily appreciate – independently of the findings of quantum mechanics – that all perception/observation/measurement involves physical interaction between ourselves and the object of scrutiny. The fact that our act of observation itself interferes with the object observed is only a further aspect of the general epistemological problem that it is impossible to know things as they are in themselves. The fact of this epistemological gap between knower and known however is perfectly consistent with realism. We can see this just by supposing that realism is true – that a real world exists which acts on our sensory apparatus to produce sense data. Of course the sense data, which are the product of a complex interaction between our nervous system and external objects, cannot give us the objects as they are in themselves, cannot bring the objects into our minds. It would be incoherent to suppose they could. So the recognition of the epistemological gap in no way *entails* positivism, as many philosophers and physicists seem to assume.

    The important point in this connection, I think, and the point that leads me to favour realism over the theory of the observer-dependence of reality, is that reality does consistently answer electron questions with electrons, and wave questions with waves, and that it refuses to answer certain other questions, for example, questions concerning phlogiston, or angels, consistently or at all. The evidence for the reality of the world is not that the appearances – the data – reveal the objects as they are in themselves (how could they?) but that the world is both selective and consistent in its answers to our questions. More-over, from a knowledge of conceptual structures alone it would not be possible to predict which questions the world would answer or what answers it would give.

The second principle which Capra includes in, but which I would omit from, the post-Newtonian model of reality is that of the primacy of process:

> [the] energy patterns of the subatomic world form the stable nuclear, atomic and molecular structures which build up matter and give it its microscopic solid aspect, thus making us believe that it is made of some material substance. At the macroscopic level this notion of substance is a useful approximation, but at the atomic level it no longer makes sense. Atoms consist of particles, and these particles are not made of any material stuff. When we observe them we never see any substance; what we see are dynamic pat-terns continually changing into one another – the continuous dance of energy . . . . At the subatomic level the interrelations and interactions between the parts of the whole are more fundamental than the parts themselves. There is motion but there are, ulti-mately, no moving objects; there is activity but there are no actors; there are no dancers, there is only the dance.[11]

This metaphor of the dance without the dancers has been widely used in the explication of the new physics. But it is a metaphor whose power to illuminate I would question. What is movement when there is nothing that moves, nothing that is the subject of motion? How is movement, which is not the movement of a substantival something, to be distinguished from a mathematical abstraction, a set of co-ordinates which plot a trajectory in abstract mathematical space? We can perhaps conceive of a pattern of 'disembodied' motion occurring in a field, where I do not use 'field' here in the physicist's sense, but only in the general sense of an arena. We conceive this on the model of a wave pattern occurring in a fluid medium. In this case the field need not be material, though it may be: it may be a liquid medium like water, or it may be a gas. But the field may also be substantival in a physical sense though non-material: it may be an ether, or it may be space itself. In any case, if the pattern of motion, which is in fact a pattern of disturbance in a field, is to be conceived as *real* motion, then the field itself must be real, concrete, substantival. If the field is merely an abstraction, then the pattern of motion which it manifests is abstract too – it does not belong to the real world.

There is in fact no way that substance, understood as that which can really, that is concretely, exist independently of any other thing, can be eliminated from the inventory of the world. Substance is built into the concept of a world: in order for a world to exist at all, it or its components must possess a concrete reality and be capable of existing independently of other things. And anything which is capable of existing concretely, independently of other things, qualifies as a substance. It is thus analytically guaranteed that a world – any world – must consist of at least one substance. Motion, as we have seen, does not qualify as substance – it cannot be conceived independently of some field of motion. Hence motion *per se* cannot constitute a world. But motion-in-a-(substantival)-field is capable of existing independently of any other thing, and hence may constitute a world. Strictly speaking it is the substantival field itself which is the substance, whether or not it is a subject of internal motion. Such a field, understood as a concrete though not necessarily material continuum, is thus sufficient to furnish a world.

The attempt to eliminate substance, in order to do justice to the fundamental status of process, system or motion is thus, I think, misconceived. A plenum ontology can in fact incorporate all the important features of the process view while still accommodating our intuitions concerning the substantivality – as opposed to the abstractness – of physical reality. The new view should, I think, accord equal ontological status to substance and process/action. These are dual aspects of reality, and are not independently comprehensible: process may be said, in the old vernacular, to 'inhere' in substance, and it is this embodiment which lends it concrete reality; but substance itself may be intrinsically dynamic, intrinsically in process, and in this case could not be understood independently of such dynamism. In the model which I am about to present I shall try to show how the concepts of substance and process are mutually informing. Motion, from the point of view of this model, is not so much a dance without dancers as a dance of ripples on the surface of a fluid: the ripples are real because the fluid is.

Certain of the fundamental principles of quantum mechanics then do point in the direction of a monistic kind of metaphysic. These are the principles which postulate a reality which is one, indivisible, holistic, and intrinsically dynamic. But physics contains a theory which answers the requirements of monism more fully without sacrificing realism and substance; moreover, in a broad quantitative way, this theory serves to explain the holism that is such a seminal feature of quantum mechanics.

The theory which provides these materials for a new monistic worldview is an extension of General Relativity Theory called geometrodynamics. Like Capra's favoured interpretations of quantum mechanics, the status of this theory within physics is controversial. The General Theory of Relativity (GTR) is experimentally and theoretically well-established, but the geometrodynamic extension of it has not so far been experimentally successful. However, it is the *ideas* of the theory that I wish to take up here, not any particular quantification of them. (Of course, the ideas of a theory are often inextricable from its mathematics, and are typically arrived at through the formalism. This is particularly true of quantum mechanics. But the qualitative outlines of geometrodynamics can, I think, be conveyed independently of the formidable mathematical structure of the theory.) Geometrodynamics (GMD) in fact expresses the vision which led Einstein to create GTR, a vision of a unified field theory which would explain the four basic fields recognized within physics – the gravitational, electromagnetic, strong and weak nuclear forces – as manifestations of a single, cosmic field. Although GMD, which achieves this synthesis theoretically, has not been experimentally verified, its basic principles stand as a viable conceptual blueprint for an ultimate physical theory, in the sense outlined in the Introductory Remarks.

It is as a metaphysic then that I wish here to examine GMD, rather than as a physics. The metaphysical archetype of substance monism finds perfect expression in GMD, and it is with the implications of this archetype that I am concerned. Almost all our thinking has to date taken place in the framework of substance pluralism. Even if physics in no way presently pointed in the direction of monism, it would, I believe, be worth exploring the implications of monistic premises. But physics does point in this direction, since its cosmology, at any rate, is avowedly monistic. It may not point *exclusively* in this direction, but the evidence is sufficient to warrant an investigation into monism. Let us call the view that we are about to examine the

Einsteinian metaphysic. There are, as we shall see, independent metaphysical grounds for accepting this view, so that even if it were not finally validated within physics for another century or two, we should still have reason to treat it seriously at present. And given its base in the well-established General Theory of Relativity, this metaphysic is certainly as viable, from the viewpoint of physics, as one built around the principles of quantum mechanics.

III THE PRINCIPLES OF GEOMETRODYNAMICS

Substance monism was introduced, in Chapter 1, to contrast with substance pluralism. Substance monism portrays reality in terms of a single, extended, universal substance, an indivisible continuum, the parts of which are logically interdependent, and conditioned by global principles. GMD rests on the monist archetype, for according to this theory spacetime is the 'stuff' of which the world is made, and the structure of spacetime is the world's physics. Space itself is intrinsically dynamic and mutable: locally it stretches, ripples and curves, and globally, it expands. Wave-like disturbances constitute electromagnetic and gravitational effects; highly curved, 'knotted-up' regions constitute matter. A given complex pattern of local curvature may be transmitted from point to point like a standing wave in a field. Energy is simply the curvature of spacetime. The parts of spacetime are logically interdependent, the properties of each determining and being determined by the rest. For this reason, spacetime is indivisible, though richly differentiated by reason of its variable curvature.

J. A. Wheeler, colleague of Einstein and founder of GMD, explained the outlines of GMD in the following terms.[12]

> Is spacetime only an arena within which fields and particles move about as 'physical' and 'foreign' entities? Or is the four-dimensional continuum all there is? Is curved empty geometry a kind of magic building material out of which everything in the physical world is made: (1) slow curvature in one region of space describes a gravitational field; (2) a rippled geometry with a different type of curvature somewhere else describes an electromagnetic field; (3) a knotted-up region of high curvature describes a concentration of charge and mass-energy that moves like a particle? Are fields and particles foreign entities immersed *in* geometry, or are they nothing *but* geometry?
>
> It would be difficult to name any issue more central to the plan of

physics than this: whether spacetime is only an arena, or whether it is everything.

The vision of Clifford and Einstein can be summarized in a single phrase, 'a geometro-dynamical universe': a world whose properties are described by geometry, and a geometry whose curvature changes with time – a dynamical geometry.[13]

The plenum concept which is central to GMD has always enjoyed an underground existence in western philosophy and physics. It appeared in strands of medieval thought, in the guise of the doctrine that Nature abhors a vacuum, and achieved its apotheosis (in a literal sense!) in the work of Spinoza, as we shall see below. According to Newton, space, though real in a metaphysical sense (it was not purely relational), was not physical: it was not a substantival medium capable of receiving and imparting physical effects. It was found necessary in the nineteenth century to augment this 'absolute' space of Newtonian physics with a substantival (though non-material) ether. The ether, which was conceived as completely filling space, was postulated as a medium for the transmission of electromagnetic effects. It was introduced, in other words, to provide a substantivalist rationalization for the notion of an electromagnetic field. No sooner had Einstein, in the early twentieth century, demonstrated the invalidity of the ether hypothesis via the Special Theory of Relativity, however, than he himself introduced, through GTR, the idea of a physically real, active spacetime.[14]

In order to grasp even the qualitative outlines of GMD then, it is necessary that we briefly examine the central ideas of GTR. GTR is a cosmological theory *par excellence*: it explains the relations of mass and energy, motion and momentum; it provides a theory of gravitation and inertia, space and time. It explains the evolutionary history of the large-scale structure of the universe. It incorporates the quantitative predictions of the Newtonian theory of gravitation as local approximations, but demonstrates the incorrectness of Newtonian predictions on the large, that is cosmological, scale.

GTR originated as a generalization of Einstein's Special Theory of Relativity. In Special Relativity (SR),[15] Einstein abolished Newtonian absolute space and absolute time: the spatial interval (distance) and temporal interval (time lapse) between two events, e_1 and e_2, is not fixed: it varies according to the reference frame in which it is measured. If A is an observer in uniform motion relative to observer B, and each measures the distance between e_1 and e_2, their measurements will not agree, unless they correct for the difference in their respective states of motion. The relativity of such measurements to the state of motion of the observer, or to the reference frame, had of course been recognized since the time of Galileo, but correction for it was routinely incorporated into calculations by specifying the absolute or true velocities of the observers in question. To specify the absolute velocities of observers in various states of uniform relative motion, it was necessary to specify an absolute rest frame. Newton had supposed that absolute space constitutes the true rest frame relative to which the absolute velocities of all observers could be determined. Einstein's innovation was to deny that such an absolute rest frame was identifiable: the state of motion of any given observer could be specified only relative to that of another. Motion – or inertial motion at any rate – was thereby irremediably relativized.

It followed then from the relativity of motion that simultaneity is not a fixed relation: events which occur simultaneously in my reference frame may not do so in yours if you are in uniform motion relative to me. There is thus no absolute spatial or temporal ordering of events within SR. This is what is meant by saying that in SR absolute space and absolute time are abolished. One consequence of the abolition of absolute space and time, or of absolute simultaneity, is that the instantaneous transmission of effects, whether by way of action at a distance or signals with infinite velocity, is no longer possible: a limiting velocity for physical signals had accordingly to be postulated. As the signal with the limiting velocity, Einstein plausibly nominated light. However, although absolute space and absolute time are abolished within SR, they are replaced by a new entity, absolute Minkowski spacetime: between any two events, the spacetime interval, which is a simple mathematical function of the spatial and temporal intervals, is invariant, which is to say, it is not frame-relative. The absoluteness of Minkowski spacetime in SR is noted less often than the relativization of Newtonian space and time therein.

The relativization of motion in SR applies only to inertial motion. Under the Lorentz transformation, the behaviour of particles is independent of the state of motion of the frame. It is accordingly impossible, from within a given inertial frame, to determine the state of motion of that frame. This is not so in the case of non-inertial frames. Accelerations are accompanied by inertial forces: the behaviour of particles is measurably affected by acceleration. The non-inertial motion of particles is therefore detectable independently of choice of reference frame. If some motions remain non-relativized, and independently detectable in this way, then evidently the nature of motion has not been fully explained in SR. Furthermore, the relativity of simultaneity and the limiting nature of the velocity of light in SR had invalidated Newton's conception of gravitation as an instantaneous action-at-a-distance force. For these reasons, Einstein was driven to push beyond the boundaries of SR.

The clue to the mystery of the physical significance of acceleration proved to be the clue to the mystery of gravitation as well. The clue was the Principle of Equivalence, which states that all 'test particles' move along the same trajectory under the action of gravity. Since the gravitational field does not affect different particles in different ways, it is not – locally, at any rate – unequivocally detectable. A certain effect is detectable, but because the effect is indiscriminate with respect to particle mass, it might as well be explained by an acceleration of the entire system of particles as by the action of a gravitational field: field and acceleration would have a locally equivalent effect on the trajectories of particles. Thus the Principle of Equivalence entails that the effects on a particle of a gravitational field are locally indistinguishable from the effects of an acceleration on the particle in question: gravitational forces and inertial forces due to acceleration are locally equivalent. In GTR Einstein explains this equivalence by postulating that motion in response to a gravitational field is just an acceleration: an acceleration caused not by the action of a force, but by the curvature of spacetime itself.[16]

In this way, Einstein identifies the gravitational field with a deformation of spacetime. The source of the gravitational field is any source of energy momentum, such as a massive body; in the case of massive bodies, mass curves the spacetime in which the body is embedded in rather the same kind of way that a brick stretches a rubber sheet on which it is placed. The trajectory of a force-free particle in flat, that is Minkowski, spacetime is that of a particle in inertial motion, but a force-free particle in curved spacetime follows the local geodesics, that is, it follows a curved path, so that its motion is non-uniform: it is accelerated. Another way of putting the point is to say that motion in a so-called 'gravitational field' is really the path of a force-free particle in a curved spacetime; it is non-uniform because the spacetime itself is not flat. The relativistic theory of gravitation is thus in effect a brilliant generalization of Newton's first law of motion effected via a radical revision of Newton's conception of space and time and hence of the underlying Newtonian metaphysic.

To the distinction between inertial and accelerated motion then, physical significance does indeed attach: it is the distinction between the trajectories of force-free particles in flat and curved spacetime respectively. Motion *per se* is thus relative in both SR and GTR, but the geometrical structure of spacetime is not. The most central conceptual innovation of GTR is this treatment of spacetime as a real, dynamic, physical entity, the geometrical structure of which provides the explanatory thrust of the theory.

The physical primacy of spacetime in GTR is reinforced in the relativist account of the evolution of the universe. On the standard model, GTR postulates that the whole universe has expanded from a point of infinite density. At this point the curvature of spacetime itself was infinite. From this initial singularity, space proceeded to expand, its global expansion somehow triggering perturbations or deformations of the local geometrical structure. This expansion entails that space is globally curved – finite but unbounded – its geometry reflecting in three dimensions that of the surface of an expanding sphere. The large-scale evolution of the universe is therefore to be discovered in the large-scale structure of spacetime.

The standard model of the evolution of the relativistic universe consists of three basic models which were proposed by Friedman in 1922.[17] The Friedman models rest on an assumption of the uniform distribution of matter throughout space. This assumption, together with the field equations of GTR, yields three basic graphs for the evolution of the universe. To understand these three models intuitively, we can adopt the rubber balloon analogy. Picture the universe as a balloon printed with uniformly distributed black dots. The black dots are galaxy clusters. As the balloon is blown up, that is, undergoes isotropic expansion, the distance between each pair of dots increases uniformly. From the viewpoint of any individual dot, the other dots would appear to be receding, as though the dot in question were located at the centre of the expansion. But this is not of course the case – there is no centre of the expansion, any more than there is a centre of the universe. The three possible ways in which the expansion may proceed are as follows.

(i) The density of matter is so low that the universe eventually escapes from its own self-gravitation and continues to expand indefinitely.

(ii) The density is sufficently high to slow the expansion down indefinitely but not to reverse it.

(iii) The density is so high that the expansion is eventually reversed: the universe suffers gravitational collapse, and contracts to its point of origin.

It is important to note in this connection that it is *space itself* which expands. Paul Davies makes this point explicit in *Space and Time in the Modern Universe*: 'the expansion of the universe is one of space itself, and must not be pictured as the migration of galaxies out into a pre-existing void.'[18] In its account of both cosmological evolution and of gravitation, then, GTR sets spacetime above the material particle as the central protagonist in cosmology: spacetime is not the passive arena of physical action, but is itself the principal actor. The theory has an overwhelming commitment to the substantivality of spacetime. Its entire explanatory thrust derives from this ontological hypothesis. To say, as philosophers such as Reichenbach and Grunbaum have said,[19] that GTR is consistent with a relationist as opposed to a substantivalist interpretation of spacetime, necessitates the reintroduction of forces and thereby cancels out the seminal theoretical innovation of GTR.[20] John C. Graves, whose account of GMD we shall shortly be examining, makes this point by saying that it is

> vitally important to recognize that this identification of space with matter and geometry with physics is the central conceptual feature of GTR. Such philosophers as Reichenbach and Grunbaum have misinterpreted the theory by attempting to keep them separate.[21]

A great deal of confusion has reigned on this question of the ontological status of space and time in GTR. One reason for this confusion is that Einstein himself was motivated by Mach's famous 'conjecture' in developing the theory. The nineteenth-century physicist had conjectured that the behaviour of a 'test particle' was to be explained in terms of the interaction between the particle and the rest of the mass of the universe, rather than in terms of local forces. To put the conjecture in context, we need to consider the problem that motivated it.[22] Newton had reasoned that, since accelerated motions are detectable in an absolute fashion, on account of the fact that they are attended by inertial forces, there must exist something absolutely at rest relative to which the test particles in question are accelerated. This 'rest frame' was, Newton believed, furnished by absolute space, where 'absolute space', as we have seen, was understood to be a space which exists in its own right but is logically independent of matter. What mode of attenuated, non-physical existence such a space was supposed to possess, Newton did not explain. Mach however denied the theoretical need for absolute space. He noted that the acceleration of test particles could be measured with respect to the distant, fixed stars. These stars in themselves furnished a rest frame. Moreover, Mach explained the results of Newton's famous bucket experiment – in which the surface of the water in a spinning bucket was seen to rotate with respect to the fixed stars – in terms of the action of the stars themselves on the surface of the water. In this way, Mach's principle involved not only the abolition of absolute space but also the appeal to holistic influence – to the effect of the rest of the universe on the trajectory of a test particle.

Einstein's well-known Machian sympathies have given rise to the impression that GTR subtends a relationist theory of spacetime. This impression is reinforced by the undoubted elimination, within Special Relativity, of absolute space and absolute time. What is less often noted in this connection however is the fact that absolute space and absolute time are abolished in Special Relativity only to be replaced by absolute (Minkowski) spacetime. The spacetime of Special Relativity is absolute in the sense that its intervals are fixed and determined, and it is logically independent of physical process. It is absolute, but not substantival. In GTR, in contrast, spacetime is not only absolute (non-relational), it is physically active: it acts on matter and is acted on by it. It is an evolving, internally differentiated physical entity. It is for this reason that it must be considered not only not relational, nor merely absolute, but substantival. The truly Machian aspect of GTR is not a relationist view of spacetime but the principle of global determinism: the universe as a whole does determine, or influence, the behaviour of its parts, just as Mach conjectured. It is not distant matter *simpliciter* which, in GTR, affects the trajectory of a test particle, but the global curvature of spacetime itself – which is partly constituted by the distribution of matter. The global curvature and closure of the universe predicted by GTR significantly affect the curvature values in local regions.

This idea of a dynamic, internally differentiated, substantival spacetime is taken, in GMD, to its natural metaphysical conclusion. GMD constitutes a true substance monism. The basic ideas of the theory were put forward – long before Einstein's name had ever been heard – in a fascinating paper called 'On the space theory of matter' (1876). The author, W. K. Clifford, was a student of Reimann. He announced the theory as one which asserted:

(1) That small portions of space *are* in fact of a nature analogous to little hills on a surface which is on average flat; namely, that the ordinary laws of geometry are not valid in them.

(2) That this property of being curved or distorted is continually being passed on from one portion of space to another after the manner of a wave.

(3) That this variation of the curvature of space is what really happens in that phenomenon which we call the motion of matter, whether ponderable or ethereal.

(4) That in the physical world nothing else takes place but this variation, subject (possibly) to the law of continuity.[23]

This simple statement of substance monism from the 1870s is echoed in the 1980s by those – few – commentators who are alive to the significance of the monistic implications of GTR. One such commentator, B. Gal-Or, who examines these implications in his *Cosmology, Physics and Philosophy*, arrives at geometrodynamical conclusions:

> from Newton we inherited the false idea that matter consists in static bits which exist and move in absolute space and absolute time; that energy is somehow something which acts upon objects, not something composing them; that gravitation is a 'single potential force', acting in perfectly 'flat' Euclidean space; that space is the 'stage' upon which physical processes are displayed to us during the 'flow of time', and that 'absolute', 'uniform' time and a 'universal now' exist. Einstein brought about the collapse of these archaic ideas . . . .
>
> Thus, no longer need we think in terms of an absolute separation between geometry, spacetime, matter, energy, momentum and gravitation . . . . Einstein's geometric theory of gravitation treats regions of space and time as governed by the curvature of spacetime geometry and the dynamic changes of this geometry is what many mean today by that old concept 'gravitation'. . . .
>
> Indeed, in the domain of the special and general theories of relativity, there is no a priori requirement to distinguish, fundamentally, between changes in geometrical properties of spacetime and changes in all other physical properties in nature. The whole world, or any part of it, can now be treated as a unified system composed of nothing but dynamically curved spacetime. . . .[24]

We are ready now to examine the central conceptual features of GMD in a little more detail. My account will follow that of J. C. Graves, whose above-mentioned book on GMD, *The Conceptual Foundations of Contemporary Relativity Theory*, offers the most philosophically sensitive account of GMD I have been able to find. Graves confirms our present observation concerning the monistic character of GMD. That he considers it a *substance* monism is clear from his comment that spacetime

> is not a passive arena, but the source and medium of all interactions, its parts both acting on and being acted upon by each other; and . . . spacetime is a unified whole, with global and topological as well as local characteristics. It is not a collection of things, but a single thing – the only thing that is really real. One could call it by such names as pure substance, or being as such.[25]

GMD is monistic in a dual sense, in that it postulates both the existence of only one kind of substance and the existence of a single substance numerically speaking: spacetime is the only kind of substance there is, and there is only one spacetime.

GMD is not only monistic however. It is holistic: the universe as a whole is not the mere sum of its parts. This shows up in the fact that the field equations are non-linear: we cannot take the sum of two effects to arrive at a total effect, nor break a total effect down into specifiable individual effects. The total effect of all the sources in the field cannot be analysed down to their individual contributions. Even the different aspects of the 'world-field' are logically interconnected – electromagnetism has gravitational effects on test particles, and gravitation has electromagnetic effects. The different fields are partially conceptually separable, but not ontologically so: they are distinct aspects of the curvature of spacetime. Moreover the other physical variables, such as mass and energy, momentum and stress, are not absolutes but are, likewise, aspects of curvature, and accordingly intertransformable.

One of the most important features of the holism of GMD is the fact that bodies are no longer precisely localizable, as they were within the framework of atomism. In other words, GMD furnishes a foundation for the principle of nonlocalizability/nonseparability/interconnectedness. 'GMD embodies the notion that a body is where it acts', says Graves.

> Insofar as the curvatures which it generates extend to the whole of spacetime, there is a sense in which each body or source is everywhere, and at the same time . . . . Since in this sense every object equally occupies the whole of space, we cannot establish identity or independence by reference to the region of space which that body, and that body alone, occupies.[26]

Holism is again apparent in the fact that the distinction between laws and initial and boundary conditions breaks down. The cosmological features of the universe – its closure and its expansion from an initial singular state – restrict the possible states of the universe at any given time, and hence the possible values of the initial and boundary conditions.

> Once again, we find an intimate connection between the local and the global features of the geometry. We cannot just make whatever local assumptions we see fit and later consider their global implications; the global conditions the local as well.[27]

The universe is, in short, a 'single, self-contained process, not one subject to external constraint'.[28]

Graves concludes his summary with a resounding statement of the philosophical significance of the GMD vision:

> It would be hard to underestimate the revolutionary and unprecedented character of physical theory based on monism. Since the dawn of modern science (and indeed long before) any attempts to understand the world had presupposed a plurality of independent things with definite properties of their own, and the possibility of understanding wholes through analysis into their parts. This presumption certainly is borne out by ordinary experience, and it has worked so well in previous science that it has become a well-established regulative principle. The principle has indeed affected the structure of our very language so completely that it is hard to find adequate expression for the new ideas of GTR. Because of this difficulty of breaking outside this framework, and the fact that any experimental tests and comparisons with classical theories have required a translation back to more familiar concepts, the true character of the theory has not been understood until recently, and then only slowly and with some difficulty.[29]

In respect of the non-linearity of its field equations, the intertransformability of its variables, the non-locality of its entities and the feedback nature of its laws, then, the GMD universe demonstrates its essentially holistic nature. In its intrinsic dynamism, too, it demonstrates the complementarity of substance and process within the GMD framework. It is noteworthy that the two broad principles in terms of which the quantum view may be characterized – those of nonlocality/interconnectedness and of intrinsic dynamism – also serve to characterize the GMD view. But what a different setting

GMD provides for those principles – it grounds them in, and explains them in terms of, a metaphysical archetype for which there are, as we shall see below, independent arguments. For from the viewpoint of GMD, quantum processes occur as local disturbances of spacetime, and, since spacetime is a paradigmatically holistic, indivisible substance (as we shall, again, have reason to see below), it follows with the greatest naturalness that quantum processes should exhibit interconnectedness. In the following two sections I shall examine (i) the power of GMD to explain both determinism and quantum holism, and (ii) the independent metaphysical justification for GMD. In the light of these arguments it might appear that quantum principles alone, unembedded in a wider substance ontology, are incapable of explaining the systemic and holistic nature of quantum reality; they might therefore be regarded as inadequate as the basis for a fully-fledged cosmology.

IV GEOMETRODYNAMICS AND HUME'S PROBLEM OF CAUSATION

In this section I propose to demonstrate the power of the GMD view of the world to explain, in metaphysical outline, both classical determinism and quantum holism. My purpose is to provide metaphysical (as opposed to empirical) vindication of the monistic alternative, by showing how the shift to the GMD framework may dissolve certain long-standing metaphysical problems in the philosophy of physics.

The problem of classical determinism, as first posed by the eighteenth-century sceptical philosopher David Hume, is as follows: why are there laws regulating the course of Nature at all? Why do events not occur arbitrarily, chaotically and unpredictably? Laws of Nature are formulated as universal statements, and universalization over an unrestricted and mainly unknown domain implies some assumption of necessity: laws, once discovered, are held to be necessary. But what kind of necessity holds them in place? Hume observed that necessity belongs to logic, not to Nature. To any given empirical state of affairs an alternative is always conceivable: such empirical states of affairs cannot be said to obtain necessarily. This holds true for states of affairs falling under causal laws, or laws of motion: whenever it is established that an event or object A is causally related to an event or object B it can nevertheless always be conceived that A could exist independently of B, and B of A. Violations of any causal connections we care to consider are always conceivable. So why do we expect the impact of the cue on the billiard ball to produce motion along a predetermined trajectory? We can perfectly well imagine ourselves striking the ball with great force yet the ball remaining stationary – even in the absence of adhesives or other impediments to motion. Whence then comes our confidence in the outcome of our action? This question of confidence may be extended to physical laws and inductive inferences in general: why, having once established a law of physics experimentally, do we expect it to hold universally? Hume voiced this doubt as follows.

> Nothing is more evident than that the human mind cannot form such an idea of two objects, as to conceive any connection betwixt them, or comprehend distinctly that power or efficacy by which they are united. Such a connection would amount to a demonstration, and wou'd imply the absolute impossibility for the one object not to follow, or to be conceiv'd not to follow, upon the other ... suppose two objects to be presented to us, of which the one is the cause and the other the effect; 'tis plain, that from the simple consideration of one, or both, these objects, we shall never perceive the tie, by which they are united, or be able certainly to pronounce, that there is a connection between them.[30]

There can be no necessary connections between, in Hume's phrase, 'distinct existences'. Cause and effect are distinct existences, that is they are independently conceivable. Therefore no necessary connections can be said to hold between them. All that the relation of cause to effect really amounts to, according to Hume, is one of contiguity and regular succession. Having once observed a number of instances of this relation, we come to associate, in our imagination, the corresponding effect with the cause in question. The supposed 'necessity' of the connection is thus purely psychological: we come, by habituation, to believe that object or event A must be associated with object or event B, but in reality their association is contingent. From an ontological point of view there is no justification for our assumption that the ball will respond to the cue in the usual way.

When Hume declares that necessary connections cannot hold between distinct existences, it is important to understand what he means by 'distinct existences'. The category of distinct existences clearly includes, for Hume, material bodies, but it also extends to stages of bodies, motions and events. He writes, for example, that 'the effect is totally different from the cause, and consequently can never be discovered in it. Motion in the second billiard ball is a quite distinct event from motion in the first; nor is there anything in the one to suggest the smallest hint of the other.'[31]

The criterion of distinct existence, for Hume, is just logical independence: if a thing can be conceived as existing independently of anything else, then it is a distinct existence. This of course strikes a familiar chord in the present context, since it is the very criterion that has here been used to identify substances. But use of this criterion did not induce us to classify events, motions or states of bodies as substances. This was because in the normal way of thinking, events and motions are seen as occurring to, or being undergone by, substances, while states are construed as states of substances. Events, motions and states, then, are defined within a substance framework, but cannot of themselves stand alone. They are not 'distinct existences'. This is not of course to say that two different events may not exist independently of each other: they will do so if they occur in distinct substances. It is clearly this that Hume has in mind when he speaks of the motion of one billiard ball being independent of that of another. But he cannot jump from this observation to the conclusion that events or states are themselves distinct existences. Indeed, even events or states located in the same substance may be distinct, in the sense of differentiable, without being logically independent: successive states of motion in a body may be distinguishable without being logically mutually independent. For in order for the state of a body at a given moment to qualify as a state of *motion*, the body must be in similar states at preceding or succeeding instants. Motion is in this sense inherently relational, and to identify a state or event as a motion is, logically speaking, to refer it to other states or events.

In the classical instances of the causal relationship however, Hume's proscription of necessary connection holds: when two billiard balls collide, the subsequent state of each is logically independent of that of the other. Whenever two or more substances are involved in a causal transaction, the outcome is logically contingent. But recognition of this logical truth raises an interesting possibility. Clarification of the notion of a distinct existence has revealed that events or states may be distinct without being distinct existences: provided they are located in a single substance they may be differentiable but logically interdependent. In other words, necessary connections may hold between them. Suppose now that, while deferring to Hume's principle that necessary connections cannot hold between distinct existences, that is substances, we deny that there are any distinct existences. Suppose we acknowledge the existence of just one

substance. The Humean problem immediately vanishes: this substance may be the subject of many events, motions or states which,
while distinct in the sense of differentiable, are nevertheless necessarily connected.

The switch to the GMD view of course constitutes just such a move:
distinct existences are abolished, but necessary connections may be
preserved. How does this work? If we think of change through time as
being ultimately analysable in terms of motion of various kinds, then
classical determinism, which prescribes the lawlikeness of change
through time, will ultimately be analysable in terms of the regularity –
the smoothness and continuity – of motion. J. L. Mackie makes this
point in *The Cement of the Universe*; he sees the heterogeneity of cause
and effect at the macro-level as being underpinned by a qualitative
and structural continuity and persistence at the micro-level.

> Qualitative or structural continuity or process, then, may well be
> something in the objects, over and above complex regularity,
> which provides some backing for the conditional and especially
> counterfactual statements that emerge in the analysis of our ordi-
> nary causal concept.[32]

The Humean question about the necessity of lawlikeness can then be
seen as the question why motion in general is smooth and continuous,
rather than arbitrary and discontinuous – chaotic. Atomism fails, as
we have seen, to answer this question, but GMD – and perhaps any
plenum ontology – can answer it. Of course, from within a plenum
framework, both the appearance of motion at the particle level, and
the appearance of particles themselves, as persisting, self-subsistent
entities, will be explained in terms of the continuous propagation of
states through the plenum (whether the plenum is conceived as field,
ether or spacetime itself). Whether it is standing waves in a field or
small areas of high local curvature ('knots') in space, which propagate, nothing of course really moves: it is the plenum itself which suffers
the continuous disturbance. Analogies are plentiful: a whirlpool may
appear to traverse a stretch of ocean. In reality it is the ocean itself
which is suffering a continuous disturbance – a disturbance which is
propagated continuously across its surface.

Now how does GMD underwrite the lawlikeness, the regularity, of
'motion'? How is the smoothness or continuity of such 'motion'
assured within its framework? Space, conceived as an indivisible
substance,[33] constitutes a perfectly elastic medium, analogous to
an ideal fluid. An impulse imparted to such a medium cannot be

contained in the neighbourhood of its source. It necessarily travels through the unresisting medium. The reason it does so is not the same as the reason that underlies Newton's first law of motion, *viz.* the mere lack of barriers to continued motion. A Newtonian particle can logically be conceived as standing still even in the absence of such barriers: its continued motion is not conceptually necessary. But a local deformation of a perfectly elastic medium is necessarily self-propagating: as each successive point in the medium curves, neighbouring points necessarily undergo corresponding curvatures, and in this way the geometrical disturbance is transmitted. Such a disturbance can no more be conceived as standing still than can a wave (discounting standing waves, which are complex intersections of waves).

Indeed, the fact that 'motion' in a plenum is necessarily continuous suggests that the primitive form of such 'motion' is wave-like. For in order to preserve its continuity, motion will have to pass from its point of origin to neighbouring points, that is to the set of points which describe a spherical shell about the origin. It will have in the same manner to pass to the next shell, and so on outward. Moreover, such expansion will presumably have to be isotropic, if we allow that the factor which predetermines the maximal rate of expansion for one direction will, given the uniformity and elasticity of the medium, be sufficient to determine the maximal rate of expansion for all directions. And given the absence of constraining or modifying factors embodied in the medium itself, there is no intrinsic factor preventing the realization of the maximal rate of expansion. What this suggests is, as I remarked, that the primitive form of motion in the plenum is *wave-like*.

The same property that may ensure that the basic form of motion in the plenum is wave-like may also ensure the conservation of motion. The self-propagating nature of geometrical disturbances within a plenum would seem to entail that such disturbances will continue to be 'carried over', or propagated, indefinitely, although as a motion becomes more and more dispersed it will tend to become less and less discernible. Nevertheless motion – or, in GTR terms, energy – would appear, in this sense, to be conserved.

In the framework of GMD then, classical determinism, with its insistence on the existence of spatio-temporal continuants and the orderly behaviour thereof, is explicated in terms of spacetime curvature, where such curvature can be seen necessarily to propagate smoothly and continuously: the orderly change-through-time that is manifested in the causal order is a function of the properties of this underlying pattern of curvature.

At the beginning of this section, however, I promised to explain not only the fact of classical determinism – of the lawlikeness of the causal order – but also the fact of quantum indeterminism – of the acausality of events in the quantum domain.

It may be the case that events at the quantum level are partially explainable in terms of diachronic disturbances propagating smoothly and continuously through space. But if they were wholly explainable in these terms, these processes would exhibit the same classical, that is causal, features as events at the macro-level. Evidently something more than the diachronic deformation of space is involved. To illustrate what this further factor could be, let us return to the rubber sheet example. I can send an impulse – a wave – through a rubber sheet just by holding it at one end and flapping it. The impulse takes time to travel from one end of the sheet to the other. The change that each point undergoes at a given moment is a result of the change undergone by a neighbouring point at the preceding moment. This is a locally induced, diachronic – 'causal' – form of change. Compare this with the case of change induced by my pinching up the opposite corners of the sheet simultaneously. The region lying between the two pinched up points will be affected at the very same time as the points themselves – the rubber will be stretched, and the curvature of the points lying within this region will reflect this stretching. The change in curvature observable at one of the points lying in this region will not be predictable from a reading of the curvature of neighbouring points at the moment preceding the change. This is a globally induced change, in which a whole range of adjoining 'effects' are brought about contemporaneously. It is a change in local conditions determined by topological factors. Another example of such a change is as follows. Suppose that B and C are points on our rubber sheet, and that C is the source of a disturbance which is transmitted in the marked direction (fig. 1a). So long as the sheet remains flat, the disturbance from C will not affect B. But now roll the sheet into a cylinder: the disturbance from C *will* now affect B, but this result could not have been predicted from a knowledge of local factors alone: the change in the state of B will have been induced partly by non-local *viz.* topological factors (fig. 1b).

From the viewpoint of GMD then, classical/causal changes are brought about by diachronic disturbances of space, and are locally determined, and hence predictable in terms of local factors. It would

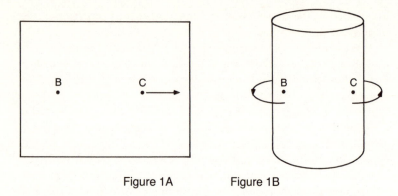

Figure 1A   Figure 1B

appear that quantum effects however might be brought about at least partly by changes in the topological structure of spacetime; in this case they could not be predicted in terms of local factors. Clearly the fluctuations in topological structure which might be responsible for quantum effects occur at the micro-level only; the topological structure of spacetime at the macro-level is relatively stable, and hence constitutes only an invariant background determinant of change. The stability of the topological structure of spacetime at the macro-level is a contingent feature of our environment. Environments which are subject to topological fluctuations at the macro-level are conceivable, and may be found in the vicinities of, say, black holes. In such environments acausal, non-locally induced changes would be as familiar to us at the macro-level as they are at the quantum level.

Why the structure of spacetime is in general more stable at the macro- than the micro-level is a question which GMD itself does not explain. The answer to this question will presumably eventually be supplied by quantum physics. But the GMD hypothesis that quantum phenomena are disturbances in the structure of spacetime does go some way towards explaining why change at the quantum level cannot be predicted from a knowledge of purely local factors. It does, in short, throw a broad beam on to the mystery of quantum indeterminacy.

V WHY SPACETIME?

The illumination of the intractable Humean problem of causation is not the only metaphysical insight which the GMD view provides. For this view furnishes the outlines of an answer to one question which both physics and philosophy have scarcely addressed, namely, *why* space and time, or spacetime? Why is spacetime the condition or framework of physical existence? Why are physical or substantival worlds invariably assumed to be spatio-temporal? Is there anything in the quality of space and of time that offers a clue to their metaphysical fundamentality? To ask why reality – substantival existence – should take *this* form, the form of spatio-temporal being, is indeed to approach the primordial question of metaphysics: why is there something rather than nothing?

Within the framework of substance pluralism there is no hint of an answer to this question; reality appears to be irremediably *ad hoc*. One philosopher – perhaps the only major one in modern times – who did seek to explain why substance takes the form it does was Spinoza. For Spinoza the task was to show that substance necessarily takes a form which is, under traditional definitions, identifiable with God. To this end he 'proves' that substance *must* have certain properties. Such 'proof' of course functions as an explanation as to *why* substance possesses those properties – if it can indeed be shown to possess them. It just so happens that the properties that Spinoza ascribes to substance are uncannily close to those that GMD ascribes to spacetime (and indeed to those that theologians have traditionally ascribed to God). Spinoza's argument thus adds further weight to the case for monism, by demonstrating the explanatory power of the monistic archetype: it explains why reality takes the form of a spacetime continuum.

For this reason I want to take a look at some of Spinoza's ideas. I do not intend fully to unravel the tortuous thread of his 'proofs' here, but only to give the general thrust of his argument. However, to accomplish even this, I need to engage with his text somewhat intensively, and it might be that readers who are not interested in Spinozist exegesis would prefer to turn to the last part of this section, where I offer a Spinoza-style argument of my own in support of the view that reality is plenic. This is a highly speculative exercise, which takes us far from the theoretical open-endedness of physics into the rarefied realms of *a priori* ratiocination. Unlike Spinoza, I do not construe such reasoning as capable of providing a 'proof' of a plenic ontology, but I believe that it can add further weight to the case for monism; it is in this un-Rationalistic spirit of modesty that I include the argument.

The whole of Spinoza's thought begins with the notion of substance. Part I of his major work, the *Ethics*, is an explication of this notion. Spinoza's conception of substance developed out of – and extended – the Cartesian concept. Descartes defined substance as that which exists by itself, but is known through its attribute(s). Thus matter is ontologically independent – depends on nothing else (apart from God) for its existence – but it is known through its attribute of extension. The Spinozist conception of substance extends this notion of independence: a substance is not only that which is 'in itself' but also that which is 'conceived through itself': 'By substance I mean that which is in itself and conceived through itself: in other words, that of which a conception can be formed independently of any other conception.'[34] The latter half of this definition is notoriously cryptic, and any interpretation calls for an examination of at least the whole of the first part of the *Ethics*. But Spinoza's basic objective was, I think, to provide a theory which, unlike the Cartesian theory, would enable us analytically to identify that which would qualify as ontologically independent. Descartes assumed that our acquaintance with bodies and minds was sufficient to enable us simply to see that they were ontologically independent in the required sense: we know substances (by acquaintance) through their attributes, and this acquaintance reveals to us that they are 'in themselves', that is, that they depend on nothing else for their existence.

Spinoza is more ambitious. He is interested in the riddle of existence *per se*: why does anything exist, and why, in particular, *this*? He wants to take Rationalism to the end of the line, and pushes on where most other philosophers had not thought to tread. He wants his theory to be rich enough to determine, in *a priori* fashion, what sorts of thing qualify as substances. This, I take it, is what he means by saying that substance is not only 'in itself', but 'conceived through itself': we can conceive in *a priori* fashion that which is in itself. Though we can *conceive* a substance in *a priori* fashion however, we can *perceive* it, or know it *a posteriori*, only through its attributes. This interpretation is consistent with the conjunction of Spinoza's definitions of substance and attribute. The definition of substance was, as we saw above, 'that which is in itself, and is conceived through itself: in other words, that of which a conception can be formed independently of any other conception'. In the very next definition, IV, Spinoza writes, 'By *attribute*, I mean that which the intellect perceives as constituting the essence of substance.'[35] I think that the phrase 'that which the intellect perceives as constituting the essence of substance' should not be taken as a circumlocution for 'that which constitutes the essence of substance'. If Spinoza had meant, simply, 'constitutes', why would he have written 'is perceived by the intellect to constitute'? The latter implies that the way a thing is perceived by the intellect is to be distinguished from the way a thing is in itself.[36] I want to take seriously, too, the fact that in Def. III substance is described as that which is *conceived* through itself, and in Def. IV, attribute is described as that which the intellect *perceives* as constituting the essence of substance. (Spinoza himself is careful to distinguish these two terms. Later in Part II, Explanation to Def. III, he writes, 'I say *conception* rather than perception, because the word perception seems to imply that the mind is passive in respect to the object; whereas conception seems to imply an activity of the mind.')

When Spinoza says 'perceives', then, I think that is exactly what he means: the intellect – by which I take him here to mean, simply, consciousness – *perceives* the attributes, and in so far as substance can be known empirically, which is to say, via perception, its essence is known through its attributes. But on this reading substance can also be known in *a priori* fashion, and this is what Spinoza means when he says that substance can be conceived through itself. To conceive substance 'through itself' is to construct certain analytic or *a priori* conditions which anything which qualifies as substance must satisfy. Or, to put it another way, substance is that which embodies certain formal, *a priori* knowable, qualities. It is these qualities which constitute the essence of substance as it is in itself, as opposed to how it is perceived. These formal qualities, which in themselves constitute the essence of substance, will then be expressed through the attributes: to the perceiver these formal qualities will be *exemplified* in the appearances, but the formal qualities will be identifiable independently of any of these manifestations.

To illustrate this interpretation of Spinoza's theory of substance, consider those attributes which Spinoza positively identifies as attributes of substance: thought and extension. Spinoza predicates extension of substance; by that I take him to mean that substance manifests itself to the perceiving intellect through extension, and this, I shall argue, implies that substance takes the empirical form of space. In light of the above interpretation then, space is not, in the framework of Spinoza's theory, knowable *a priori*. In this respect Spinoza's theory differs from Kantian theories according to which space is an 'inner sense', or, as Kant says of space and time together, 'forms of perception, belonging to the subjective constitution of our own mind, apart from which they cannot be predicated of anything what ever'.[37] For Spinoza, space is real – substance really is extended substance. Space is not merely a feature of 'transcendental psychology' – it is one of the aspects, or faces, through which substance reveals itself to us. The truths of Euclidean geometry may be *a priori* verifiable by us if they are understood purely formally or abstractly. But to understand the Euclidean system as a set of propositions concerning the structure of (physical) space, we have to have learned through experience the meaning of its primitive terms, *viz.* point and line, and hence the meaning of extension. (To the objection that a point is an ideal, not an empirical, object, it may be replied that a point is an idealization of an empirical object, and hence the notion of a point is apprehended partly *a posteriori*.) If our knowledge of points and lines is *a posteriori*, then we cannot be said to conceive space 'through itself'. Space therefore cannot be identical with the essence of substance as it is in itself, though, as I shall argue, it expresses or embodies the formal qualities which do constitute the essence of substance.

A similar argument may be mounted in relation to thought considered as an attribute of substance. The mind of course knows itself immediately, and in that sense it can apprehend itself independently of experience of the external world. But this is not, I think, the sort of *a priori* knowledge that Spinoza has in mind in speaking about conceptions which can be formed independently of any other conceptions. It is not *analytic* that reality or substance should express itself through mind. A non-selfconscious mind may be capable of apprehending the truths of logic and other analytic truths; it may be capable of discerning the formal qualities which necessarily constitute the essence of substance; but without having experienced thought consciously, it will not be able to say that the essence of substance will be expressed through the attribute of thought. It does not know what thought is, and cannot prefigure it for itself working only from analytic premises. After it has consciously experienced thought, however, that is, after it has become self conscious, it may recognize that thought is the kind of property which satisfies the formal, analytic conditions which characterise the essence of substance. In this sense, then, thought, though known immediately, is not conceived 'through itself', or *a priori*. It has to be experienced before it can be known. It cannot therefore be identified as the essence of substance, though it may be such as to exemplify the formal qualities which do constitute that essence.

What then are these formal or abstract qualities invoked by Spinoza in his construction of an *a priori* and analytic conception of substance? All that Spinoza has to build on, in constructing this concept, is the definition of substance as that which is ontologically independent. That is to say, Spinoza's task is to conceive substance through itself; this part of the definition of substance is thus clearly of no help in forming a conception of the essence of substance. All that remains in that definition, then, is the specification that substance exists 'in itself'. However, it should also be noted that when Spinoza speaks of substance, he means the substance of which the real or concrete world is made. 'Concrete' here does not imply 'material': a concrete world is an actual world, and as such it may be constituted of mind, or spirits, or ether, or space, or matter. Concreteness is to be understood as standing in contrast to abstractness: abstract entities, such as propositions, and numbers, etc., could not qualify as substances for Spinoza. They are not part of the furniture of an actual world. Despite certain esoteric controversies in the philosophy of modal logic,[38] I shall adhere to this Spinozist assumption in all subsequent discussions of substance.

Using only this minimal definition of substance, together with the Principle of Sufficient Reason – which is tantamount to a principle that for any given fact about the actual world an explanation is always possible – Spinoza seeks rigorously to establish the following theses in Part I of the *Ethics*. The first thesis is that substance has *necessary existence*:

Prop. VII.	Existence belongs to the nature of substance.
Proof	Substance cannot be produced by anything external (Corollary, Prop. VI), it must, therefore, be its own cause – that is, its essence necessarily involves existence, or existence belongs to its nature.[39]

The second thesis is that substance is '*absolutely infinite*', that is it has an infinite number of attributes, each of which is infinite after its kind:

Prop. XI.	God, or substance, consisting of infinite attributes, each of which expresses eternal and infinite essentiality, necessarily exists.[40]

The third thesis is that only this substance exists, that is, that this substance is *One*:

Prop. XIV.	Besides God no substance can be granted or conceived.[41]

Lastly, the one and only substance is not only self-realizing and infinite, but *indivisible*:

Prop. XII.   No attribute of substance can be conceived
                from which it would follow that substance can
                be divided.

Prop. XIII.   Substance absolutely infinite is indivisible.[42]

In short, Spinoza argues that anything which satisfies the definition of substance will necessarily exhibit certain formal properties, *viz.* self-realizability, infinitude, unity and indivisibility. These properties together anticipate a property which Spinoza himself does not explicitly invoke (but which Leibniz does), namely the property of *plenitude*.

Since Spinoza never makes it explicit that he is, in Part I, tackling the job of 'conceiving substance through itself', that is, putting together an abstract conception of substance derived deductively from the definition of substance, commentators have in general overlooked the fact that he ascribes these perfectly definite properties to substance in addition to ascribing the explicit attributes to it. They have assumed that substance is to be characterized exclusively in terms of the attributes, and hence that these constitute the essence of substance. But if this were the case, what would the status of these other, abstract properties be: they would not constitute the essence of substance, but nor could they be seen as contingent to substance. In any case, Spinoza himself quite explicitly describes these properties as 'properties of substance': in the first note to Prop. X in Part II, he says, 'the proposition is evident from the other properties of substance – namely, that substance is in its nature infinite, immutable, indivisible, etc.'[43]

A rich, analytic account of the essence of substance, then, is constructed by Spinoza. Substance is whatever instantiates these essential – abstract – properties. These abstract properties themselves will be 'expressed' through the attributes of substance. This 'expression' idiom is prevalent throughout the *Ethics*; the thesis that the attributes express (rather than constitute) the essence of substance is explicit in passages such as 'By *God*, I mean a being absolutely infinite – that is, a substance consisting in infinite attributes, of which each expresses eternal and infinite essentiality.'[44] Also 'Thought, therefore, is one of the infinite attributes of God, which expresses God's eternal and infinite essence.'[45] The attributes then, according to this interpretation, can only be known *a posteriori*, through acquaintance. Spinoza posits attributes in addition to those with which we are acquainted, but we cannot form any conception of these others beyond the requirement that they satisfy the formal conditions.

The attributes thus are as they are because they express the logically predetermined nature of substance: the nature of substance is not to be inferred from them. It is in this sense that substance is conceived through itself – it is conceptually independent of the attributes, though it is known *a posteriori* through them.

Thought and extension then are the two attributes of substance to which we have empirical access. Spinoza often alludes to 'extended substance' in order to refer to substance under the attribute of extension. Extended substance will have to exhibit unity, indivisibility and infinity. Since matter does not exhibit these qualities, and since Euclidean space does, we are forced, I think, to the conclusion that by 'extended substance' Spinoza implicitly refers to space.

Individual bodies are, for Spinoza, merely modes or modifications of extended substance. In light of the above interpretation, this entails that they are modes or modifications of space. How could space be locally modified in such a way as to give rise to the appearance of individual bodies? That the appearance of individuality is merely an appearance is clear if it is accepted that bodies are continuous with space, which is itself indivisible. Bodies are not discrete chunks of substance, but are distinguished from one another (and from the space with which they are continuous) only by their qualitative state – or, specifically, as Spinoza says, by their state of motion: 'Bodies are distinguished from one other in respect of motion and rest, quickness and slowness, and not in respect of substance.'[46] This may be understood in geometrodynamical terms, as suggesting that bodies are merely local disturbances in the 'fabric' of space – wave-knots, or complex dynamic configurations in the substantival medium.

The point of this detailed interpretation of Spinoza's theory of substance is to illustrate the way in which Spinoza arrived, in purely Rationalist fashion, at a plenic view of reality. He argued on purely metaphysical grounds that reality had to take plenic form: the plenum is the embodiment of plenitude, which is the analytic essence of substance. His work suggests, too, that the empirical form which answers to the plenum blueprint is space. If his arguments were accepted, they would constitute an explanation for the fact that reality takes a spatial form. This deep explanatory power would in turn argue in favour of his monistic premises.

I have not here offered Spinoza's argument for the thesis that plenitude constitutes the essence of substance, for the reason that it never appears in a unified and explicit form. There are separate arguments for the separate properties which make up the composite property of plenitude. I can however offer a Spinoza-*style* argument for this thesis, using only the tools that Spinoza used, namely *a priori* reasoning, the Principle of Sufficient Reason, and Spinoza's own definition of substance. The role of the Principle of Plenitude, as it emerges from this argument, will be important in our later discussion of the way in which telos is embodied in the universe.

We begin then by taking over the Spinozist definition of substance as that which is in itself and conceived through itself, where this is understood as that which is ontologically independent and subject to certain *a priori* conditions which are antecedent to – and partly determine – its empirical manifestations. We take as primitive the adjectival notion of substantivality or concreteness – in other words, we take over the assumption, mentioned earlier, that substance is the stuff of which any real or concrete world is made. We also avail ourselves of the Principle of Sufficient Reason (PSR), not in the strong form apparently invoked by Spinoza,[47] but in the intuitive form according to which a sufficient reason, or explanation, is required for its being the case that some actual state of affairs obtains. I do not intend to offer an *a priori* justification for assuming this principle here, but will trust on the one hand to its intuitiveness, and on the other to the fact that it constitutes the methodological *sine qua non* of science: it is a principle which any theoretical enterprise would be hard pressed to do without.

If we have acquired a primitive understanding of substantivality through our own experience of an actual substantival reality, then there is one synthetic fact of which we may be certain, namely the fact of actual concrete existence, or substantivality, *per se*: we know empirically that something substantival actually exists. Since it is analytic that only that which is substantival may be actual, it follows that the fact that something substantival actually exists is equivalent to the bare fact of actuality *per se*. It may now be asked of this bare fact of actuality *per se*, whether it is open to PSR? Is it a 'state of affairs' that calls for explanation? I cannot see why it should not be so regarded. The fact that there is something – whatever it may be – rather than nothing, seems pre-eminently to call for explanation. But two types of explanation might be offered here. It might be argued that there is something rather than nothing because there is some particular thing – some substance – which, on account of its peculiar properties, is self-actualizing, and therefore necessarily actually exists. This kind of explanation would discover the sufficient reason for actuality *per se* in the properties of a particular thing. Alternatively, it might be argued that the reason why there is something rather than nothing is con-nected with the nature of actuality itself – that actuality necessarily manifests or expresses itself, or that, *qua* mode, it necessarily occurs.

Since, in the present context, we do not wish to beg any questions about what it is that actually exists, but want to take it as given only that something does so, the question, 'why is there something rather than nothing?' should here be understood in the second sense, and accordingly provided by PSR with an answer of the second kind. I shall therefore assume here that, by adhering to PSR, we can infer from the given fact that some unspecified substantival thing actually exists that there is in principle a sufficient reason for this bare fact of actuality. We need not, for present purposes, be apprised of the reason in question, but only assured that it exists.

Assuming then that such a reason exists for the fact of actuality *per se*, which is to say, assuming that there is a sufficient reason for the actual *existence* of something – any thing, whatever it might be – then this would also appear to be a sufficient reason for the existence of *every* logically possible thing. For if it is the fact of actual *existence* that we are explaining, then the explanation will not distinguish between the actual existence of *this* thing and the actual existence of *that* thing. The fact of actual existence, the fact that a thing is actual, as opposed to merely abstract, is the same whatever the thing in question happens to be. A sufficient reason for the fact of actual existence in the case of one particular thing, then, will be a sufficient reason for the fact of actual existence in the case of any and indeed every thing with which it is logically compossible. A sufficient reason for the sheer fact of the actuality of substantivality then appears to entail a sufficient reason for unconstrained actual substantivality. And since sufficient reason for X ensures that X obtains, it follows from the present argument that, in the actual world, substantival existence is unconstrained. In other words, according to this argument, the actual world must exhibit quantitative plenitude. For *external* constraints can certainly not be imposed to mitigate the maximizing effect of the sufficient reason for actual existence *per se*: such constraints would have them-selves to be actual, and therefore would not qualify as external to substantival actuality. Nor is there anything self-contradictory in the notion of actuality itself that would entail the operation of internal or logical constraints on actual existence. It would thus appear to follow that actual existence is subject to no quantitative limits. This con-clusion in itself furnishes a logical – not quantitative – constraint on actual existence: the actual world must be the *fullest* possible world.

The fullness here ascribed to the actual world is not a maximal *qualitative* plenitude, or plenitude of forms, but a plenitude of quantity – a maximization of the sheer amount of concrete or substantival existence, abstracted from the forms which this existence assumes.

One objection to this argument is that it assumes that '(actual) existence is a predicate'. Such an assumption is generally regarded as a sin in itself, but it is compounded in the present context by the fact that, if (actual) existence is a property, then the same argument which has here been used to derive a plenitude of existence may be used to derive a plenitude of any property whatever. The property of redness, for example, is one of which instances are known empirically to exist; by the above reasoning it could be shown that since there must exist a sufficient reason for the fact of redness *per se*, and since a sufficient reason for the fact of redness *per se* is a sufficient reason for the presence of redness in this thing and that and any other thing, it follows that everything must be red. Is this not a *reductio ad absurdum* of the argument to plenitude?

I think not. When we ask the question, why is this thing red, or why is there redness at all, the kind of answer we are seeking is an empirical one, preferably a causal explanation, but at the very least an explanation in terms of the compatibility of redness – whether in a given particular, or in general – with other particulars or properties present in the world. These empirical and causal factors *explain*, but they also *constrain*: they indicate the place to be occupied by redness in the jigsaw of the already pieced-together world. Clearly the explanation for the fact of existence *per se* would not be of this order – it would explain the fact of existence not in terms of particulars and properties, but in transcendental terms. An explanation of this order would not limit the scope of existence in the process of explaining it. The argument to plenitude then cannot, I think, be generalized to ordinary empirical predicates.

A further objection that might be brought against the argument to plenitude is as follows: substantivality and actuality are modal rather than ordinary concepts, and as such they fall into the same category as the concept of abstractness. Hence if the argument to plenitude works for substances, it must also work for abstract entities. Such an argument must demonstrate the necessity of a plenitude of abstract existence.

I think this conclusion is true, if realism with respect to abstract entities is granted. A plenitude of abstract existence cannot be understood in the same way as a plenitude of substance, however: there is no scope for *quantitative* plenitude in the abstract domain. Abstract entities are non-duplicatable; there is just one of each kind. A plenitude of abstracta, then, will consist in a manifold of all possible abstract entities. In other words, all possible abstract entities will achieve existence, *in abstracto*. But there is nothing objectionable or far-fetched in this; it is exactly what Platonists already believe.

The argument to plenitude, as it has been developed here, is not, as has already been pointed out, an argument to qualitative plenitude, to a plenitude of forms, or to a 'great chain of being'. It is evident that the totality of possible forms does not constitute a co-instantiable set. Plenitude in a quantitative sense however is achievable; the sheer quantity of existence can be maximized without logical difficulty. This is accordingly how the requirement of plenitude may be understood in the present context.

Returning now to our original argument, let us consider what kind of ontology is logically prescribed by this requirement of plenitude. Of the two broad ontologies that we have here defined, *viz.* substance pluralism and substance monism, which is better adapted to realize the Principle of Plenitude? In the pluralist world the principle would be satisfied if all numerically possible individuals were actualised. In other words, the fullest world, from a pluralist point of view, would be a sardine-tin world, into which individuals were packed as tightly as possible. In monistic worlds, in contrast, the Principle of Plenitude would be satisfied if the single world-substance took the form of a plenum.

The quantitative possibilities of existence afforded by the monistic ontology can in fact be shown to be greater than those afforded by the pluralist one. For however individuals were multiplied, an ontology of discrete individuals would fail to match the fullness of a plenum. Their very discreteness, the very specificity of the forms they embody, imply limitation. Where such discreteness and limitation are, there are gaps. The ontology which leaves no gaps, no 'spaces between', and which accordingly achieves maximal fullness, is simply the ontology of the plenum. Hence the monistic ontology seems best to satisfy the requirement of plenitude.

I have already enumerated the formal properties which I take together to make up the property of plenitude in Spinoza's system. They are:

Unity: to be a plenum is to be one, a single substance.
Continuity: a plenum is a continuum, in the sense that it harbours no

discontinuities – no gaps or edges – since where such gaps are present, fullness is not achieved.

Indivisibility: a plenum is indivisible because divisibility implies the capacity of the medium in question to harbour discontinuities – the kind of discontinuity that is involved when a part becomes detached from the whole. A plenum thus does not consist of parts which are themselves capable of becoming detached and existing independently.

Unboundedness: boundaries indicate the presence of limitations. A traveller in a bounded medium would in due course arrive at an edge – her movement would be obstructed. In an unbounded medium, in contrast, her movement could continue indefinitely, unimpeded. (Infinitude rather than unboundedness was included in the list of formal properties of Spinoza's substance, but my reasons for substituting unboundedness for infinitude in the present definition will become clear.)

How would an entity satisfying the requirement of plenitude be empirically manifested? We know that a pluralist ontology may be empirically manifested by way of a set of discrete material bodies or particles. But the plenum obviously does not take the form of a *material* continuum. The only empirically identifiable entities which satisfy the conditions for plenitude are space and time, or, since these can be united in a single manifold, spacetime. Physical spacetime is a continuous, indivisible and unbounded unity. The requirement of plenitude seems naturally to direct us to the conclusion that substance takes the form of spacetime; spacetime is thus, according to this argument, necessarily substantival; 'nonsubstantival spacetime', is, from this viewpoint, a *contradictio in adjecto*.

This conclusion has a double significance. For I have tried to show, by means of purely *a priori* argument, *why* substance takes the form of spacetime, but also, *a fortiori*, *that* substance takes this form. If the argument is right it resolves, at one stroke, the long-standing dispute between the relationists and the substantivalists with respect to the status of spacetime. It achieves this by suspending the usual assumption of substance pluralism, and instead arguing directly from the concept of substance.

This result, together with the result that we obtained in relation to the Humean problem, suggests that certain of the major and seemingly irresolvable problems of metaphysics are in fact only problems *for a particular metaphysic*. The existence of such 'anomalies', in the

Kuhnian sense, might have alerted us, long ago, to the need for a 'paradigm switch', but the in-place paradigm was so deeply submerged, so thoroughly identified by us with the structure of thought *per se*, that it was in general not recognized as a paradigm, as one model amongst others, open to revision or replacement.

I have argued that Spinoza arrived at the conclusion that substance necessarily takes the form of space. But Spinoza's notion of time is relatively *ad hoc*. He seems to have felt that the being of time is more contingent than that of space, and that substance is, in essence, outside time: existence in itself is eternal, that is non-temporal. 'By eternity, I mean existence itself, insofar as it is conceived necessarily to follow solely from the definition of that which is eternal' (Part I, Def. VIII). And in the Explanation to this Definition, he writes, 'Existence of this kind is conceived as an eternal truth, like the essence of a thing, and therefore cannot be explained by means of continuance or time....'[48]

On my own interpretation of Spinoza's theory of substance, space is not in any case of the essence of substance, but is rather merely an appearance, a manifestation of that intrinsically non-empirical essence. But Spinoza seems to have felt that time is non-essential in an even stronger sense – that it is not even a real manifestation of the essence of substance. The material world would be perceived by the perfect intellect *sub specie aeternitatis*. Had Spinoza not harboured this preconception concerning the nature of time – and a preconception is what it is, for it does not , I think, follow from his argument – he might have recognized that time is itself an extension. Time exhibits unity, indivisibility and infinitude – and hence is as much a manifestation of the essence of substance under the attribute of extension as space is. Had he recognized that substance takes the form of spacetime rather than of space alone, he would have paved the way for a *dynamic* theory of substance. As it was, motion was introduced into the essentially static plenum in a thoroughly *ad hoc* and contingent manner – simply by axiom in Part II of the *Ethics*.

If the time component of spacetime is admitted along with the space component, and substantival existence is accordingly understood in terms of becoming rather than of timeless being, then it follows that plenitude should be understood as the tendency of the world-substance to *become* full, to *seek* fullness. Subject to absolutely no constraints on its actualization, space, on this view, comes into being and unfolds in time. Since there is nothing to impede its actualization in any direction, the Principle of Sufficient Reason suggests that it will spread out smoothly and continuously in all directions: it will undergo an isotropic expansion. The cosmological model which reflects this metaphysic is of course that of an expanding spherical three-space – the standard model for the General Theory of Relativity. Current astrophysical evidence suggests that the expansion will then be succeeded by contraction and collapse. This evidence points, in other words, to the third of the three Friedman models which we examined in Section III. The metaphysical argument which has been developed in this section is not sufficiently powerful to choose between the model of indefinite expansion and that of collapse or oscillation; it does not predict the specific effect of local curvature on global curvature. It suffices only to show that the Principle of Plenitude, together with the given definition of substance, implies that reality takes the form of dynamic spacetime, a spherical, finite but unbounded space that expands in time. But this in itself is no mean feat for *a priori* metaphysics.

These metaphysical arguments, while having suggested that spacetime must be globally curved, have not thrown any light on why this global curvature gives rise to variable local curvature, and hence to the phenomenal world of matter in motion. Physics is presumably needed to explain this step in the development of the GMD view – perhaps by demonstrating how a transition from infinite to finite curvature must be accompanied by intense local turbulence and disturbance.

Our Spinoza-style defence of at least certain salient aspects of the geometrodynamic view of the world hopefully demonstrates that this view embodies significant metaphysical insight. We tend to regard the Principle of Plenitude as a quaint relic of a pre-scientific era of thought. But we discover how quickly the notion of plenitude springs to life again the moment we begin to consider those metaphysical questions which Newtonianism removed from the philosophical agenda.

Chapter 3

System and substance: alternative principles of individuation

I SYSTEM AND SUBSTANCE

Twentieth-century humanity finds itself then, if Einstein's vision is in outline correct, not standing on the brink of an infinite abyss of whirling atoms, but rather eddying in an all-pervasive medium, a medium analogous to a fluid, in which the currents and waves are 'forces' and the vortices are 'matter'. We ourselves are complex ripples propagating in its depths. Substantivally speaking we are identical with the universe: it is into *its* substance that the pattern that is *our* signature is written.

But what is the status of our apparent individuality from this viewpoint? Are individuals really real, or does individuality belong exclusively to the realm of appearances, with no basis in ontology? What principle of individuation, if any, does GMD prescribe?

This question is fundamental to the articulation of GMD as a metaphysic, for a metaphysic is partly constituted by the principle of individuation which informs it. In the framework of Newtonian atomism, things were individuated in accordance with the substance criterion: true individuals were conceived as substances, where, as we have seen, substances were understood to be ontologically auton- omous entities, their identities logically mutually independent. The criterion of identity for substances was spatio-temporal: an entity qualified as a substance only if it was demarcated in space and time, enclosed within a physical boundary, discrete from all other physical things. Substances were considered to be simple or compounded out of other, constituent substances. A simple substance was one which could not be divided into parts which would themselves qualify as substances. Newtonian physics, as we saw in Chapter 1, took over the classical notion of atomism, according to which the simple substances that collectively constitute the world are small, individual parcels of matter called atoms. Atoms stand in causal relations to one another, but these relations are logically contingent, imposed from without; the atoms themselves could exist independently of such relations. Relatedness does not, in other words, belong to their essence; logically speaking, the entire universe could consist of a single atom, and its uniqueness would make no difference to its identity.

Not only relatedness, but motion, is an extrinsic feature of the manifold of atoms: motion is, as we have seen, introduced into this manifold via some external force or source of agency. This lack of intrinsic dynamism is one of the hallmarks of the mechanism which characterized the Newtonian worldview: atoms in themselves are inert, static, passive. Substance and being are logically primary in this scheme of things; motion, change, process, unfolding or becoming-in-time are secondary and *ad hoc*, depending on extra-physical devices such as the First Cause or the Unmoved Mover for their appearance on the scene. Complex substances, including macro-objects, are construed as aggregates of the simple, indivisible atoms. The nature of such an object may be exhaustively understood in terms of the intrinsic nature of the unit or simple substances which constitute it, and their arrangement in space and time. Objects are thus 'built' out of atoms, in much the same way as houses are built by us out of bricks. This anthropomorphic building brick model is central to the worldview of classical physics: the world must, logically speaking, have been built from the ground up, the artefact of a behind-the-scenes bricklayer. It must accordingly be explained and understood in like manner, in terms of units and layers (theoretical levels), its identity a function of the arrangement of its parts.

Motion, change and process are conceived, from this point of view, as *happening* to substance. Substance is logically prior in the order of reality because process may be analysed as a series of states of a substance, but substance cannot, from this viewpoint, be construed as a series of phases of a process. In similar fashion, substance is portrayed in the pluralist tradition as logically prior to relation, since substances may be conceived independently of relations, but relations may not be conceived as holding in mid air, so to speak, independently of their relata, the substances which constitute the terms of the relation.

In the wake of the transition from Newtonian to post-Newtonian physics however, the old view of the world as made up of an aggregate of discrete, logically mutually independent individuals is, as we have seen, no longer tenable. Looking at reality from the Einsteinian viewpoint, the physical substrate is now seen to be a dynamic continuum – a spacetime manifold of variable local curvature. Material bodies no longer possess an absolute substantival identity, but are rather reducible to areas of high local curvature in spacetime. If individuals are to retain any objective status within the domain of concrete reality, a new criterion of individuality will have to be found. For according to the old criterion, discreteness and unity were functions of the divisibility and separability of substance: a thing qualified as a discrete unity if it was a separate chunk of substance. On the new view, substance is a fluid continuum which cannot be carved up into separate chunks. Therefore discreteness and unity, if they are to have any status from this viewpoint, must be functions of something other than mere substance. They must, in fact, be functions of form, pattern, organization. But what kind of form, pattern or organization is constitutive of true unity, true 'discreteness'? A rock is a stable geometrical configuration within space, so its identity, in so far as it has one from the new point of view, is a function of form. But the true individuality of the rock has vanished with the substance criterion of individuality; the rock is identifiable, but it is not, ontologically speaking, a true unity, a truly discrete entity. If true individuality is to be retained in the new scheme of things, it must be a function of a very special kind of form. One such alternative criterion of individuality is implicit in General Systems Theory. This is a theory which has flourished in the philosophical gap left by the perceived demise of a substance metaphysics: if the individuals with which we epistemically populate our world are not substances, what are they? The answer furnished by GST is, of course, that they are systems. But what is a system? How is a system to be distinguished from something which is merely aggregatively constituted?

According to Stafford Beer, one of the founders of cybernetics – the theory of engineering systems – a system is any cohesive collection of items that are dynamically related.[1] Yet this is scarcely illuminating, since on our old mechanistic model material objects like rocks are composed of items – atoms – which are both cohesively and dynamically related, in the sense that they are chemically bonded together. Yet the dynamic relations which hold between the individual atoms are extrinsic, contingent, causal relations, which in no way inform the identity of the atoms themselves. On the old mechanistic model, then, a rock is a mere aggregate, the sum of its constituent atoms together

with certain extrinsic laws of physics. A more searching account of the
nature of systems is clearly required.

In an earlier adumbration of cybernetics than that of Beer, J. C.
Smuts offers the following description:

> Taking a plant or animal as a type of whole, we notice the funda-
> mental holistic character as a unity of parts which is so close and
> intense as to be more than a sum of its parts; which not only gives a
> particular conformation or structure to the parts, but so relates
> and determines them in their synthesis that their functions are
> altered; the synthesis affects and determines the parts so that they
> function toward the 'whole'; and the whole and the parts therefore
> reciprocally influence and determine each other and appear more
> or less to merge their individual characters.[2]

On this account the nature of the parts is not independent of the
nature of the whole: parts and whole logically codetermine each
other. This holism is the broadest characteristic which can be used to
distinguish systemic from aggregative unities. In more recent times,
Gregory Bateson, following Ross Ashby, encapsulated a more specific
aspect of the notion of a system when he said of biological systems that
they are

> describable in terms of interlinked variables such that for any
> given variable there is an upper and a lower threshold of tolerance
> beyond which discomfort, pathology and ultimately death must
> occur. Within these limits, the variable can move (and is moved) in
> order to achieve adaptation.[3]

This definition brings out the flexibility of (organic) systems, their
ability to perform their functions under variable internal and external
conditions; but it also brings out their capacity to maintain a steady
state, that is a state that is subject to only minor though continuous
fluctuations. This stability is a dynamic stability: the system is
capable of maintaining its structure over a long period of time by
means of a constant exchange of energy with the environment, but
this exchange places the system in a permanent state of disequilibrium. This disequilibrium is confined within limits, and it is the
fluctuation within fixed limits which provides the flexibility mentioned above, and thus the margin for adaptation: the system has the
capacity to exist within a range of environmental conditions. The
disequilibrium moreover leaves energy available for the work the
system must do in maintaining itself.

While Bateson's account of the nature of systems emphasizes the notion of the steady state, it does not bring out the peculiar fashion in which such stability is typically maintained, namely via feedback loops. In a feedback loop, a given state of the system reacts on itself to produce a further effect. That is to say, it is the value of the variable in question itself which triggers an effect or series of effects which serve in turn to alter that value. One example of a feedback loop[4] would be the partially controlling effect of a population of birds on a population of caterpillars: as the number of caterpillars in the population increases, so does the number of birds which feed on them; but as the number of birds increases, the population of caterpillars is diminished. There is a feedback relation between the variables B (birds) and C (caterpillars) such that the value of B determines the value of C, but the value of C in turn determines the value of B. The bird–caterpillar system is in this respect self-regulatory: it can regulate the values of its state variables without the aid of external controls or constraints. This is an example of negative feedback, and negative feedback mechanisms produce a condition known as homeostasis: the ability of a system to maintain the values of its state variables within fixed limits. (It was to homeostasis, as the central feature of a living system, that Bateson's description pointed.)

The classic biological example of homeostasis is the homeostasis of body temperature: a rise in body temperature triggers reactions – sweating, panting, flushing – which serve to lower the temperature again; a drop in temperature triggers reactions – shivering, rubbing, movement – which help to raise it again. However it should be noted that homeostasis in organisms is rarely a function of a simple negative feedback loop, but is rather a complex effect of many different interacting variables. Positive feedback loops, in contrast to those conducive to homeostasis, consist in feedback mechanisms which serve, not to correct deviations from a steady state, but to amplify such deviations, that is, the system reacts on itself to amplify the deviations in the values of its state variables. One example of positive feedback is the phenomenon of eutrophication in a pond ecosystem: as the water becomes eutrophied, organisms begin to die, adding to the existing organic matter suspended in the water; this further eutrophication in turn causes more organisms to die, which further eutrophies the water, and so on. Positive feedback mechanisms are involved in the processes of growth and death – the major changes to which organic systems are subject. Negative feedback networks tend to typify the functioning of the organic system in its normal mature states.

Another feature of biological systems worth noting is that they incorporate mechanisms known to cybernetics as regulators: regulators help to regulate the internal environment of the system, in order to maintain homeostasis. A regulator blocks the transmission of 'variety', that is of fluctuation in the values of environmental variables, from the external environment to essential variables of the system. As Ashby explains, regulation in biological systems can take place in two kinds of ways.[5] One way of blocking the flow of variety from the source of the disturbance to an essential variable of the biological system is via the interposition of a physical barrier, for example the shell of a tortoise, the bark of a tree, the human skull. The other form of self-protection is via skilled counteraction on the part of the organism. The organism gathers information about the impending disturbance, prepares for its arrival, and then meets it with a complex and mobile defence, for example the fencer who relies on his skill in parrying to keep the values of his essential variables (such as blood volume) constant. It is the function of the nervous system in animals to obtain information in this way about environmental disturbances, with the aim of preventing the flow of the information contained in these disturbances to the essential variables of the organism. Regulators then are mechanisms deployed by systems for the maintenance of homeostasis.

One other feature of biological and other systems which must here be emphasized is that of equifinality. Von Bertalanffy explains equifinality thus:

> In most physical systems, the final state is determined by the initial conditions.... Vital phenomena show a different behaviour. Here, to a wide extent, the final state may be reached from different initial conditions and in different ways. Such behaviour we call equifinal.[6]

Equifinality is exemplified in the growth of organisms: an individual typically achieves the size characteristic of its species regardless of (reasonable) deviations in its initial size, and of temporary setbacks to its growth occasioned by nutrient deficiency. Equifinality, like most of the other systems properties we have just examined, is not a characteristic of closed systems, that is, systems which are such that no material enters or leaves them. It is exclusively a feature of open systems, that is, systems which import and export material, and therefore involve material turnover. 'Living systems are open systems, maintaining themselves in exchange of materials with environment, and in continuous building up and breaking down of their components,' writes von Bertalanffy.[7] A closed system has at its disposal only that amount of energy which is present in its initial state. It will accordingly 'wind down,' in conformity with the Second Law of Thermodynamics. A closed system is a one-way-street. An open system, in contrast, is a case of all roads leading to Rome. Open systems achieve the same final state from different initial conditions because their development of a steady state is independent of initial conditions.

The phenomenon of equifinality is related to that of goal-directedness. If a system is such that it will predictably find its way to a specifiable state, regardless of initial conditions, then it can be said that the realization of that state is a goal of the system. The goals that can be defined for non-living systems are not in general 'entertained' in any sense by the systems themselves, but are projected onto them by external designers or programmers. The status of the 'goals' that may be defined for living but non-conscious systems is, as we shall see below, more problematic.

The paradigmatic instance of the open system exhibiting self-regulation, homeostasis, equifinality and goal-directedness is of course the organism. However, numerous instances of purely mechanical self-regulating systems exist, from the simple negative feedback mechanism of the classic Watt governor[8] to the sophisticated electronic mechanisms of advanced servo-engineering. Such systems may be designed for many different purposes, and the purpose one assigns to a particular system may depend on one's own interests and purposes. For example, from a motorist's point of view, the purpose of a governor in an automobile engine is to limit speed; but from the point of view of the automobile-parts manufacturer, the governor may also be regarded as a device for wearing out metal. There is then a certain relativity of purpose, on account of the fact that the machine cannot, so to say, speak for itself: it does not itself in any sense entertain the goals or purposes in question. Whatever else it might be, however, whatever other project the governor may embody, it is not a system for maintaining and renewing itself: the prevention or repair of wear and tear to itself is not, from anybody's point of view, one of its effects. The same may be said for sophisticated servo-mechanisms: their behaviour may exhibit goal-directedness, but the goal in question is not the maintainance or self-realization of the machine itself.

II SELF-REALIZATION

It is in respect of this essential purpose or project of self-realization that mechanical systems such as governors and servo-mechanisms differ from organisms. For an organism is not merely a device for controlling state variables such as blood temperature, volume and oxygen levels, in the same way that a governor is a device for controlling speed. The control of speed is not related to the viability or continued integrity of the engine; the control of blood temperature, volume and oxygen levels is however related to the viability or continued integrity of the organism. In other words, in the case of the organism, the goals of maintaining a steady state in respect of these state variables are subsidiary to the general, overarching goal of self-maintenance: an organism is, first and foremost, a system for effecting its own maintenance, repair and renewal. The regulation of internal variables is not effected for its own sake, as the regulation of speed or the tracking of a target is effected for its own sake by the governor or by a cybernetic tracking device. Rather, this regulation is effected because the stability of these variables is essential to the perpetuation of the system as a whole. An organism, then, is a system devoted to its own realization; to this end it satisfies its own energy requirements, grows, repairs or renews its own tissues, and reproduces itself.[9] In short, while most mechanical systems could be described as machines for wearing themselves out, the organism is a 'machine' for self-realization.

If self-regulating cybernetic systems constitute a special category of form or pattern, self-realizing systems clearly constitute a superspecial one. And in this category of form or pattern may lie the key to a new principle of individuation, a new criterion of discreteness and unity. However, before elaborating further on the distinction between self-regulating systems in general and self-realizing/self-maintaining systems, let me first consider an objection. The goal of self-maintaining systems, I have said, is not merely to maintain the values of their state variables within fixed limits, but to maintain and perpetuate the system as a whole. But, it may be objected, how are we to define the system as a whole except in terms of its state variables? And in that case, what does the idea of maintaining the system as a whole add to the idea of maintaining the values of the state variables? This objection rests on an equivocation in the use that has so far been made of the term 'self-maintaining'. For when it is said of a system S that it maintains itself, this may mean either that S remains in a steady state as a result of its own intrinsic self-regulating mechanisms, or it may mean something more than this, namely that (i) S maintains its own fuel supply, that is, procures its energy requirements by its own efforts, and that (ii) it does not depend on an external command signal for its direction. If a system is self-maintaining in the latter sense, that is, if it is self-fuelling and self-directing, then it will have to be a special kind of system, with very special characteristics. To say of a system that its overarching goal is self-maintenance then, is not merely to say that it regulates its own state variables but that its state variables are themselves of a peculiar kind. It is this fact, rather than the mere fact of self-regulation, that induces us to describe the system as self-maintaining.

If self-regulation is not a sufficient condition for self-maintenance, it may be asked whether it is a necessary condition: could something which failed to qualify as a system yet qualify as self-fuelling and self-directing? The answer, I think, is no. In order to fuel itself, a thing would have to be capable of reacting to its own fuel levels. In other words, it would have to incorporate a feedback mechanism such that a significant lowering of the fuel level would trigger a series of events which would lead to the restoration of the optimal fuel level for the system. (Hunger in the higher animals follows this pattern.) The status of self-direction is less clear: in order to be self-directing, a thing would *a fortiori* have to exhibit goal-directedness, and this, as we saw, is a characteristic of certain kinds of systems. But whether or not goal-directedness could in principle be understood in non-systemic terms is a question I would prefer to leave open.

Returning now to a further elaboration of the distinction between living and non-living systems, let us examine biologist Jacques Monod's succinct characterization of life in terms of three criteria: teleonomy, autonomous morphogenesis and reproductive invariance.[10] To say that organisms are teleonomic is to say that they are endowed with a project or purpose, and that this project or purpose largely determines their activities. To say that organisms experience autonomous morphogenesis is to say that they construct themselves in accordance with directions from within, rather than being formed under the exclusive action of external forces (that is, they grow). And to say that they are characterized by reproductive invariance is to say that the source of the information which directs the construction of a living being is always another living being of the same structure. Monod defines the teleonomic project of living beings as 'consisting in the transmission from generation to generation of the invariance content characteristic of the species.'[11] (Note that the transmission of the invariance content still allows for variation in the individual, and hence for flexibility and adaptation in the species as a whole.) All structures, performances and activities contributing to the success of the essential project are called by Monod 'teleonomic'.

Two questions may be addressed to these criteria. Firstly, do they indeed demarcate living from non-living systems? Secondly, are they fully captured in the single notion of self-realization? In reply to the first question, we may say that while non-living self-regulating systems are teleonomic in that their behaviour is determined by a goal, their goal is not in general that ascribed by Monod to living systems, *viz.* the transmission of essential structure from one 'generation' of system to the next. Since the other two criteria are subordinate to the first, they too constitute conditions not generally satisfied by non-living systems. Indeed these two criteria represent strategies for implementing the teleonomic project of transmitting essential structure from generation to generation of the system. So we may see this project as being the most fundamental characteristic ascribed by Monod to living systems. Is this characteristic captured in the notion of self-realization?

Surely it is. Reproduction is only one strategy for self-maintenance, and so self-maintenance/self-realization in fact constitutes a broader criterion for life than that suggested by Monod. Were an organism to devise strategies for its own individual perpetuation, reproduction would be rendered unnecessary. However, reproduction offers the scope for the multiplication and variation necessary for natural selection to be operative and hence for evolution to occur. It is hard to see how organisms would originate in a non-reproductive context. (However if the earth (biosphere) itself qualifies as an organism, as has been suggested by scientist James Lovelock in his book *Gaia*,[12] then this is clearly one organism which did not originate as a result of reproduction, nor hence in the context of evolution as we understand it.[12] But this is clearly a very special case.) Reproduction remains in principle only one strategy for implementing what I would take to be the basic teleonomic project of self-realization.

To describe organisms as intrinsically self-realizing I think brings out in an intuitive fashion the really seminal difference between organisms and other self-regulating systems, a difference which can become blurred in the more technical definitions. The categorical difference between organisms and other individuals – systems or substances – is that organisms, by their activity, define an interest, or a value, namely their own. Other systems may be designed and constructed for the purpose of producing a particular effect, but this purpose is definable only relative to the intentions of the designer. In a deserted post-holocaust world, mechanical devices such as type-writers and bicycles, and even cybernetic devices such as governors and guided missiles, would return to the estate of mere objects, their purpose having vanished from the world with the agents who designed them. Such systems do not embody their purpose in them-selves: their purpose is superadded to their existence, and can be subtracted from it without the things themselves ceasing to exist, or ceasing to be the things that they intrinsically are. Organisms differ from such systems in as much as they do embody their purpose in themselves; for an organism, to exist is to possess self-interest. Unlike the machine, which can exist as a durable material structure indepen-dently of fulfilling the purpose for which it is made, the existence of the organism coincides with its purpose, for its purpose is to exist. Its purpose is not, like that of the machine, contingent to its existence. It is not defined relative to some external designer who may or may not exist. Since the existence and the purpose of the organism coincide, interest enters the world, ontologically speaking, in the shape of the living system. (The term 'living system' may denote not only individ-ual organisms, but ecosystems, and in some cases even communities. We shall postpone consideration of these questions to chapter 4.)

Perhaps the peculiar quality of self-realizability will be brought out more clearly if we consider what a mechanical system would have to be like in order to satisfy this condition. Consider an engine that runs on oil. Suppose moreover that the engine is automatic, that is requires no driver or engineer. This engine has been programmed with certain command signals, one of which is to move about in search of fuel. The engine incorporates a feedback mechanism such that the lowering of its own fuel levels stimulates this command. It also incorporates an oil detecting device such that the detection of oil triggers the release of a vacuum hose directed toward the source of the oil; the hose remains in place till the tank is filled or the source exhausted. The energy that the machine supplies to itself is used to sustain its mobility, so that it can continue to supply itself with fuel. It is also used to obey other command signals, which concern the maintenance of the machine – the replacing, renewing and repairing of parts. These activities require complex capabilities on the part of the machine: the capacity to process substances and perhaps to transform them into other substances and to fashion and fit them to the requirements of its structure. Such activities would require a high level of organization in the structure of the machine, and the complexity of the structure will complicate even further the task of self-maintenance. Such a complex system must be designed for flexibility, otherwise a fault or dysfunction in one minor part will bring the whole intricate mechanism to a halt. To keep such a complex body in good order would, under normal conditions, require continuous maintenance, for such complexity will otherwise rapidly break down under the principle of entropy. Of course there are exceptional conditions in which the complex structure might remain intact indefinitely without maintenance, for example if it is frozen or placed in a vacuum. But a being whose purpose is to exist must be capable of existing under normal conditions, and these are highly entropic. The continued existence of such a complex machine then is guaranteed only for as long as it actively maintains itself. If its goal is self-maintenance, then it is in this sense that its existence coincides with its purpose.[13]

With the set of commands necessary for the machine to repair and maintain itself, it might be possible to construct a new machine. This might in fact be the easier strategy for the machine to deploy – reproduction. Reproduction is the perpetuation of form or structure by means of renewal rather than repair; it is self-maintenance not in the substantival sense of 'self', but in the structural sense: it is the same form or structure which is perpetuated.

A machine which satisfied the criterion of self-realizability then would be a very special kind of machine. It would be an engine which was not used by anyone for any purpose, and hence would not be attached to or incorporated in any other structure, as ordinary engines are attached to vehicles or industrial machines. The self-realizing engine is 'used' by itself. Its purpose is self-referential. Its goal is its own continued existence, its own 'survival'. That purpose does not disappear even if we, its supposed designers, do. This 'oil guzzler' *exists for itself*, in a way that typewriters and guided missiles could never do: its material being (its body) depends for its continued existence on its continuous self-maintaining activity (its function).

Could such a 'machine' in fact exist? Could it in principle be designed and built by us? I think not. The level of interconnectedness of parts required for its self-monitoring function would presumably require structural holism, and holism entails that the parts cannot be given independently of the whole, since the nature of the whole conditions the parts. In this case, we cannot start with an assemblage of parts and piece them together to construct the whole. The whole must be created whole. And the whole can presumably only be created whole by the wider system, of which its existence is a function. It seems improbable to me that such holistic creation could be simulated, for example in a laboratory. For this reason I doubt that 'life' could be created in a 'test tube'. However, if holistic creation were to be achieved by artificial means, the self-realizing system which would result would not have been pieced together in mechanistic fashion, but would have come into existence whole as a function of a specially created environment. As it is arguable (see Chapter 4) that self-realizing systems arise only in environments which are themselves self-realizing systems, however, the artificial creation of the kind of environment capable of giving rise to a self-realizing system may pose the same problems as the creation of a self-realizing system did in the first place.

With the appearance of systems-for-self-realization then, this ontologically new quality – the quality of being-for-itself – enters the world. The quality of being-for-itself is informed with a special quality of purposiveness, special because it is self-referential: the purpose embodied in such systems is simply to exist. I shall call this special purpose embodied in self-realizing systems *telos*. The notion of telos is not independent of the notion of *self-interest*. A being whose purpose is to perpetuate itself is a being with interests – we can identify what is good and bad for such a being. It cannot be said of a rock that certain things are good for it and certain things bad for it, for a rock has no interests, no identity that it is actively seeking to preserve. It cannot be said even of an artefact like a servo-mechanism that things are good or bad for it, for although there may be factors which favour or hinder the fulfilment of its goals, *it* has no interest in the realization of those goals. A servo-mechanism is a being-for-others, not a being-for-itself; what it does or what happens to it may accordingly matter to others, but will not matter to it. A self-realizing being, however, is one which, through its nature, defines a self-interest. What happens to it matters to it because it is actively seeking to preserve its own integrity, its identity. And this self-referential activity is constitutive of the notion of *agency*. Agency, which is also a function of being-for-itself, is generally contrasted with causation. The present thesis – that with the appearance of self-realizing systems, telos and self-interest enter the world – is not committed to denying the causal genesis of such systems. It does not insist that organisms may not evolve under the action of 'blind' causal influences. (This position is somewhat qualified, however, in Chapter 4, Section V.) What the thesis principally points to is that with the appearance of self-realizing systems, something new, something qualitatively, indeed categorically, different from the rocks and clods of clay and grains of sand that populate the class of substances, enters the world. For the rocks and clods and grains possess only a contingent – substance – unity, a contingent individuality, shaped by external forces, and entirely at the mercy of the same. A rock is no way self-affirming, demarcating and preserving its own identity; a rock is just a lump of matter, arbitrarily hewn out, waiting to be worn away by wind and rain. It is only an individual by chance, and its individuality does not 'matter' to itself. It in no way resists causal inroads into its own accidental 'integrity'. A self-realizing system, in contrast, having once come into being, by whatever means, actively determines and preserves its own perimeters, thereby creating an objective unity. Such self-affirming activity marks off the self-realizing being as an *agent*, as opposed to a mere link in a causal chain, with no interests or purposes of its own to dictate its action.

The notion of being-for-itself then is a package which includes the notions of telos, self-interest and agency. On the present account, a being may be said to be endowed with telos, self-interest and agency even if it is not in the ordinary sense conscious at all. The criteria for these features are systems-theoretic rather than intentional. My claim is that we can only convey the categorical distinction between inanimate objects and self-realizing beings by way of these concepts which signal a transition from one 'order of being' to another.

A further categorically new feature of such beings, which needs to be emphasized here, is their power of self-envaluation: a being with self-interest – which is to say, a being with an interest in its own perpetuation – is a being which values its own existence. Again, this value which the being in question may be said to have for itself may not be a function of consciousness, or conscious awareness. Rather, it is constituted by the being's actively seeking to maintain itself in existence. Self-realizing beings, in other words, embody value, just as they embody telos. To be actively self-maintaining is just what it is, on this account, to be valuable to oneself. Such activity is the primitive form of value, the preconscious form in which value first enters the world. It is not that an organism seeks to maintain itself because it values its existence, but rather that seeking to maintain itself is constitutive of its valuing itself.

Since the very existence or continued existence of such beings is mute testimony to the value that they possess for themselves, I propose that such beings be described as intrinsically valuable.[14] Is this justifiable? In what sense, if any, is a being which values itself thereby rendered intrinsically valuable? Does my valuing myself render me valuable, any more than my valuing a piece of fool's gold renders it valuable? In the case of the piece of fool's gold, my valuing it is perfectly consistent with its not possessing any value of its own – any innate, objective value. Other valuers, X,Y,Z, may assign different values to the piece of fool's gold, and it may be that none of these evaluations is the 'correct' one, since the piece of fool's gold may have no independent value. It may be valuable only relative to external valuers, and these may disagree in their evaluations of it. The object itself is thus not rendered valuable by the fact that I or others value it. How, then, does my envaluation of myself possess a different status and significance from my envaluation of the fool's gold? How, if at all, does my valuing myself render me innately or intrinsically valuable?

The difference in this case is that, since it is I who value myself, I, unlike the fool's gold, am not dependent for my value on the existence of some external valuer. Whether or not such external valuers exist, and whether or not they agree on the value they assign to me, I have a certain independent value, namely that which I assign to myself. This is my intrinsic value. Notice that this account of intrinsic value in no way severs the conceptual link between value and valuer. But it spotlights a case in which this relativity of value to valuer does not entail outright relativism with respect to the value of the thing in question. For in this case the value that the being in question possesses is inalienable: it is independent of any that other valuers may assign to it. Indeed, this value is inextricable from the very existence of the being in question, since it is constituted by that being's activity of maintaining itself in existence.

To summarize, then, value as well as agency, self-interest and telos, is involved in the quality of being-for-itself which is the peculiar feature of self-realizing systems. Telos and value, and to a lesser extent agency and self-interest, have traditionally been understood as functions of human consciousness: it is human beings who evaluate, and entertain purposes. Neither telos nor value is, on this traditional view, objectively 'in the world', that is, outside of human consciousness. On the present thesis, this of course is not the case. Telos and value are 'in the world', though only in beings which belong to a special category, the category of self-realizing systems (a category which at present, as far as we know, includes only living systems). Telos and value, as well as agency and self-interest, are a function not of human consciousness but of self-realizability.

The new criterion of individuality that was the goal of the present inquiry should by now be clear: it is, of course, self-realizability. Self-realizing systems show an objective unity, an objective distinctiveness, which is not based on substantival separateness but on a very special kind of form. Notice that even within a substance ontology, self-realizing systems would qualify as objective unities, and hence as individuals, though of a different order from substances. Indeed, such systems have a less contingent individuality than compound substances such as rocks within the pluralist substance ontology. However, when the pluralist ontology is abandoned, a non-substantival criterion of individuality is positively needed. The principle of self-realizability furnishes such a criterion, operable within the framework of substance monism.

It should be noted that the special form in terms of which individuals are individuated, under the principle of self-realizability, is a *dynamic* form. Individuality, under the new principle, is a functional concept: the existence of an individual is not independent of its function, because the function of the individual is to maintain its existence. Individuals, from this point of view, are intrinsically dynamic; a principle of motion and change is thus in this sense built into the new ontology at the level of individuals as well as at the cosmological level. Contrast this with the ad hocness of motion and change in the atomist ontology: atoms were construed as intrinsically inert, and dynamism was a contingent feature of the metaphysic.

A final point that cannot be overemphasized in the present connection is that the unity and distinctiveness which characterize self-realizing systems, though objective, are not absolute. Self-realizing systems are open systems and hence cannot exist independently of their environment. A self-realizing system cannot constitute the sole item in the domain of a possible world. As Bateson[15] has put it, the unit of survival, under natural selection, is not, as Darwin thought, the breeding individual, or the family group, or the species. The unit of survival is an organism-in-its-environment. If the environment fails to survive, so does the individual. And the local environment may itself be a self-realizing system, which may in its turn be part of a wider self-realizing system. The unity of such an objective whole, then, does not preclude that whole itself being a part of a greater whole. Indeed, self-realizing systems are typically embedded in such hierarchies of systemic unity and integrity. The systemic point of view then does not permit the division of the world into mutually independent units. Rather, it provides a principle of individuation according to which intrinsic individuality is consistent with – indeed entails – intrinsic interconnectedness.

III SELFHOOD

How can we begin to cash out this systems-theoretic principle of individuation within the Einsteinian framework of a geometro-dynamic world? Clearly it is a principle which could operate within an atomistic ontology also, provided subsets of the atoms were arranged in systemic structures. But within the framework of substance pluralism the systemic principle of individuation would be contingent and dispensable, not fundamental to ontology. Within the framework of substance monism, in contrast, this principle *is* fundamental: if individuals are to be granted any ontological standing, then the criterion of their individuality must, as far as our present analysis has shown, be the systemic principle.

In illustrating the system-theoretic principle of individuation in geometrodynamic terms it will be useful to employ again the hydro-dynamic analogy. Suppose we are seated at the prow of a boat observing a tracery of ripples and eddies on the surface of the water. Most of these disturbances smooth out and fade away with the swell, or melt into the wake of our vessel. But occasionally we observe complex and unusual configurations on the surface, and within the confines of these, small whirlpools or vortices which travel around apparently autonomously, maintaining their structure. Like the more transient eddies and swirls, these are merely disturbances of the water, rather than self-existing entities capable of being excised from the medium in which they occur. But unlike the transient formations, these are not merely part of the ebb and flow of things. The self-maintaining vortices resist the causal ebb and flow, maintaining a stable structure through variable conditions. But even while we ob-serve their relative independence of 'wild' causal influences, we are aware that this independence is itself a function of their geometrical dependence on the complex wider structures in which they are em-bedded. This holistic dependence creates a relative independence in the face of external causal conditions. The 'autonomy' of the self-maintaining system is thus acquired at the cost of a geometrical or functional dependence on a special environment. This 'autonomy' then is not the same as that which attaches to the notion of substance: it is in no way a capacity to 'stand alone'.

I propose to call this special kind of individual, whose autonomy and integrity are a function of its interconnectedness with its environment, a 'self'. For in objectively separating itself out from the general flux, by directing its activities preferentially towards maintaining its own existence, such an individual introduces a true self-other distinction over and above that which is established by means of spatio-temporal demarcation.

Spatio-temporal demarcation, however, is not irrelevant to the identity of selves, but a necessary component of it. For two self-maintaining systems which share the same form or pattern are nevertheless distinguishable in terms of their position in space and time. It is true that selves need not be fully localized within a closed boundary: they may in principle be more scattered in space and time than material bodies are. However, the 'thisness', the haecceity, of a given self is still a function of its location. The criterion of 'thisness' is thus the same for both substances and selves. What makes a particular substance *this* one is just that it is the one that is here, now, and what makes a particular self *this* one is the same. On the other hand, what makes *this* individual (that is the individual at this point in space and time) a *substance* is that is it fully enclosed within a physical boundary – it has substantival unity. And what makes *that* individual (that is the individual at that point in space and time) a *self* is that it is a self-maintaining system.

Let us not overlook the radical nature of the switch imposed on our perception of the world by the systemic principle of individuation. Set in a geometrodynamic framework, this principle renders inanimate matter a mere backdrop to the true individuals, the only individuals that appear on stage, the selves. Organisms and other self-maintaining systems move around in a differentiated but indivisible continuum. Rocks and clods of clay and grains of sand are not really things in their own right, but merely knotty bits of the underlying continuum. Matter is in general properly described in mass terms: earth, rock, sand, water, sky, air, etc. The only things that objectively stand out against this background, the only individuals that genuinely populate this world, are the selves. This view, so strikingly in contrast with our present view which perceives living systems as complex, epistemically rather awkward things built out of simple, much more straightforward, fundamental things, was anticipated by Aristotle. Aristotle entertained a basically biological –

though not ecological – ontology: the world was composed of individuals whose unity was understood, after the fashion of the unity
of organisms, in functional terms. But despite this limited degree
of functionalism, Aristotle's metaphysic does not develop in a
holistic or systemic direction, but stops short at an emphatic form of
individualism – a pluralism of discrete biological individuals. The
concrete relations in which these individuals stand to one another are
entirely external to their identity, and in principle such individuals
could be rearranged or reshuffled at will. There is no anticipation here
of the concept of ecology, or of the indivisibility of systems. For an
account of individuation which chimes with the present analysis and
also falls within the framework of substance monism, we turn again to
our inspiration, Spinoza.

IV CONATUS IN THE COSMOS

The idea of self-interest (an interest in self-realization) as an
informing principle of 'selves' is then one which again resonates
deeply with the thought of Spinoza. Spinoza inherited from scholastic
philosophy a concept known as that of the 'conatus'. The conatus,
according to the Schoolmen, is the impulse for self-preservation or
self-maintenance, and also for existential increase, or self-realization.
Under the scholastic interpretation, the conatus consisted in the
unfolding or motion of a thing toward an independently or externally
defined form or goal (where the external author of such a form or goal
was of course presumed to be God). Spinoza took over the notion of
the conatus as an impulse for self-maintenance and self-realization.

> Everything, in so far as it is in itself, endeavours to persist in its own
> being.
>   ... no thing contains in itself anything whereby it can be
> destroyed, or which can take away its existence...; but contrari-
> wise it is opposed to all that could take away its existence....
> Therefore, in so far as it can, and in so far as it is in itself, it
> endeavours to persist in its own being.[16]

Furthermore, Spinoza thinks, this conatus, this 'endeavour,
wherewith everything endeavours to persist in its own being' is
'nothing else but the actual essence of the thing in question'.[17] David
Bidney explains this identification of conatus with the essence of the
individual as follows:

> [the] conatus or effort of the individual is identical with [its]

whole essence; it is not merely a part of its nature or function. The nature of a thing is not shown by its static perfection of form; and it is not defined by reference to some end which it tends to realize. The nature or essence of a thing is rather expressed by its actual functions and power to continue in existence.[18]

For Spinoza the 'goal' of self-preservation was not imposed on things by an external author, and it was for him perfectly consistent to suppose that things could both possess conatus and yet be subject to 'efficient' or mechanical causation: the conatus could be acquired accidentally, that is mechanically, and then in turn serve as an efficient cause of the motion of the individual in question. 'The essence of a thing is simply its force of motion or activity, *no matter how acquired*, and no separate form is required to account for its present motion or its continuation in the future.'[19] The conatus is a principle, or form, which, while it may have causal origins, once established becomes a force or drive which enables individuals to resist causal affronts to their integrity.

The notion of the conatus then is effectively equivalent to that of self-realizability, except in so far as the former lacks systems-theoretic connotations. Spinoza's view that the 'nature of a thing is not shown by its static perfection of form'[20] applies directly to selves as opposed to substances. And the idea that the 'nature or essence of a thing is rather expressed by its actual functions and power to continue in existence'[21] anticipates my claim that, in self-maintaining systems, purpose and existence are inextricable: selves exist only in so far as they fulfil their purpose. Or, as we might say, their essence is to exist.

The difficulty with enlisting the support of Spinoza here is that in Spinoza's doctrine the scope of the conatus appears to be wider than the scope of the principle of self-realizability as I have defined it: everything, according to Spinoza, possesses conatus. When Spinoza speaks of 'things' or 'individuals' he tends to be thinking of organisms anyway, and this is confirmed by his explicit identification of the conatus with life in the *Cogitata Metaphysica*: 'we understand by life the force by which things persevere in their being.'[22] But, as Bidney points out, he also identifies the conatus with the principle of inertia, where this clearly applies to all material things, animate or inanimate: 'the universal conatus in all things is identical with the essence of those things and is nothing other than the effort or force of each thing to continue in its form of motion and rest, whether that form be innate or acquired accidentally; it is inertial, efficient power.'[23]

Why does Spinoza declare that all things – material objects as well as living beings – exhibit an impulse towards self-preservation? What he may have in mind here, I think, is the fact that a rock, once constituted, will, if left to itself, remain in existence. That is to say, provided no disintegrating external forces are applied to it, it will retain its substantival unity. Logically speaking, there is no reason why the identity of the rock should be preserved in this fashion: it could just as well split apart as remain intact. In this weak sense then, the rock is 'self-maintaining'. But really it is misleading to put it this way: the rock does not in any sense by its own activities maintain its integrity; rather, its integrity is maintained. What maintains it? The laws of physics. In other words, in order to explain why a living system remains in existence we refer to the activities of the system itself; in order to explain why a rock remains in existence we refer to the nature of the universe at large.

I think the reason that Spinoza overlooks the seminal distinction between animate and inanimate things in this connection lies deep in his doctrine of mind/body parallelism. For Spinoza every physical manifestation of substance corresponds to a mental manifestation. The level of organization of a given structure dictates the level of 'mind' which it attains. The level of organization achieved in a human body, for instance, accounts for the high level of consciousness present in us; the comparatively low level of organization present in a pebble accounts for its correspondingly low level of 'mind'. In the light of this mind/body parallelism, it is arguable that Spinoza considered all material bodies to be in a certain sense 'alive', and for that reason endowed with conatus.

I have not as yet ventured to defend an enlarged conception of mind according to which beings normally regarded as unconscious are considered as endowed with mind. However the fact that I have imputed telos, agency and the power of self-envaluation to certain kinds of unconscious beings suggests that an enlarged, systems-theoretic conception of mind is indeed implicit in my account of selfhood. While conceding this – and without wishing to enter into a defence of it here – I nevertheless wish to point out that the notion of mind with which I am implicitly working is applicable only to self-realizing beings, or selves. It does not extend to objects such as rocks. This is not the place to weigh the merits of Spinoza's mind/body parallelism, but only to signal the deviation of the present view from

Spinoza's in respect of the scope of the conatus. Conatus is understood, in the present context, as inhering only in selves; it can accordingly in no way be seen as equivalent to inertia.

A further question which Spinoza himself does not explicitly address, but which springs very naturally from his thinking, is the question whether or not the universal substance is itself self-realizing. Does it exhibit conatus? Spinoza's failure to consider this is, I think, tied to his failure to develop a *dynamic* theory of substance: conatus, as the impulse towards self-realization, is manifested in becoming rather than in being, in an unfolding-through-time rather than an established manifold. This being so, conatus could not find expression in the static manifold of Spinozist space.

This question whether or not the cosmos constitutes a self-realizing system is certainly one which arises within our geometrodynamic theory of substance. It was argued in Chapter 2 that the essence of substance is to seek plenitude, and that it was for this reason that substance takes the form of an expanding space. Plenitude was understood as the impulse to achieve fullness, sheer maximal existence. The impulse towards plenitude then is plainly a very literal expression of the 'force of existence' or 'power of activity' in the cosmic context. Our account of the essence of substance *per se* accords very well with Spinoza's statement that 'the essence of a thing is simply its force of motion or activity'. The principle of plenitude is a straightforward translation into a cosmic context of the principle of the conatus.

However, while our account of spacetime undoubtedly entails that it is self-realizing, it is not clear whether it entails that spacetime constitutes a system. It was suggested earlier in this chapter that self-realizability was to a certain extent supervenient on systems-theoretic properties, but this cannot be assumed to hold when the self-realizing being in question is the cosmos itself. The cosmos is undeniably a special case. Can geometrodynamic spacetime, which has already been characterized as a substance, and shown to be self-realizing, also consistently be described as a system?

I think it can, though it is, predictably, no ordinary system. But nor was it an ordinary substance. This was apparent not only in the fact that it was intrinsically dynamic, but also in the fact that it was indivisible and holistic: the parts were conditioned by the whole – the local curvature being (partly) a function of global curvature. (I say 'partly' because local influences are also effective; the total effect, however, at any given point in spacetime, cannot be accounted for in terms of local influences only.) In Chapter 2 we had not yet reviewed the properties of systems, and were accordingly in no position to deal explicitly with the question whether geometrodynamic spacetime, despite its substance status, also qualified for the title of system. We are now in a position to tackle this question, where doing so will involve examining the implications of the holistic indivisibility of space.

The indivisibility of geometrodynamic space into self-subsistent parts was explained in Chapter 2. That the 'parts' of space cannot be excised and made to stand alone is an intuitively compelling point, but theoretical justification for the point is harder to find. Space is represented, in mathematical terms, as a point construct. The reason for denying its divisibility then must lie not in mathematics but in physics or metaphysics. GMD, *qua* metaphysics, does I think provide a justification for the indivisibility of space. For any region, s_i, of geometrodynamical space will have a non-zero curvature. This curvature will be a function of the curvature of the wider region of space, S_I, in which s_i is embedded. 'Excise' s_i, and it will not retain its curvature, any more than a patch of the surface of an inflated balloon will retain its curvature after excision. In his book, *The Conceptual Foundations of Contemporary Relativity Theory*, Graves voiced – and replied to – this objection to the indivisibility of space as follows:

> One might still argue for a form of atomism on the following grounds: The various tensors used to characterize different curvatures are all functions of the points in space-time. Thus it is really the individual points, rather than space-time as a whole, that are the substances, and the curvatures are their properties. Spacetime is nothing but a general term for the totality, as regions are the names of less inclusive collections of these points, and overall curvatures should be regarded as statistical effects. This might be true if there were no connections between the local and the global structure of spacetime, in which case the properties of one point would be logically independent of those of any other point. But . . . this is not so. There is an intimate connection between the local and the global features, so that the latter influence the former as well as vice versa. Because of this we must consider space-time as our sole substance, albeit not an internally homogeneous one.[24]

It was the indivisibility of space which led us to the conclusion that space was one substance, but it is the holistic grounds of this indivisibility which lead us now to ask whether space is systemic. I think that a deeper examination of the meaning of holism will in fact reveal that from a geometrodynamic viewpoint space is indeed systemic in nature. In an article entitled 'The logic of systems', systems analyst Angyal presents the following account of holism.

> Wholes ... cannot be compared to additive aggregations at all. Instead of stating that in the formation of wholes something more than a summation of parts takes place, it would be more correct to state that summation does not play any part whatsoever in the formation of wholes. In summations the parts function because of their inherent qualities. ... On the other hand, when a number of parts constitute a whole, the parts do not enter into such a connection by means of their inherent qualities, but by means of their position in the system. The formation of wholes is therefore not additional to the aggregation of parts, but something of an entirely different order. In aggregates it is significant that the parts are added; in a system it is significant that the parts are arranged.[25]

It is the positional values of the 'objects', rather than the objects themselves, which constitute the system, and these positional values are inherently relational – they cannot be defined independently of the framework (system) within which they are located. Applying this analysis to space, it is the positional values of the 'points' rather than the points themselves which make up the system of geometrodynamical space. The positional values of the points of geometrodynamical space are their curvature values. On this broad logical criterion for systems then, a geometrodynamical space will qualify as systemic.

Angyal's analysis, however, suggests that the 'objects' could exist independently of their 'positional values', even though those positional values themselves are inherently relational and hence could not 'exist' independently of the other positional values which define them. Applied to space, this would imply that the points of space could exist independently of curvature – that the 'arrangement' of the points into specific curvatures is contingent to the fact of the existence of space. On this view space would be inherently atomistic. But our account of the logical origins of spacetime in the formal nature or essence of substance implied that the curvature of space was entailed by the nature of substance – that an expanding spherical space was the form that substance necessarily assumed. According to this argument, then, curvature is intrinsic to the nature of a physical or substantival space: the curvature cannot be abstracted from the notion of physical space. It follows that since the positional value (the curvature) of each point in space is inherently relational, each point itself is inherently relational in the sense that it cannot exist independently of the other points. Geometrodynamic space, then, is not a construct of atomistic points, but is intrinsically a holistic continuum.

In this seminal respect then – that it to say, in respect of holism – geometrodynamical space is indeed systemic. Since it is also unquestionably self-maintaining, it satisfies the twin conditions that I proposed as prerequisites of selfhood. However it is, as we would expect, a rather special sort of self. For self-maintaining systems, as we observed earlier in this chapter, are, for reasons of entropy, generally held to be *open* systems. Open systems, we recall, are those which are subject to import and export of materials, and involve continuous substantival turnover, a building up and breaking down of their components. It is this exchange of materials with their environment which prevents them from 'winding down' into a state of maximal entropy. The cosmos as a whole however would appear to be ineligible for open system status, for the simple reason that there is no environment to which it can stand in relation. It would appear to be the original closed system. But the requirement of openness sprang from an essentially mechanistic assumption – the assumption that the energy for work, for growth, for expansion, must come from without. This mechanistic assumption – that things possess no intrinsic principle of dynamism – is closely related to the assumption of entropy, that is, that systems, left to themselves, without input of energy from without, will wind down, will cease to be able to do work, to grow, to expand.

Does the cosmos as a whole, then, fall within the scope of these two principles of mechanism and entropy? Does the cosmos create and maintain its structure without importing energy from outside itself? Is it a closed though self-maintaining system? Clearly, if we drop the Newtonian assumption of a transcendent and divine First Cause, the universe can be seen to have created itself without the assistance of an external force. In this respect it lies beyond the scope of the mechanistic principle. But from whence does the organization manifest in the universe come? How is it maintained? Physicists as yet have no unequivocal answer to this question. As Paul Davies explains in *God and the New Physics*, the present view is that the initial state of the universe was one of thermodynamic equilibrium, that is, a high-entropy, low-order state.[26] As a result of the gravitational effects of the expansion of space, temperature differentials developed, and these reduced the entropy – increased the levels of organization – in the universe. On this view, order followed, purely via the laws of physics, from an earlier state of disorder. However this scenario leaves open the question of the degree of organization of the initial gravitational field, the energy of which generated the development of cosmic order. Was this field in a state of low or high entropy? How is entropy even to be quantified in relation to gravitational energy? There is no agreement amongst physicists on these questions. However, whether order/information was already present in the singularity which yielded the initial state of the universe, or whether it evolved out of an initial state of pure disorder, it would appear that the cosmos is capable of generating and maintaining its own structure – which is to say, of realizing itself – without the assistance of external agencies. The systemic requirement of openness appears in this special case then not to apply.[27]

In its broadest contours then, the geometrodynamical universe combines the logical features of both systems and substances. At the highest level of generality, system and substance are, as we should expect them to be, complementary rather than mutually exclusive principles of individuation. The universal substance is a self, a being endowed with conatus, possessed of an impulse for self-preservation and self-realization. We shall now turn our attention to the normative implications of this hypothesis.

Chapter 4

Value in nature and meaning in life

I THREE LEVELS OF VALUE

It was argued in the previous chapter that the primitive form of value is the interest-in-self-realization that is embodied in a self, or a self-maintaining system. This argument rested on an (undefended) assumption, namely that value is indeed conceptually tied to the existence of a valuer. In other words, in order for an entity to possess value, it must be at least potentially valuable for, or relative to, a valuer. This assumption leads us to exclude from consideration the kind of theory which assigns value to objects which are beyond the purview of possible valuers. I am content that this should be so, not because I have a ready refutation of such theories, but because my purpose here is simply to give content to the notion of intrinsic value in certain limited contexts. There may be other contexts in which the notion of intrinsic value is understood differently, and there are certainly complex and important fields of ethics, notably the field of inter-human interaction, that are not exhausted by the account I offer here. I accordingly make no claim to exhaustiveness for the value theory which follows. My aim is to develop a theory which prescribes a particular normative stance to Nature. The stance in question is basically ecocentric, but ecocentrism as I prescribe it is understood as having a bottom-line significance – it rests on a fundamental moral principle, though this principle is not necessarily one to which all other moral principles may be reduced. With these qualifications in mind, then, I propose to identify three levels of value, where the value in question is in each case relativized to a valuer, or self.

The first level of value is derived from the intrinsic value that attaches to the cosmos as a whole on account of its status as a self. Just as every part of my body matters to me, since I matter to myself, so every part of the universal self or system matters to it – every part possesses a value which it inherits from the value of the whole. We may call this value which attaches to everything *qua* part of the universal self, the 'background value'. Like the background radiation in physics, the background value is universally distributed, permeating organisms and inanimate objects alike, even apparently 'empty' stretches of spacetime. The background value, then, attaches to things *qua* particulars, that is *qua* regions of spacetime, rather than to things as instances of sortals or natural kinds. Our world, the world of physical reality, is an expression of selfhood, of a cosmic will-to-exist, and as such has a meaning, and a value, that would not attach to a purely 'blind' and contingent world. There is in this sense an element of affirmation and fulfilment in the existence of every physical thing. Even the rocks and clods of clay and grains of sand call forth a certain reverence in the light of their participation in this great act of self-realization on the part of the cosmos. (The significance of the intrinsic value of the universal self will be subject to closer examination in Section VI.)

However, while this background value evokes a generalized sense of reverence for the physical world, it does not, at first sight at any rate, appear to have any further normative significance: it does not prescribe one kind of action rather than another. The Conservation Laws in physics guarantee that no action of ours can destroy physical reality: one form of energy may be transformed by us into another, but the energy itself, or the spacetime which it animates, cannot be destroyed. It is only the second level of value which furnishes normative indicators. The second level of value is identifiable as the intrinsic value embodied in individual selves or self-maintaining systems. This is the value that was explained in the previous chapter. It attaches to things not merely *qua* particulars but *qua* selves. Does the fact that individual selves possess a built-in value in this fashion entitle them to a degree of respect over and above that to which they are entitled on account of the background value that accrues to them *qua* particulars? Does recognition of intrinsic value imply recognition of entitlement to respect?

Surely it does. If something is characterized as intrinsically valuable, then it is simply analytic that, other things being equal, it should not be destroyed or prevented from existing. It has a *prima facie* claim to our moral consideration. Even when intrinsic value is analysed, as it is here, in terms of the value that the being in question has for itself, this value-for-itself, once recognized, must set the being apart from the other objects of our attention. In acting upon such a being we are entering into the field of values, whether we like it or not. In Kantian terms this being is an end-in-itself, rather than a mere means to ends of ours, and we are morally obliged to treat it as such. We may choose to disregard this obligation, but in this case we are choosing to be immoral. Identifying certain entities as intrinsically valuable, then, does not in itself provide an answer to the question, 'Why be moral?', but it does point the way to certain *prima facie* moral duties.[1]

This second level of value, *viz.* intrinsic value, is, like the first, objective and absolute, in the sense that it inheres in the things which possess it and is not relativized to the needs and desires, or interests, of external observers or agents. But this, as we have seen, is not to say that intrinsic value does not have its base in the interests of living – or self-realizing – beings.[2] In this sense it is still, in a way, 'subjective', but this element of subjectivity in no way leads to the tenets of moral subjectivism. Since the value does inalienably inhere in the beings which possess it, and is not merely projected on to them from some external point of view, it qualifies as part of the 'furniture of the world' – any description of the world which aspires to objectivity and exhaustiveness must include reference to it. Intrinsic value must accordingly, as I have indicated previously, be included in the realm of 'fact' – the traditional fact/value dichotomy is inapplicable to it. This claim to facthood, or objectivity, is consolidated when we appreciate that, although such intrinsic value is a function of the interests of the self which possesses it, it is in no way arbitrary or variable, as values formulated from a subjectivist standpoint are. It is analytically impossible for something to qualify as a self and yet to choose not to value itself. Intrinsic value is thus built into selfhood, and may in this sense be considered objective.

Although it is not my purpose here to offer critiques of other value theories, I would like to make one comment about the use that is made of the notion of intrinsic value in utilitarian theory. In utilitarianism the intrinsic value of pleasure or happiness is asserted on the grounds that conscious beings do as a matter of fact universally desire/value pleasure or happiness – the hidden premises here being that what is universally desired is objectively desirable, and that what is objectively desirable is intrinsically valuable. The idea that objects, or more accurately, beings, may themselves be intrinsically valuable (where such value clearly cannot be a simple function of desire) is foreign to utilitarian theory.

The omission of beings themselves from the realm of the intrinsically valuable is, prima facie, anomolous, for we might well ask why value should be accorded to a psychological state if the being which is the subject of that state is itself without value. Indeed, the doctrine that happiness is an intrinsic good – with creatures being the almost incidental vessels of happiness – has led to the well-known and fatal disrespect for personal (and animal) autonomy within the framework of utilitarianism.[3]

The idea that beings themselves may be intrinsically valuable has found wide contemporary currency only within the recent literature of environmental philosophy, and most particularly in that branch of environmental philosophy known as Deep Ecology. The term 'Deep Ecology' was coined by Norwegian philosopher Arne Naess, who outlined the broad principles of the Deep Ecology movement in a brief paper in 1973.[4] The tenet of Deep Ecology that has attracted the greatest attention has been the intrinsic value thesis, the view that '[t]he well-being and flourishing of human and nonhuman Life on Earth have value in themselves (synonyms: intrinsic value, inherent value). These values are independent of the usefulness of the non-human world for human purposes.'[5] Other norms of Deep Ecology that will be discussed in the course of this chapter include biocentric egalitarianism, the principle of richness and diversity of life-forms, and the restriction of human consumption in accordance with 'vital needs'.

Returning now to our discussion of the various levels of value, I have pointed out that to acknowledge the validity of intrinsic value in the present sense is to dissolve the traditional fact/value dichotomy. This dichotomy does become applicable however in relation to the *third* level of value. The third level of value is derived from the second. For if an individual values itself, it will assign positive and negative values to at least some of the elements of the world in which it finds itself. Each self furnishes a point of view from which the instrumental value – positive, negative or neutral – of all the elements of its environment can in principle be determined. The value of these elements is, broadly, a function of their *utility* for the self in question. Elements of the environment which promote the self's interest-in-self-realization possess positive value in relation to it, while elements which oppose its interests possess negative value. The value thus ascribed to any environmental variable is objective relative to the interests of a particular organism – that is to say, it is a fact about the world whether or not that variable promotes those interests. But the value itself is not absolute – it is not *in* the environmental element itself. That element possesses the value in question only *relative to* the particular organism. The third level of value, then, is relativist though objective. If we suppose each self to furnish a distinct reference frame, then it can be said that the third level value of an environmental element, e, will differ from frame to frame, as its utility for different selves varies. Of course, if e happens itself to be a self, then it has a fixed intrinsic (second-level) value which does not vary from frame to frame, though frame-relative values may be assigned to e in addition to its intrinsic value. Human beings, for instance, possess a fixed intrinsic value, on account of their status as selves, but their relative value will vary from viewpoint to viewpoint across species: the utility value of the human being is presumably positive for, say, the domestic rat, and exceedingly negative for the Blue Whale.

It should be emphasized that the determination of this relative, third-level value is not subjective, in the sense of being a matter of arbitrary preference: the utility of one species relative to another is entirely determinate, and this is so regardless of whether or not members of the species in question are consciously aware of such values. A self furnishes a viewpoint even if it is not in the ordinary sense conscious at all – it may, for instance, be a single-celled organism, which has attained only the most rudimentary level of sentience. Nevertheless, since it is a self-maintaining system, its activities define an interest, and that interest is either served or subverted by particular environmental variables. Indeed the very concept of sentience is inextricably tied to that of value: an organism is adapted to perceive, or to be sensitive to, environmental factors which are relevant to its well-being. Nor is sentience detachable from action, or response. A simple organism such as an amoeba is sensitive to light because light *matters* to it, and the value of the stimulus is expressed in the positive response of the organism to it. Action at its most primitive level is *towards* some environmental stimuli, and *away* from others, and perception develops to serve these values. The value of a given environmental factor for a particular organism is thus objectively determinable even when the organism in question is not itself conscious of that value. Furthermore, an organism, such as a human being, which is conscious of values, may be mistaken in its evaluation of a particular environmental factor. Its subjective or insufficiently informed estimation may not match the objective utility of that factor. An example of this kind of subjective error would be the belief of a human patient that a drug which will in fact prove lethal to her is beneficial. The point that I have been illustrating, then, is simply that the third level of value, though relative, is perfectly objective. Clearly the third level of value corresponds to a utilitarian schema, the difference being only that the class of beings relative to whom the third level of value is calculable is wider than the class of beings to whom utilitarians traditionally attribute moral considerability. The reason for this is that utilitarianism, as we have seen, discovers intrinsic value in psychological states and relativizes utility to these. It is therefore only relative to beings capable of experiencing those states that evaluative frames of reference can be defined within utilitarianism.[6] The third level of value, in contrast, is relativized not to states of consciousness but to individual conatus. It follows that reference frames for the third level of value can be defined for all self-maintaining beings.

II DEGREES OF INTRINSIC VALUE

The first level of value, as defined above, is presumably unquantifiable – we cannot know the degree to which the universe values itself. Value at the third level is in principle quantifiable, though the practical difficulty of working any kind of utilitarian calculus is well-known. But what about value at the second level? Do different selves possess different degrees of intrinsic value? Or do all selves value their existence to the same degree?

On the face of it, the answer to the last question would appear to be no. If the value of a being resides in its self-maintaining activity, then the measure of its intrinsic value would seem to be the degree of its power of self-maintenance. A little unicellular organism 'wants to live', and 'wants' to with all its might, and in this sense values its existence as highly as does a 'higher' animal. But it is plain to see that the 'might' of the amoeba is limited – its power of self-maintenance is slight beside that of, say, a mammal. The reason for this is that power of self-maintenance is in general linked with degree of complexity. Complexity of organization in a living system tends to indicate the capacity of the organism in question to survive in a wider range of environmental conditions than less complex organisms could accommodate. It tends to indicate the capacity of an organism to utilize resources, make the most of opportunities and get out of trouble. This is not to say that simplicity, too, does not sometimes make for adaptability – if the needs of an organism are minimal, then it is likely to be able to make do in a wide range of conditions without needing to exercise ingenuity at all. But greater complexity does confer greater autonomy, in the sense that the more complex the organism, the more capable it is of taking stock of its surroundings and actively adapting them to its own needs. A unicellular organism cannot take precautions against or exploit any interferences or disturbances in its environment. It may be capable of withstanding extremes of, say, temperature, but it will be entirely causally subject to more complex forms of variety. Such autonomy as is possessed by more highly organized beings is, as we have seen, a definitive component of self-realization. The greater the complexity of a living system, then, the greater its autonomy; the greater its autonomy the greater its power of self-realization, and the greater its power of self-realization, the greater the intrinsic value, or interest-in-existence, it may be said to embody.

However, this thinking, which introduces a hierarchy of values into the domain of selves on the grounds of degree of self-realizability, may in the end have to be modified in the light of ecological considerations. The notion of value applicable to selves may turn out to be less clear-cut than our three-tiered analysis would suggest.

As I explained in the previous chapter, self-maintaining systems are open systems – they maintain their structure and hence their identity by importing energy from the environment. Because it is the purpose of such a system to maintain itself, and because this purpose is of its essence, it may be said of such a system that it has *needs*. Given the logical connection between needs and the requirements of self-maintenance, it follows that the needs of an organism are of its essence. Let me explain what I mean. A rock clearly has no needs, since it is not actively seeking to maintain itself. A non-self-maintaining system such as a Watt governor may be said to 'need' fuel, in the sense that without fuel it does not continue to operate, but since it is no part of its purpose to continue to operate, or to maintain itself in existence, this 'need' is no part of its essence. The identity of rocks and Watt governors thus makes no reference to elements of their respective environments, that is, their identity is structural not relational.

Let us examine in a little more detail what it means to say that the identity of a self-maintaining system is relational. The essence of a self, *qua* self, is its power of self-maintenance, its conatus. But the essence of a particular *kind* of self, for instance a Blue Whale, is its power to maintain itself in a particular way, that is through specific kinds of interaction with elements of its environment, for example through consuming krill. To exist by eating krill is part of what it is to be a Blue Whale as opposed to, say, a hippopotamus; its particular ways of maintaining its existence are written into its structure and into its behavioural repertoire – the Blue Whale is a device which perpetuates itself by eating krill, sieving seawater, etc. Take away these specific modes of self-maintenance, defined through its needs, and you take away its Blue Whalehood. The identity of the Blue Whale is thus irreducibly ecological – it cannot be exhausted by anatomical and physiological inventories; it essentially involves reference to specific elements of the environment.

To draw this distinction between the – relational – identity of selves and the – nonrelational – identity of other objects may seem to go against the geometrodynamic account of physical particulars outlined in Chapter 2. It was shown there that, from a geometrodynamic point of view, the identity of *all* particulars is relational, since particulars are to be explained in terms of topology and the topology of any given region of space is at least partly a function of the curvature of the surrounding space. Certainly at the purely physical level the identity of selves and other objects is equally relational if we adopt the geometrodynamical viewpoint; that is to say, *qua* physical structures at any given moment their identities are equally relational. But the point here is that, while an account of its physical structure may be sufficient to identify an object, such as a rock, or stuff, such as water, it is not sufficient to identify a self, such as a Blue Whale. It is precisely the extra – ecological – dimension that distinguishes the self from mere objects and stuffs, and this ecological interrelatedness is a function of its telos.

A question concerning the symmetry of the identity relation arises here. If it is true to say that the Morning Star is identical with the Evening Star, then it must also be true to say that the Evening Star is identical with the Morning Star. Identity is symmetric. Does this mean that if we say that the identity of a Blue Whale 'involves' the elements e_1, e_2, for example brine and krill, then we must also say that the identity of e_1 and e_2 'involves' Blue Whales? Surely not. The relation that obtains here is less one of identity than of constitution: it is a part/whole relation. When it is said that e_1 and e_2 are involved in the identity of the Blue Whale, what is meant is that they help logically to constitute that identity. The identity of the whale is partly logically constituted out of the relations that hold between the whale, *qua* body, and e_1 and e_2. This relation of constitution or part-to-whole is not necessarily symmetric, though it can be. It is not symmetric for the variable e_1, since brine is clearly not constituted out of any relation that salt water has to whales, that is, brine is not dependent on whales for its existence. But this relation may be symmetric for e_2, since the dependence of whale on krill may be reciprocal: the krill may need the whale to regulate its population in a reliable manner. If it is indeed a fact that the whale is functionally adapted to krill, so that krill and only krill will meet its need for food, and that the krill population is functionally adapted to whales, so that whales and only whales can 'cull' that population in the manner required for its perpetuation, then it can be said that the identities of whale and krill are ecologically interconnected – mutually logically constitutive of each other. It is a fact about the 'web of life' that in general the ecological dependence of one kind of organism on others is reciprocal, with the result that the identities of most selves are logically interconnected with those of others.

Now this whole issue of identity and the logical inter-connectedness of selves arose apropos of the question of intrinsic value: do different degrees of intrinsic value attach to different selves? The answer ventured earlier was that to those selves with greater powers of self-maintenance, a higher degree of intrinsic value accrues. But in light of the logical interconnectedness of selves, it appears that the allocation of 'marks' or 'grades' is no longer so clear-cut. If an A-grade being, such as a whale, is logically interconnected with D- or E-grade beings, such as krill, then it has to be admitted that either the whale is not as high-grade as we thought or the krill are not as low. Either way, the logical connection between the parties begins to close the value gap: a flow of intrinsic value, from one self to others, commences. When we consider the extreme complexity of the relations of ecological interdependence in Nature, we see that the pathways of this flow may be intricate indeed. The intrinsic value of a given self may ultimately be a function not only of its own power of self-maintenance, but also of the intrinsic value of the many other species of organism on which that power depends. In this way the original hierarchy of selves, in respect of intrinsic value, is broken down. Indeed, given the dependence of most organisms on features of the total biosphere – such as oxygen or soil – which are the products of other organisms, which in their turn depend on the animal and vegetable residues of other organisms, such a web of pathways for the transmission of intrinsic value is established, that it would in most cases be misguided to try to assign higher and lower values to specific kinds of organisms. The effect of the multiple refractions of intrinsic value through the network is to average-out the value which attaches to any particular organism. Thus while at first it appears that the whale embodies a higher intrinsic value than the krill, due to the whale's immensely greater powers of self-preservation, a deeper understanding of the whale's identity and its place in the scheme of things may redress the initial judgement.

The intrinsic value of a given self, then, is a dual function of its relative autonomy, or power of self-maintenance, on the one hand, and its interconnectedness, or dependence on other selves, on the other hand. Both aspects of the self are real, and neither can be wholly reduced to the other, and both components of its value are relevant for normative purposes. If we were faced with the choice of taking the life of an individual whale and that of an individual krill, then we should spare the whale, because viewed as an individual its relative autonomy is its more important aspect, and the whale plainly possesses a greater power of self-maintenance than does the krill. But if the choice is between whale and krill as species, then it is a toss-up, because viewed as species they are mutually inextricable, and it therefore makes no sense to assign a higher value to one or the other.[7]

The thesis of 'biocentric egalitarianism' is, along with that of intrinsic value, one of the major tenets of Deep Ecology, as I mentioned earlier. In their book, *Deep Ecology*, Devall and Sessions write:

> The intuition of biocentric equality is that all things in the biosphere have an equal right to live and blossom and to reach their own individual forms of unfolding and self-realization within the larger Self-realization. This basic intuition is that all organisms and entities in the ecosphere, as parts of the interrelated whole, are equal in intrinsic worth.[8]

Again, as this quote makes clear, the thesis of biocentric egalitarianism is put forward in Deep Ecology on largely intuitive grounds – it is presented as an axiom of their moral theory by proponents of Deep Ecology (though others have attempted to provide some justification for it).[9] I have here tried to show that biocentric egalitarianism is in fact *entailed* by the thesis of interconnectedness, which I have sought to establish on independent grounds, and which figured as the first principle in Naess's outline of Deep Ecology. This principle, as stated by Naess, involved

> [r]ejection of the man-in-environment image in favour of the *relational, total-field image*. Organisms [are seen] as knots in the biospherical net or field of intrinsic relations. An intrinsic relation

between two things A and B is such that the relation belongs to the definitions or basic constitutions of A and B, so that without the relation, A and B are no longer the same things. The total-field model dissolves not only the man-in-the-environment concept, but every compact thing-in-milieu concept except when talking at a superficial or preliminary level of communication.[10]

This clearly corresponds to the scenario of ecological interdependence – the web of interconnected selves – that I outlined in Chapter 3. My concern here has been to show how a form of biocentric egalitarianism flows from this metaphysical premise. If, as I argued in Chapter 2, the premise is justified, then so is this ethical corollory of it.

The problem of justification arises again for another principle affirmed by Deep Ecologists, namely the principle of diversity or multiplicity of life-forms.[11] Naess and Devall and Sessions regard the richness and diversity of life as an independent value, and there is even the suggestion that the value of life itself derives in part from its innate tendency to produce a proliferation of forms. The normative implication is that all steps should be taken by us to preserve and promote that diversity of forms. This is a principle which I accept, and which will in fact typically prevail in cases of conflict of interests between competing selves. If the parties to the conflict are, say, a feral cat and a potoroo, then the relative scarcity of potoroos will ensure that, as referees, we would decide in the potoroo's favour, despite the fact that cat and potoroo are equal in intrinsic value. Such preference for the rarer party may prevail even when it is a much less complex creature than its competitor. Such an interest in preserving the greatest possible diversity of life-forms does not appear to be explained by appeal to their intrinsic value.

But perhaps it can. The success of life on Earth has been partly due to its capacity to adapt to ever-changing physical conditions. Glacial conditions call forth one set of forms, tropical conditions another. So long as there is a limitless supply of potential new forms on which to draw, life is secure.[12] Diversity is thus a requirement for the continued self-realization of life, and as such it is entailed as a normative principle by our account of intrinsic value. But there is another sense in which the norm of diversity is entailed by the requirement of self-realization, for a being realizes itself not only by maintaining its physical integrity, but also by actualizing all the potential ways of being, all the possible modes of expression that are open to it. Plenitude is achievable not only in a quantitative but in a qualitative sense: 'greater being' may be attained not only by expanding in size but by proliferating one's modes of being. Diversity can therefore be seen as a global expression of the impulse towards self-increase, the conatus.

Another question which needs to be considered before we proceed to the next section concerns conflicts of interest between human and non-human organisms. If a redback spider is ultimately as valuable as a human child, how could we justify choosing to kill the redback to protect the child? The first point that needs to be made here is that the primary duty of any self is towards itself – this is a metaphysical imperative, in the sense that self-maintenance is constitutive of self-hood. However self-maintenance is not interpreted here in such a way as to encompass greed, cruelty, exploitativeness etc., but merely involves the satisfaction of 'vital needs', to borrow the relevant expression from Deep Ecology.[13] Vital needs are those which a self is entitled to satisfy in order to secure its own flourishing. We are not of course to understand 'flourishing' here in a narrow egoistic sense, as in for example, becoming rich and famous, being a star or a celebrity. We are rather to understand it in a physical, emotional and spiritual sense, involving freedom from disease and chronic physical and psychological tensions. It may be thought of as consisting in a state of inner harmony and integration of the personality, which is expressed in a positive and creative attitude to life's challenges. To achieve such a state of flourishing is the built-in goal of any self, and if it has to destroy plants, beetles, other animals, to achieve this, then it is entitled to do so – on the understanding that other selves are also in their turn entitled to destroy it – if they can catch it! Recognition of the equality of selves then does not require that one starve, that one adopt a totally 'hands-off' approach. But it does require that one refrain from thwarting the interests of other selves if it is not necessary to one's flourishing to do so.

Returning now to the case of the redback and the child, it is perfectly arguable that the duty of self-maintenance extends to one's own family – as biological and psychological extensions of oneself, one's nearest kin fall within the scope of this duty. Nor would it be stretching the principle to apply it, more tenuously, to all members of one's own species. In the scenario of the redback and the child, it seems to be perfectly legitimate to protect the child at the redback's expense, since the child may be seen as an extension of one's own 'family', or as belonging to the 'family of humankind'. This kind of species loyalty need not degenerate immediately into the anthropocentrism to which Deep Ecology is (rightly) so opposed, but the line that needs to be drawn here is admittedly fine. Certainly our commitment to our own species cannot legitimately exceed the intention to universalize the state of flourishing indicated above; that is, the commitment can be to the satisfaction of vital needs only. But even this needs qualifying, because the species as a whole must share the respect for the biosphere that is incumbent on the individual, and over-population is not an expression of such respect. So species loyalty – a limited prejudice in favour of members of one's own species in unavoidable, life-and-death conflicts – is ethically proper for a species whose population is ecologically viable.[14]

Where the value of a being is made the measure of its moral considerability, arithmetic is introduced into morality. Morality may then ossify into a soul-less calculus, as the case history of utilitarianism testifies. But the arithmetic of intrinsic value is clearly deviant: as we shall see in the next section, the many possums which inhabit a forest each possesses the same value as the forest itself, where the value of the forest is, in part, the 'sum' of the values of all the possums. Indeed there are overtones of transfinite arithmetic here, since infinity multiplied or increased by any number is still infinity. Perhaps the implication is that the intrinsic value attaching to all selves is infinite. Since any choice of base value for selves seems entirely arbitrary, this transfinite option in fact looks quite attractive! However the point here is just to demonstrate that an ethic based on intrinsic value is in no danger of degenerating into a mechanical calculus. The response that an appeal to intrinsic value aims to evoke is a generalized respect rather than a tendency to quantify.

III IDENTIFYING SELVES

The question that follows on with the greatest moral urgency from the previous section is, what kinds of things qualify as selves – as autonomous, self-realizing beings? The paradigm instance of the self is, of course, indisputably, the organism – from primitive amoeba to highest mammal. At the other extreme it has been claimed in Chapter 3 that the cosmos as a whole possesses the power of self-realization, and hence qualifies for selfhood. But other systems remain to be considered, specifically eco- and social systems. In this connection problems of demarcation abound. How are ecosystems to be defined? Are inanimate elements to be included among their constituents? What of rivers, lakes, dunes, rock formations? What of 'the land', and how does it differ from the ecosystems which it supports? And what about societies? Do they qualify as selves in their own right? How is society to be defined, and how is a society to be distinguished from a community (a particular) on the one hand, and a culture (a universal) on the other? And what is the relation between a particular society and the ecosystem in which it is embedded?

These latter questions concerning the status of societies I shall postpone until the next section. It is to the status of non-human systems that we shall now turn. Devall and Sessions use a broad brushstroke on this question: the objects of intrinsic value include not only organisms, they write, but also things which 'biologists classify as "non-living"; rivers (watersheds), landscapes, ecosystems'.[15] Is this right? Are forests, mangrove swamps, mallee plains, dunefields, all beings in their own right? Are they autonomous, self-realizing systems, embodying telos and constituting ends-in-themselves?[16] Perhaps so. The definitive characteristic of self-systems is that it is *by their own efforts* that they procure the energy for their self-maintenance. To the extent that an ecosystem is adapting, or has adapted, a region to satisfy its own requirements, we can say that it is a self-realizing system. Mature, integrated ecosystems are systems which have proceeded through a succession of developmental stages to a climax community, the conditions for which have been prepared by the earlier stages themselves. This cybernetic view of ecosystem development is, at any rate, the view taken by most ecologists today. In the updated version of his classic text *Fundamentals of Ecology*, Odum defines the strategy of ecosystem development as follows:

> Ecosystem development, or what is more often known as ecological succession, involves changes in species structure and community processes with time. When not interrupted by outside forces, succession is reasonably directional and, therefore, predictable. It results from modification of the physical environment by the community and from competition-coexistence interactions at the population level; that is, succession is community-controlled even though the physical environment determines the pattern and the rate of change and often limits how far development can go.
>
> (p. 444)[17]

In other words, Odum confirms the idea that ecological succession is a holistic phenomenon, involving a self-organizing strategy on the part of the ecosystem. He emphasizes that this does not mean that ecosystems are 'superorganisms', since they employ different strategies of self-organization from those of organisms. (They do not, for instance, use the strategies of reproduction or predation.) They do however involve a superorganismic level of cybernetic organization.

Since an ecosystem modifies its environment to meet its own needs it may be regarded as a being which, to a certain extent, supplies its own energy requirements. It does not roam around in search of food, like an animal. Nor is it passive, like a servo-mechanism waiting to be switched on. True, it relies on the sun's being 'switched on', but it cannot utilize the sun's resources until it has by its own activity released some of the stored but as yet unavailable energy in the abiotic environment. The 'passivity' of the reception of sunlight on the part of the ecosystem is as illusory as that of the plant: a plant will grow toward a light source, whereas a servo-mechanism placed out of reach of a powerpoint will not move closer to it.

If it is accepted that ecosystems are to a certain extent self-realizing beings, the next question to consider is that of demarcation. Where does one such system end and another begin? Does the entire system of life on earth itself constitute a single ecosystem? Let's consider that question first. The resounding answer from ecologists during the last twenty-five years has of course been yes. Ever since Rachel Carson launched the current wave of the environmental movement in 1962[18] we have been aware that DDT sprayed in North America turns up in the bodies of fish as far away as Antarctica, and that disturbances occurring within a local ecosystem can have incalculable repercussions on life everywhere. One scientist who has drawn from this insight the conclusion that the biosphere deserves to be regarded as a self-realizing being in its own right, is James Lovelock. In his by now widely cited and influential book *Gaia, A New Look at Life on Earth*, he argues that the biosphere as a whole constitutes a system which has adapted and continues to adapt the terrestrial environment to its own advantage, that is to the advantage of life.[19] Gaia – Greek Earth goddess and the name Lovelock chooses for the global ecosystem – acts on the environment to produce the basic conditions in which life can flourish. It actively maintains those levels of oxygen and nitrogen in the atmosphere which are necessary for life but which would be negligible in an inanimate world. A relatively constant mean surface temperature – just within the margins of tolerance for organisms – is also maintained, despite drastic fluctuations in the sun's output and the geologically early changes in atmospheric composition.

The regulation of chemical composition – control of salinity levels in the oceans, for instance – is another of Gaia's functions. Lovelock discusses still others.

In his explanation of Gaia's systemic nature, Lovelock employs the analogy of the thermostat. He does not bring out the distinction between self-regulation in the cybernetic sense and self-realization in the sense of autonomy or the capacity of a being by its own efforts to maintain itself in existence. However, what he does say clearly implies this distinction, and lends support to the conclusion that the global biosphere to a certain extent qualifies as a self.

Many local ecosystems also exhibit a marked though relative integrity and autonomy, though the smaller the system the more tenuous its demarcation becomes: is a pond system, for instance, distinct from the forest system in which it is situated? Well-defined boundaries are not available on this, or indeed on larger, scales: a mature natural forest undoubtedly constitutes a relatively distinct ecosystem, and an established heathland undoubtedly constitutes a different one, even though the forest may thin out gradually – through a belt of open woodland – into the treeless heath. Despite the lack of precise boundaries, however, it is arguable that to the extent that such systems actively promote their own particular forms of growth and development, they qualify as – fuzzy – individuals with specific needs and specific ways of satisfying them. It follows that such ecosystems can qualify, up to a certain point, as selves.

What of inanimate features of the landscape, such as rocky outcrops, and in particular dynamic features, such as rivers? On the face of it a river appears to be a purposive entity, cutting deep passes for itself through solid rock in answer to its imperative to reach the sea. But if a river could truly be said to have a purpose, this would surely be to transport rainfall from higher to lower altitudes. Its purpose would not be self-realization. If it were, rivers would surely *avoid* the sea, wandering for as long as possible across the land! They would resist the causal push to break their banks and spread out amorphously into floodplains, since to do so is to lose their identity as rivers! Rivers are thus not autonomous in the required sense: they are dynamic but non-purposive, and accordingly fail to qualify as selves. This is not to say that a river may not be an important feature of an ecosystem, on which the viability of that ecosystem may depend. And it may itself support a relatively self-maintaining streamside and aquatic ecosystem. In this respect a river, *qua* body of water, may resemble other inanimate features of a landscape, such as rocky outcrops: while not themselves qualifying as selves they may be indispensable component configurations of ecosystems that do, and in that sense possess a derivative intrinsic value. On the other hand, such entities may occur in wholly lifeless landscapes, and in those cases I think the intrinsic value that accrues to organisms would not accrue to them. They would of course, like all other parts of reality, inherit the background value that springs from the selfhood of the cosmos as a whole.

In many tribal cultures, 'the land' is regarded as a being, usually a benign and maternal being. Does anything in our discussion so far correspond to this concept? Is 'the land' simply the ecosystem which is supported by a particular bioregion? But such a region will normally support a number of diverse local systems. If these add up to a single larger system, is it this 'mother system' which is the referent of the term 'the land'? Intuitively – and I think this is ultimately a matter for intuition rather than precise definition – I would say no. The concept of 'the land' seems to include the geomorphic features of the landscape – the rocks, mountains, plains – not merely incidentally to the organic features, but as presences in their own right. The land in all its manifestations – organic and inorganic, present and primeval – is revered and sanctified in a way that apparently cannot be justified in terms of the intrinsic value of self-realizing systems. On the other hand, a deeper probe into this concept may reveal an essential link with life after all. Primal peoples perceive the land, in all its massive materiality, as the source, the ground, the womb, of life. It is sacred under the aspect of Mother, the great body from which all life springs and on which all life depends for its sustenance. It is under this – carnal – signification that the great land-forms are perceived, and when they are viewed in this light their sanctity is of course related to the intrinsic value of life.

This recognition of the selfhood attributable to wider systemic wholes raises a further question concerning the distribution of intrinsic value, a question that was not addressed in the previous section: what degree of intrinsic value should be attributed to systems at different theoretical levels, for example organisms, local ecosystems and the global ecosystem, respectively? In Section III it was argued that the value attaching to organisms was a dual function, of their power of self-realization on the one hand and of their interconnectedness on the other. Does the same analysis serve for ecosystems?

How in cases of conflict should the interests of organisms be weighed against those of ecosystems, for example in the competition between rabbits and native Australian ecosystems?

In so far as individual organisms are components of ecosystems, and in so far as a given ecosystem typically consists of a multitude of such components, it would seem that the value of the ecosystem as a whole must outweigh that of individual organisms: it would be patently foolish, and wrong, to burn down an entire forest to spare the life of a single possum. However, this kind of thinking, obvious as it is to common sense, is fraught with traps: is an ecosystem necessarily a more complex self-realizing system that an individual organism? Very simple systems, like very simple games, may be constructed out of complex components or players – the complexity of the components does not entail a commensurate complexity for the system. So on the complexity criterion of intrinsic value, it does not necessarily follow that higher order systems such as ecosystems are of greater value than their components. But more importantly the principle of interconnectedness which led to an averaging out of the values of individual organisms applies in the relation of system to subsystem. Organisms, *qua* components or subsystems of the wider ecosystems in which they evolved, stand in a holistic relation to those wider systems.

In systems theory the relation of part to whole is not linear or additive but holistic – the part helps in the usual way to condition the whole, to make it what it is, but the whole also helps to shape the part. The part cannot be given independently of the whole. In this sense the part in some measure takes on, or mirrors, the character of the whole. The possum then, to a degree, mirrors its native forest. As long as the possum lives, echoes of the forest's voice remain. To the same degree that the possum mirrors the character of the forest, it inherits the intrinsic value of the latter. Its intrinsic value is thus a function of its interconnectedness not only with other selves, but with other levels of system. And just as the nature of the possum mirrors that of the forest, so the nature of the forest mirrors that of the possum, since the possum helps to make the forest what it is. The effect of all this refraction of value is thus only not an egalitarianism of selves but of systems. Of course in most cases of conflict between individual organisms and ecosystems, this systems-egalitarianism will not produce moral anomalies. The reason for this is that the principle of scarcity – derived from the principle of diversity – usually decides the issue. The organism will typically be more numerous than the ecosystem: there are many possums to a single forest. However, when the possum in question is not just any old possum, but, say, a Leadbeater's, on the edge of extinction, and if sacrificing one forest in a heavily forested region will, for some reason, save it, then the sacrifice of the forest may be justified.

IV ARE SOCIETIES SELF-REALIZING SYSTEMS?

We have been looking at the way intrinsic value is distributed across the non-human world. It is now time to look at the intrinsic value of human beings, at the status of societies, and at the relations between human individuals and societies on the one hand, and societies and the ecosystems in which they are embedded on the other.

As organisms we already of course possess intrinsic value. But as organisms we are subsystems not only of our local ecosystems but of the cultural systems in which we live. Our intrinsic value, then, will be a function not only of ecology but also of culture. But do cultures qualify for intrinsic value? Let us look at the background to this question a little more fully. If human beings lived, like the other primates, in communities but not within cultures, then the situation *vis-à-vis* intrinsic value would be straightforward. We would be constituted by our ecological relations with other organisms within our ecosystem and would therefore possess the same degree of intrinsic value as they. We would be just one species amongst others, as the proponents of biocentric egalitarianism insist. It is true that we are – partly – constituted by the ecological relations in which our pre-cultural primate ancestors stood to the elements of their environment, so that to this extent we are on all fours, so to speak, with other organisms in respect of intrinsic value. But there is nevertheless a significant difference between our case and theirs. While their structure and behaviour are fully functions of their ecological relations, our behaviour, if not our structure, is a function not only of ecology but of culture. Unless it can be shown that culture itself is a function of the wider ecosystem in which it develops, then the web of interconnections that locks our identities into those of all our fellow-beings in Nature is rent; our identity is partly a mirror to Nature, but partly too a mirror to a principle distinct from that of Nature – the principle of culture.

The opposition between Nature and culture has been a traditional assumption of western thought, leading to the view that places humankind outside Nature. It is this view which has spawned the whole gamut of anthropocentric values. The literature of Deep

Ecology – and those of many non-Occidental spiritual and philosophical traditions – enjoin us to develop 'ecological consciousness',
recognizing our inalienable interconnectedness and oneness with the
whole of life. This literature however has largely overlooked the role of
culture in shaping human identity, and the relation of culture to
Nature. Clearly these questions have to be studied before the thesis of
interconnectedness – with all its normative implications – can be
sustained in the human case.

To broach these questions, let us backtrack a little. What is culture,
and why is it problematic in the present connection? It is problematic
because the global ecosystem, or Nature, is physical and concrete,
composed of particulars, while culture is abstract, a system of representations or symbols, composed of forms or universals. Ecosystems
consist of individuals and their interactions; a culture is a way of life,
abstracted from the community which practises it. Culture is the
creation, at a symbolic level, of a context for a shared life – it involves
representation of the world, enabling *communication* about the world to
occur, with the limitless possibilities for co-operation that this opens
up. The fundamental form of symbolic representation is language,
but other forms – pictorial, sculptural, architectural, musical, dra-
matic and ritualistic – also exist.

I am claiming then that the quality of human-ness is as much if not
more a function of such symbolic representation as it is of direct
physical, ecological pressures. This claim has been substantiated in
the present century by many philosophers and psychologists and
other social thinkers, who have shown that the processing of experience into intelligible conceptual, perceptual and emotional structures
depends, in the human case, on language acquisition: children deprived of language, as, for instance, those raised by wolves in the wild,
have been found to be completely inhuman, in the sense of lacking
human thought and feeling structures – and non-lupine too, for that
matter, in the sense of lacking the thought and feeling patterns
characteristic of wolves. Their experience is ordered purely around
the stimuli of hunger and, in adolescence, sexuality. Their world is
dissociated, chaotic and fragmented at all levels of experience. It is
inferred that without language the genetically programmed, specifically human structure of experience fails to be realized. Yet language
acquisition depends on culture, on living in structured association
with other human beings. The human capacities for rationality and
abstract thought, with the powers of emotional differentiation and
imaginative activity which attend these, thus turn out to depend on

the kind of sustained and co-operative human interaction for which culture provides the framework.

Indeed it may be argued not only that culture is the prerequisite for the blossoming of those genetically in-built powers associated with human-ness, but is itself one of the principal genetic endowments of human beings. On this view, culture (or 'nurture') is in no way opposed to Nature, but is itself a direct expression of human nature or instinct, the genetically transmitted, biological constitution of the human species. Of course to accept this view requires a wider interpretation of 'instinct' than is sometimes accorded to it. Mary Midgley, in her book *Beast and Man*, draws a distinction between open and closed instincts, in preparation for defending the thesis that the disposition to build a culture is innate to human nature:

> Closed instincts are behaviour patterns fixed genetically in every detail, like the bees' honey dance, some birdsong, and the nest-building pattern of weaver birds. Here the same complicated pattern, correct in every detail, will be produced by creatures that have been carefully reared in isolation from any member of their own species and from any helpful conditioning. Such genetic programming takes the place of intelligence; learning is just maturation. Open instincts on the other hand are programs with a gap. Parts of the behaviour pattern are innately determined, but others are left to be filled in by experience .... So 'programming' includes a number of strong general tendencies, for example, to get home, to seek water, to hide by day, and to avoid open spaces. And the more complex, the more intelligent creatures become, the more they are programmed in this general way rather than in full detail.[20]

Midgley goes on to explain how the disposition to build a culture as the shared context for human social life may be seen as such an 'open instinct', its instinctiveness accounting for its universality, its openness accounting for the diversity of cultures that anthropologists and historians have disclosed. Midgley quotes Konrad Lorentz in support of her claim concerning the innateness of culture to human nature:

> To appreciate how indispensable cultural rites and social norms really are, one must keep in mind that ... contemporary man is by nature a being of culture. ('Contemporary man' here does not of course just mean twentieth century man, but man in his present evolutionary form.) In other words, man's whole system of innate activities and reactions is phylogenetically so constructed,

so 'calculated' by evolution as to need to be complemented by cultural tradition.... Were it possible to rear a human being of normal genetical constitution under circumstances depriving it of all cultural tradition – which is impossible not only for ethical but also for biological reasons – the subject of the cruel experiment would be very far from representing a reconstruction of a pre-human ancestor, as yet devoid of culture. It would be a poor cripple.[21]

The case of the wolf children cited earlier as an example of the consequences of language deprivation would of course serve equally well as an illustration of culture deprivation, and would bear out Lorentz's conclusion. Either way it may be concluded that humanness is at least mediated, at most constituted, by culture. It is worth noting the extent to which this view is at variance with the liberal view of the relation between individual and society that was outlined in Chapter 1. Within that broadly Newtonian framework, society was seen as an aggregate of logically mutually independent human atoms. A Hobbesian 'state of Nature' – pictured as a war of all against all – was taken seriously as a logical possibility, and indeed as the starting-point and main problematic of social theory. The fallacy of this liberal thinking has, as I have remarked, been amply demonstrated in the present century. The impact of 'social conditioning' and the difficulty of drawing lines between the effects of nature and of nurture have been fully acknowledged. In this sense it is no longer controversial to state that a human individual is essentially a cultural being, and that culture is an emanation of Nature.

While this undoubtedly confounds the old atomistic, liberal view, it does not immediately validate the ecological view that is here in question. For though culture may be an emanation of Nature, in the sense that it has natural causes, it may nevertheless be a metaphysical one-way-street, in the sense that it does not feed back into Nature, is not itself an active part of its eco-matrix. It is conceivable that ecological pressures could create in a species a feature which, being abstract and symbolic rather than physical, was ecologically inert – unable to feed back into its immediate ecosystem. If culture is inert in this way, then we, *qua* functions of culture, would be inert to the same degree – not full participants in Nature. In this case, the traditional western view of the human condition, which sees us as detached observers of Nature, logically distinct from it even though causally dependent on it, would be redeemed. Is culture then an epiphenomenon, or is it in fact ecologically functional, ecologically interconnected with the rest of Nature?

Although the cultural dimension of a society is abstract and symbolic, there is a sense in which a culture may be ecologically informed with elements of its environment. For instance, the peculiar quality or essence of certain American Indian or Australian Aboriginal cultures reflects the relation of the societies in question to specific beings or elements of their respective ecosystems. These cultures may be essentially buffalo or kangaroo cultures, let us say, physically, technologically and spiritually centred on those particular animal species. To sever the connection between such societies and the species around which their cultures are constellated would be to destroy the identity of those cultures. Typically the dependence of such societies on their local ecosystem is mutual – their interaction with their environment contributes to the viability of the ecosystem. The role of such cultures, with their pointedly value-laden belief systems, is precisely to generate such interaction – to channel social action in ecologically sustainable and beneficial directions. Despite its abstractness, then, a culture may act as a naturally selected instrument of Nature, or participant in the local ecosystem. The society which practises such a culture, tied to a particular region and a particular set of ecological relations, may thus qualify as a self-maintaining system – since it successfully perpetuates its own social structures by means of its belief-system – and thus as a holistic subsystem of the local ecology.

However, systems of symbolic representation are not in principle tied to specific regions and specific sets of ecological relations, but may be applied to the wider world. When a society takes this wider world – the world in general – as the object of its system of symbolic representation, then its essential relationship to a particular geographical region is cut. Its discourse and its belief systems will become more abstract, and accordingly more remote from action. In Australian Aboriginal cultures, beliefs about kangaroo spirits were, we hypothetically supposed, the naturally selected mechanism whereby Aboriginal behaviour was conditioned to contribute to the maintenance of the kangaroo population: beliefs, in this case, were inextricable from actions. But when a system of representation is generalized to apply to *any* region, or to the world in general, then it is no longer an instrument of the local ecology – the link with particular actions or patterns of interaction with a specific environment is broken.

So to generalize the system of symbolic representation – to develop the power of representation as an end in itself ('knowledge') rather than as a medium of interaction with a specific environment – is precisely to step back and, by breaking the link between belief and action, to make humankind the observer of Nature, the spectator rather than the immersed participant. This ability to step back and think, observe and understand relatively independently of intention or action, is what gives us freedom to choose. Since thought at this level of abstraction does not flow on inevitably into specific actions, it can construct alternative scenarios, and hence the possibility of choice of action.

A culture built on a generalized system of representation in which thought is relatively independent of specific actions (that is, 'knowledge' is 'disinterested, 'objective') and is not applicable only to the elements of a particular bioregion (that is, knowledge is 'universal') will not be interconnected, *qua* culture, with any particular local ecosystem. Belief in kangaroo spirits has given way to much more universal, more abstract beliefs, such as belief in gravitation or atomic matter. Since such a system of belief is not logically informed with the elements of any particular ecosystem, it does not fit, Chinese-box-wise, into the wider systems of Nature.

Our identity as human beings is, as I have remarked, demonstrably as much a function of our culture as it is of our ecological relations. So if our culture is not a regional one, ecologically integrated with the elements of a particular environment, then to that extent we as individuals are not ecologically integrated either. Having stepped back from a particular ecological role we have indeed to a certain extent stepped out of Nature – and this standing outside is mirrored in our freedom to choose how we shall live.

Of course, given the freedom of choice, we can *choose* to make culture an instrument of Nature. With the level of *objective* knowledge already attained we can readily recognize our physical dependence on general forms of life such as vegetation and soil micro-organisms. It would be possible, in light of this knowledge, consciously to build a reverent or conservationist attitude into the concepts of these life-forms – in the sense that these concepts could acquire an emotive charge, a connotation of preciousness, as the concept of, say, mother-hood tends to have. If such attitudes were built into the very concepts of the elements of the global environment, then the resultant culture would be determined by its system of representation to prescribe ecologically positive patterns of interaction with the environment. But the very fact that we can choose whether to make our culture an instrument of Nature in this way, or else to make knowledge an end-in-itself, thereby rendering culture an epiphenomenon of ecology, might be thought to demonstrate our lack of real interconnectedness. The power of choice in itself reflects our independence – our apartness.

To this it may be rejoined that this 'freedom' may really only be a function of error. A true apprehension of Nature reveals the depth of our physical groundedness in Nature, and therefore does entail a careful attitude toward our finite resources. But, more importantly, it may be argued that a correct representation of the world will reveal its telos, its selfhood, and this in itself will entail an attitude of respect towards Nature, a particular set of values. This is of course the argument of this entire book – that the right cosmology will dispose us towards a benign pattern of interaction with the environment. A culture based on such a representation would indeed be an instrument of Nature, and as a function of this culture our own identity would be logically integrated with the global ecosystem.

On this view then we become disconnected from Nature when culture malfunctions, that is, when our system of abstract representation delivers up a misleading or erroneous picture of the world. When this occurs we start to act 'out of sync' with our environment. This kind of malfunctioning can and does happen within ecology – it does not constitute a counter-example to ecology. The genetic programme of an individual organism can go awry, maladaptive mutations can arise, entire species can evolve into evolutionary cul-de-sacs. In all these cases beings perform in ways that run counter to both their own interests and those of the beings in adjoining ecological niches. They are accordingly no longer viable, no longer self-realizing. Their ability to act anti-ecologically is not 'freedom' and does not place them above Nature. They are merely dysfunctional. Their lack of fit with the environment will inevitably result, sooner or later, in their being 'written out' of Nature, eliminated by natural selection.

Let me put the point another way. Assuming that Nature does indeed embody a spiritual principle – that it is a self, possessed of conatus and imbued with intrinsic value – then we can say that, in order to be viable, any culture must include a representation, at whatever level of abstractness, of this conative aspect of Nature. Such a representation will in turn entail attitudes to the environment which will ensure that culture *is* an instrument of Nature, and that we are fully interconnected with the whole. If our culture misrepresents

Nature as being dead, blind, without a purpose or spiritual principle, then it does indeed cut the cord to Nature – but through malfunction, not through transcendence. We are in this case in the same position as the organism whose genes have betrayed it so that it can no longer function as a self-realizing system integrated with the wider systems of Nature. The price of this failure of interconnectedness is ultimately of course extinction.

V SUMMARY OF ARGUMENT SO FAR

In section VI I draw the final – and by far the most speculative – conclusions of this book. I offer them completely undogmatically, as much in a spirit of hope and wonder as of conviction. Before turning to these last ideas, however, I want informally to lay out the structure of the argument so far, to bring to light the key conceptual relationships

> Substance is an indispensable category in any metaphysic, since substance is defined as that which is capable of constituting a world, where a world is understood to be a concrete as opposed to an abstract thing. (Process metaphysics, which focuses on 'the dance rather than the dancers', fails if it does not admit a substantival something in relation to which the process unfolds. If there is no substantival dimension to the world, then the actual world – or the actual world-process – is indistinguishable from the same world *in abstracto*.)

> Two broad archetypes of substance metaphysics are available: the atomistic and the plenic. Atomism is the base of the worldview that has come to be known as Newtonian. Plenism underlies some of the main approaches to a worldview in contemporary physics, notably Einstein's cosmology. However we are not here judging atomism and plenism on the particularities of their respective scientific vehicles, for in their broad outlines they may be evaluated on their metaphysical merits. The version of plenism advanced here however includes a dynamic principle – the plenum is conceived as *intrinsically* dynamic, essentially unfolding or becoming. In this way process, which is entirely extrinsic to atomism in any modern variant thereof, is built into plenism, so that the virtues of a process perspective are – via the geometrodynamic model – assimilated into a plenum metaphysic.

> In the framework of atomism the criterion of individuation is purely spatio-temporal and substantival. Substances are the basic

individuals. The ultimate ontological units are the atoms, or simple substances. Complex substances (material bodies) and arrangements of substances (the cosmos) are aggregates of these.

In the framework of plenism substance cannot be plural so the criterion of individuation cannot be substantival. An alternative principle of individuation which is applicable within this framework is functional and systemic – certain wave-forms or constellations of motion within the substantival continuum distinguish themselves from their surroundings by actively maintaining their own structure in the face of the external ebb and flow which otherwise shapes local configurations in the field. By this intrinsic activity they create a genuine – ontological – self/other distinction, though their individuality in no way implies their separability or discreteness from the substantival matrix. Indeed this individuality connects them to their environment with even stronger ties of dependence than do their mere substantival or topological ties. *Qua* self-realizing systems they need and actively seek out specific environmental elements, where this renders their relation to the environment one of ecological interconnectedness.

The paradigm instance of the self-realizing system – or 'self' – is the organism. But the geometrodynamic universe as a whole also qualifies for selfhood.

A self-realizing being is one which, by its very activity, defines and embodies a value (*viz.*, its value-for-itself.) Since self-realization is a function of ecological interconnectedness, the property of intrinsic value is likewise a function of such connectedness.

The *prima facie* degree of intrinsic value possessed by a particular self will be commensurate with its degree of power-of-self-realization, which will generally be a function of its degree of organizational complexity.

The complexity of environment required for the emergence of self-realizing systems must itself in general be maintained in existence against the entropic inroads of the wider environment. In other words, selves in general require specialized environments in order to form, and these environments themselves constitute wider self-maintaining systems.

The relation of part to whole in a self-realizing system is systemic/holistic rather than linear/aggregative. The components of systems are characteristically involved in feedback loops, in which part conditions whole and whole conditions part, and so on. Thus each part, through its action on the whole, which in turn conditions other parts, helps to shape the other parts of its parent system. This is a form of indirect ecological interdependence between components of a system. Thus the relations of ecological dependence in which a self stands to other elements of its environment may be directly reciprocal, as in the example of whale and krill, or indirectly reciprocal – mediated by the network of interdependencies which hold between the parts of a system.

Holistic nesting of a self in a wider self-system means a relative identification with that system. Because the self stands in relations of ecological interdependence (direct or indirect) with the elements of that wider self, those elements (or its relations to them) are logically involved in its identity. Individuality in this framework is thus, again, a relative matter – it is a function of involvement in a wider system, the identity of which is implicated in the identities of each of its participant subsystems. The individual is thus in a very real sense a microcosm of the wider self in which it occurs.

Due to this logical interaction of the identities of selves both with other selves within the parent system and with the parent system itself, the *prima facie* differentials in the intrinsic values of different selves will 'average out', and an effective egalitarianism in respect of intrinsic value ensue.

These are the main stages of the argument so far. However certain clarifications may still be called for. It would appear that ecological interconnectedness and selfhood, as here defined, could occur within an atomistic framework: selves would still be irreducibly ecological entities whether they were disturbances in a plenum or aggregates of atoms. Since the normative principles which I have outlined here have followed from this ecological principle of individuation rather than from the fact of substantival or topological interconnectedness *per se*, it might be asked why I need to appeal to the plenic paradigm in order to advance these normative principles.

The first point to make in response to this question is that though selves in the present sense would appear to be definable within an atomistic framework, they would not be the basic or primary individuals therein. They would accordingly be *reducible* to the primary individuals, *viz.* the substances, and ultimately, the atoms. In other words, the 'true' individuals would be the substances of which the selves were composed, and since these would be without intrinsic value, the intrinsic value of selves would presumably itself be reducible.

The important point here however is that, contrary to first appearances, an atomistic universe could not, I think, be so arranged as to constitute a self-realizing system. The reason for this is that in an atomistic framework the relation of part to whole can only be aggregative, never holistic, since it is a definitive characteristic of the substances which could constitute the parts of the atomistic whole that they are logically independent of any other entities. The parts – which is to say in this case the atoms – can be given independently of the whole. This means that although the whole is a function of the parts, the parts are in no way a function of the whole. Given that the relation of part to whole in a self-realizing system must be holistic, it follows that a self-realizing world cannot be built out of atoms. Furthermore, it is unlikely that selves could be constructed at all, at any level of system, in an atomistic world. The reason for this is that a self is a holistic part of a wider whole, and as such the dynamics of the wider whole are reflected in it. Selves which were holistic parts of wider systems could conceivably be constructed in an atomistic framework up to the level of Gaia. But what in this case would the parent system of Gaia be, and how would its dynamics be reflected in the nature of Gaia? The parent system would have to be the cosmos, but the atomistic cosmos is inert, dead – it has no intrinsic dynamic which the nature of Gaia could reflect. Besides, within atomism Life, like the universe as a whole, is built from the ground up out of atoms, and there is no intrinsic relation between one part and another or between any part and the whole. Gaia then cannot be a holistic part of the cosmic whole in an atomist world. But this means that Gaia itself cannot be a self-realizing system. The implication of this in turn is that Gaia cannot play parent-system to the local ecosystems which compose the biosphere, and these local systems will thereby be disqualified for selfhood. And so it goes on down through the levels of system, the web of ecological interconnectedness unravelling as the holistic part/whole relationship does.

In the geometrodynamic world, in contrast, the cosmos is a self, and so it makes perfect sense to suppose that Gaia, *qua* self, reflects the cosmic system. But to this our earlier objection – that if ecological interconnectedness is granted, topological or substantival interconnectedness is not needed – may be turned around and levelled again. For while it may be true that in a geometrodynamic world the cosmos is reflected in Gaia, it is equally true that in such a world the cosmos is reflected in the moon, which is not a self. In other words the objection is that if topological/substantival interconnectedness is granted, ecological interconnectedness is no longer needed to ensure that Gaia is a holistic part of the cosmic whole. In a geometrodynamic context everything whatsoever stands in a holistic relation to the cosmic whole. So the appeal to selves and to ecological interconnectedness is, in this context, superfluous.

Is there a difference then between the moon and Gaia in their respective relations to the cosmic whole? The kind of difference for which we are looking would be analogous to that between a frog and a rock in their respective relations to a limnological system. Both rock and frog are substantival parts of the system, but the animate element, the frog, reflects the system in the sense that it is conditioned by it, whereas the inanimate element, the rock, is given independently of the system. Both Gaia and the moon reflect the cosmos in the sense that they are substantivally and topologically conditioned by it. But unlike the moon, Gaia reflects the *essential* dynamic of the cosmos *qua* self-realizing system.

This calls for explanation. Topological and substantival interconnectedness *per se* could obtain in a *geometrostatic* universe, by which I mean a world consisting of a substantival continuum – space – internally geometrically and topologically differentiated, but frozen, unchanging. (This is in fact the kind of world that is entailed by Spinoza's axioms in his *Ethics*, Part I.) Such a world would be holistic – all parts would reflect the whole – but it would not be a self, since a self is a process, involving an unfolding, a becoming, in time. For the same reason such a world could not contain selves. It could however contain the moon, and the relation between cosmos and moon would not be significantly different from their relation in a geometrodynamic world. But a geometrostatic world could not contain Gaia.

The suggestion is then that Gaia differs from the moon in its relation to the cosmic whole in so far as Gaia reflects an aspect of the cosmos which the moon cannot – namely the essential dynamic of the cosmos, which is, of course, its will-to-exist, the conatus. The conclusion of the argument is that true selves can exist only in a universe which is a self-realizing system, and that only a substantivally holistic – as opposed to atomistic – world can be a self-realizing system. If selves exist, then, the scope of selfhood must extend all the way up to the cosmic level. If the cosmos is not in fact a self-realizing system, then the appearance of selfhood at the biological levels must be illusory – organisms must indeed be machines, built from the ground up, as Descartes believed.

The universe seen as a self-realizing system which is internally interconnected in an ecological – and therefore also in a topological and substantival – sense, I call the *ecocosm*. If the microcosm is the small, and the macrocosm the large, the ecocosm is 'the pattern that connects' the small and the large.[22]

The human implications of the relation in which selves stand to the ecocosm will be explored in the final section.

VI MEANINGFULNESS

We have already traced in this chapter some of the normative implications of the thesis that biological systems – organisms, ecosystems, the biosphere as a whole – possess intrinsic value. The normative thrust of this thesis is that we should adopt a bio- or eco-centric ethic, and learn to 'tread lightly' on this earth, taking from it only what we must to satisfy our 'vital needs'. In this our normative conclusions chime with those of Deep Ecology.

But the thesis that we, as human selves, stand in a holistic relation – a relation of 'oneness' – with the cosmos itself, promises more than a list of ethical prescriptions. It promises a key to the perennial questions of who we are, why we are born, what is our reason for living, etc. In short it promises to throw light on the *meaning* of life.

Deep Ecology approaches this question of meaningfulness too. For in Deep Ecology the main emphasis is not only on the thesis of intrinsic value, but on that of a form of human 'self-realization' which springs out of 'ecological consciousness'. (Indeed some writers place the *main* emphasis of Deep Ecology on this thesis of self-realization.)[23] Naess invokes the *Bhagavadgita* to explain his concept of self-realization:

> He whose self is harmonized by yoga seeth the Self abiding in all beings and all beings in Self; everywhere he sees the same.[24]

He goes on to explain:

> Through identification, higher level unity is experienced: from identifying with 'one's nearest', higher unities are created through circles of friends, local communities, tribes, compatriots, races, humanity, life, and, ultimately, as articulated by religious and

philosophic leaders, unity with the supreme whole, the 'world' in a
broader and deeper sense than the usual . . . .

This way of thinking and feeling at its maximum corresponds to
that of the enlightened, or yogi, who sees 'the same', the atman,
and who is not alienated from anything. The process of identification is sometimes expressed in terms of loss of self and gain of Self
through 'self-less' action. Each new sort of identification corresponds to a widening of the self, and strengthens the urge to further
widening. This urge is in the system of Spinoza called *Conatus in suo
perseverare*, striving to persevere in oneself or one's being . . . . It is
not a mere urge to survive, but to increase the level of acting out . . .
one's own nature or essence, and is not different from the urge
toward higher levels of 'freedom' (*libertas*). Under favourable circumstances, this involves wide identification.[25]

Clearly for Naess *Self-realization* (which I italicize henceforth to distinguish it from the self-realization which here is taken to qualify
systems for the status of selfhood) involves the identification of the
small human self – the personal ego – with ever wider wholes, up to
the level of the cosmos as a whole. This identification is not, for Naess,
a purely psychological affair, but is grounded in a recognition of the
metaphysical fact of interconnectedness. The biological fact of ecological interconnectedness is taken to be a model of a deeper kind of
interconnectedness which permeates the entire physical realm, from
micro- to cosmo-levels. Naess appeals to Spinoza, and other writers
appeal to eastern worldviews, such as those of Buddhism or Taoism,
to vindicate their metaphysical preferences. But it has not been part of
the programme of Deep Ecology to undertake any kind of thoroughgoing justification for such a metaphysic of interconnectedness.[26]
Given such a metaphysic as a base however, the 'identity' of the
human self with the cosmos is in some sense an ontological given, and
the recognition of this identity, which Naess takes to be a good in its
own right, is constitutive of *Self-realization*.

In this section I want to explore the relation between the human
self and the cosmos in the context of the particular metaphysic of
interconnectedness that I have tried both to develop and in part to
justify in this book. I also want to throw light on *why* recognition of
this relationship of 'oneness' should confer meaning on life. In this
particular metaphysic of interconnectedness – which involves the ·
concept of what I have called the ecocosm – there are two ways of
viewing the universe: under the aspect of substance, and under the

aspect of self. When the universe is viewed under the aspect of substance, the relation in which it stands to me, when I am viewed as an extended region of spacetime, is the holistic one of geometrodynamical interconnectedness: I am topologically conditioned by the universe, and it is topologically conditioned by me. When the universe is viewed under the aspect of self-realizing system, then the relation in which it stands to me, when I am viewed as a self, is the equally holistic one of ecological interconnectedness: its selfhood conditions mine, my selfhood conditions its.

Let us look first at the significance of my geometrodynamical interconnectedness with the universe viewed as a seamless substantival unity. Certainly it implies that I am 'one with' that universe, in the sense that I am structurally and substantivally shaped by its geometry, as it is, in a small way, by mine. But in this respect I am no different from any other physical thing, indeed any other region of spacetime, occupied or unoccupied. Does my oneness with the universe retain its meaningfulness in light of this? When we ask for the meaning of life, do we expect an answer that will apply just as well to amoebas and rocks and gases and unoccupied regions of spacetime? If meaningfulness hinges on specialness, then our substantival unity with the geometrodynamical world appears to offer little antidote to futility.

However, this conclusion may be too hasty. Being human is different from being amoebic, or being a rock or a gas or a region of spacetime, in so far as we alone amongst these entities can *grasp* our unity with the greater whole. There is nothing unique in our relation to the universe, but it makes a difference to us, to our experience, if we are *aware* of this relation – and it may be this difference that makes the difference, that invests our lives with a greater meaning. Why does awareness of our unity with the cosmos make a difference to our experience? As human beings we are endowed with self-interest, self-concern, self-love. (Since we are viewing ourselves merely as regions of substance rather than as selves in the present context, I here appeal to self-love not as our essence *qua* selves, our conatus, but simply as a contingent given of human psychology.) When we recognize the involvement of wider wholes in our identity, an expansion in the scope of our identity and hence in the scope of our self-love occurs. This appears to be the meaning of *Self-realization*, according to Naess' account of it, and it leads, as he indicates, to a loving and protective attitude to the world – an extension of our loving and protective attitude to our own bodies. Naess points out the preferability of such conservationist protectiveness springing from the heart, as it does in this case, rather than from an intellectual apprehension of the intrinsic value of Nature and a rational appreciation of its consequent entitlement to moral consideration. This attitude of protectiveness, based on identification with Nature, marks the shift from an ethics of duty, grounded in the recognition of the intrinsic value of selves, to an ethics of care.[27]

The benefits of this transition from self-love to *Self-love* are considerable. It offers a conclusive cure for alienation, replacing alienation with an ineffable sense of at-homeness in Nature, and a disposition to live in harmony with it. It relieves the mind of the tyranny of personal desires, and allows one to cultivate the peace and joy of 'unattachment' in something like the Buddhist sense of that term. It is perhaps the kind of state that Spinoza was pointing to in his doctrine of the 'intellectual love of God'. According to Spinoza, the unique vocation of the human mind was, simply, love – not personal love based on emotional need or sensual desire, but 'the intellectual love of God or Nature'. Because of Spinoza's dry style and (unavoidably) austere life, the doctrine of the intellectual love of God has acquired a stern, ascetic reputation – it is seen as the kind of love that a mathematician might have for Platonic circles. But Spinoza distinguished three kinds of knowledge: sensory (common sense, opinion), abstract or theoretical (science, metaphysics), and intuitive (what we might describe as gestalt insight). It was through the third kind of knowledge that we arrived at the intellectual love of God or Nature – not through rational deliberation but through intuitive insight into our identity with the pattern of Nature. On my understanding of Spinoza, this love of Nature is no pale intellectual shadow of love, but the real thing. Understanding our involvement in the grand scheme of Nature, our whole perception of ourselves and our role in the world is transformed. We experience life differently, and the love that was narrowly beamed inwards onto our personal egos is beamed outward, illuminating everything around us, drawing it into the circle of our own concern, our own being. This loving of the world is a blissful state which warms and animates everything around us. It spills over into a real and robust love of people in their full emotional and physical richness, of other beings, of lands, and skies, and the furthest reaches of the night. It bursts the bars of the personal heart, and vastly expands our sense of self. To whoever can achieve such a whole love it is, as Naess claims, joy.

Self-realization as Naess describes it, then, would appear to correspond, in the ecocosmic framework, to a recognition of our geometrodynamic interconnectedness with the universal substance, and a consequent expansion of our self-love to embrace it. This would also appear to correspond to Spinoza's notion of the intellectual love of God.

However, in Deep Ecology identification with the universe – sustaining the widest possible identification – is taken as a sufficient end-in-itself, with little regard for the nature of that universe beyond the fact of its internal interconnectedness. There seems to be an assumption in the air that the universe is a great and magnificent thing, worthy of being identified with, but any explanation of its nature or any justification of this assumption is hard to find. No secular reason is given for supposing that the universe is in any sense alive, or that it promotes life within it, or that life dances to the tune of any particular purpose or telos; indeed no indication is given of what any of these ideas would mean in a secular context. For all that Naess or any other Deep Ecologists, so far as I am aware, have shown, the universe could be, like the geometrostatic universe, internally interconnected but nevertheless quite meaningless, devoid of telos or intrinsic worth. The reason given for loving it is just, at bottom, that it is an extension of ourselves.

Various arguments can be brought against this position, and in order to have more than merely intuitive force the doctrine of *Self-realization* really has to rest on a more positive and articulated view of the universe, a view which provides independent grounds for loving the universe. If the universe were in fact a blind and neutral entity, like the geometrostatic world, or worse, a self-destructive one, then identification with it may actually weaken our self-love by revealing us as less meaningful then we thought we were. I think that Spinoza's notion of the intellectual love of God is, perhaps unlike Naess' notion of *Self-realization*, informed with the assumption that our love for the universe – premised on an understanding of its worthiness – feeds our love for ourselves-who-are-identifiable-with-it; that is, I do not think Spinoza's view is based exclusively on the assumption that self-love feeds our love for the universe-which-is-an-extension-of-us. Certainly Spinoza conceived the universe as a great and worthy being and was at pains to articulate its nature. He demonstrated that it satisfied the standard theological criteria for divinity – oneness, indivisibility, infinitude, etc – which is why he used the names 'God' and 'Nature' interchangeably. But Spinoza was opposed to teleology (though he ultimately failed to escape it in his account of the conatus)[28] and would have refused to attribute telos to his universal substance. In the terms of my argument, then, he failed to show that the universe was a self, and hence to supply grounds for attaching intrinsic value to it. His universe, though one, indivisible, eternal and self-creating, may in the end be no more edifying to be one-with than the geometrostatic universe indicated above.

Let us concentrate for the moment however on the Deep Ecological notion of *Self-realization*. If the universe with which the personal self is to identify is not shown to be a self-realizing system, then the following objection may be levelled at the claim that identification with Nature will produce a spontaneously loving and protective attitude to the environment. Nature in itself, the objection runs, is not only creative but destructive. New life arises from the often violent destruction and deterioration of the old. Planets are born out of the shattered remains of blown-out stars. Elementary particles are constantly created and annihilated in the endless dance of energy at the micro-level. This is the nature of our larger Self, the 'law' of its being. To love oneself is to attempt to realize one's true nature, the 'law' of one's being. To love the greater Self then, to give expression to its presence in us, will be to do as it does, that is, to destroy as well as to create. Humanity the exploder and wrecker will in this case be seen to be expressing its interconnectedness with Nature just as legitimately as humanity the worshipful or loving conserver.

This objection can be pushed even further, as we shall soon see. Before we pass on, however, there is another, even deeper objection which may be brought against the doctrine of *Self-realization* when that doctrine is not tied to the view of the universe as a self, a being possessed of its own conatus. According to this objection, if the universe is viewed as an internally differentiated, internally dynamic universal substance, then the destruction of particulars (particular objects, organisms, ecosystems, planets) is of no consequence to it. Change – the Buddhist *anicca* – is the underlying principle of such a reality: everything comes into being and passes away. For a particular to be destroyed is just for it to be reabsorbed into the universal flux, of which it is in any case just a momentary manifestation. If this universal flux constitutes our larger Self, then these particular comings-into-being and passings-away are of no concern to us, for the identity of our Self remains constant throughout. Indeed this Self may be relied on to give rise to new particulars, new manifestations: it is the ever-self-renewing fountainhead of all wonders and beauties. If we lose a species or two, a forest, a dune field, even Gaia itself, there is no reason for grief, for we are at one with the inexhaustible source of such forms-of-being, and are therefore not diminished. Indeed we might even point out that those who struggle to preserve the particulars are acting precisely from an un-*Self-realized* point of view, for they are seeing the objects of destruction as discrete entities, logically un-connected with the whole and for this reason irreplaceable. Conser-vationists are, from the point of view of this objection, acting from atomist premises.

There is something that rings true in these objections. The same chest-beating self-importance often lies behind the urge to conserve, protect, tend, look after things as lies behind the urge to blow every-thing sky high. There is nothing in our western mind-set that is prepared just to leave things – including our own aggressive tend-encies – alone, let things arise and pass away in their own time. There is no acceptance of ourselves as a natural phenomenon – or a natural disaster, perhaps – on a par with ice-ages and interplanetary col-lisions. But this zen-like surrender to our own natural tendencies turns the whole argument for *Self-realization* on its head.

To avoid these objections, and to bring to fruition what Spinoza was reaching for in his doctrine of the intellectual love of God, we have to view the universe with which we are to be identified not only under the aspect of substance, but under the aspect of self. We have to consider the implications not only of our substantival but of our ecological interconnectedness with the ecocosm. Availing ourselves of the full extent of our theory of the ecocosm supplies immediate replies to the above objections.

To the first objection, that if the universe is not a self, then ident-ifying with it might actually weaken our self-love by diminishing our sense of the worthiness of what we are, the reply is now clear cut: the universe is itself a self, possessed of its own grand telos and immeasur-able intrinsic value. There is no risk that identifying with it will diminish us, or cause our self-love to dwindle.

To the second objection – that creativity and destructiveness are symmetric principles of the universe, equal 'laws of its being', so that being true to the universe as our greater Self involves giving ex-pression to both these tendencies – we may reply as follows. In the context of the ecocosm, creation and destruction are not symmetric principles. Selves exhibit an asymmetric will-to-exist. This is their conatus, their determination actively to resist destruction and to expand their being. Since the ecocosm is a self, its essential principle is the conatus. As vehicles of the conatus, selves are anti-entropic, where this must ultimately be as true of the cosmic self as of others. (See Chapter 3, Section III for our discussion of the scope of the principle of entropy.) Positive and negative forces do not balance out in a self-realizing world: positive forces prevail. Thus in attempting to realize our greater Self – the ecocosm – we should attempt to do what it does, that is we should do our utmost to preserve and enrich, rather than to destroy, our environment.

However, this way of putting the objection, and the reply, is relatively superficial. Really to follow through on the argument would be to demonstrate that unless we allow that the universe is itself a self, it would be self-defeating for me to attempt to identify with it: the whole project of *Self-realization* would be incoherent. For suppose that the universe with which we proposed to identify was not a self, but that the 'law of its being', or underlying principle, was one of random flux, or even self-erosion. Then, since as a self the law of my own being is self-realization, my impulse will be to realize the potentialities of whatever I identify with. In other words, when my self-love is extended to things with which I have reason to identify, it will incline me to try to realize the 'law of their being'. If the law of their being happens to be, say, self-erosion, then my love of the thing in question will incline me to promote its erosion. In this way self-love, or the will-to-self-realization, can come to entail self-destruction, which is self-defeating. It therefore follows that a self may only consistently identify with beings which are also selves. Naess' doctrine of *Self-realization*, on this reasoning then, actually requires that the universe be a self. As soon as it is admitted that the universe is a self, the second objection to the doctrine of *Self-realization* dissolves.

The third objection – that the arisings and passings-away of particulars are of no concern to my larger Self because its continued existence is consistent with, indeed entails, this internal flux – cannot be dealt with until we have examined the way in which I, as a self, am related to the ecocosm.

It was pointed out earlier that when the universe is viewed only under the aspect of substance, and I am identified merely as a particular region within its universal extension, then my relation to the universe is no different from that of a rock. But as a self, my relation to the universe viewed as an ecocosm is entirely different from that of a rock. I am related as subsystem to a nested series of parent-systems, up to the level of cosmic self. I stand in the relation of ecological part to whole. The rock, not being a self-realizing system, is not a part of the ecological order, and hence does not stand in the relation of ecological part to cosmic whole. This is not of course to say that rocks do not contribute to ecosystems. They do, but as their nature is given independently of the ecosystem to which they may contribute, it cannot be claimed of a rock that it is a holistic part of that ecosystem, that is that it is ecologically interconnected with it. For in order for this to be true, the rock would not only have to help shape the ecosystem, but would have itself to be shaped by it, and this is not the case. As a holistic part of the universal substance, a rock topologically shapes and is shaped by the whole in this way. But as the rock does not influence, and is not influenced by, the *selfhood* of the universe (except in so far as without the property of selfhood the universal substance, and hence the rock, would not exist), it cannot be seen as a holistic part of the order of selves, that is the ecological order. I, as self, in contrast, reflect and am reflected in the higher order self-realizing systems.

But in which way do I reflect the higher-order selves in which I am nested? The general characteristic which distinguishes a self is of course its conatus, its power of self-realization, the will-to-exist. So the way in which any self reflects the dynamics of a wider self at the most general level is through its conatus. The conatus of the individual, by helping to shape the wider system, helps to sustain the conatus of that system, and the conatus of the system, by maintaining that specialized environment in existence, provides the conditions for the emergence of self-realizing forms. It is the dynamics of the conatus which is reflected up through the levels of systems.

As ecological part then it is through my conatus that I mirror, and am mirrored in, the wider systems of Nature. It is through my conatus that I, and other selves, achieve oneness with the ecocosm. Recognition of the fact that my conatus unites me with the ecocosm, which is thus seen to be my greater Self, in itself expands the scope of my conatus: my will-to-exist now encompasses the wider systems of Nature. The expanded self-love that I experience in this case is not a passive contemplative matter, as is Spinoza's intellectual love of God. Since I am ontologically at one with Nature, my conatus actually feeds the cosmic conatus, actually helps to maintain the ecocosm in existence! It is in this human participation in the cosmic process that the meaningfulness of our relation to Nature may be found: through our awareness of our interconnectedness with it we experience a love for this great self, a love which is actually constitutive of, or a tributary to, its own conatus, its own will-to-exist.

But how does this work? Animals and plants are holistic parts of the ecocosmic order too, so their self-love, their will-to-self-realization, must reinforce the cosmic conatus in the same way that ours does. Each organism, in fulfilling its conatus and achieving a state of flourishing, is helping to maintain the ecosystems further up the line, and each system, by maintaining itself in place, is preserving the conditions in which the organism can achieve self-realization. So if animals can contribute to the self-maintenance of the ecocosm without being aware of their unity with it, and acting only out of their own narrow self-interest, why can't we? Why can we not fulfil our cosmic role just by looking out for ourselves, following the path of egoism, and through our own flourishing helping to secure the self-realization of the wider systems?

Why? Because following the path of egoism does *not* lead to flourishing, and hence does not help to sustain the ecosystems in which we are embedded. A viable human being is, for reasons explained earlier, one who is informed with a viable culture. A viable culture is, for reasons also explained earlier, an eco-sensitive culture. Human beings who are products of non-viable cultures are not viable individuals, and non-viable individuals cannot be described as flourishing.

But how are these statements to be justified? Many people who live in cultures which are not eco-sensitive, and are therefore presumably non-viable, give every appearance of flourishing. They appear to live long, healthy, successful, productive lives. Indeed has not our non-viable western culture, with its unprecedentedly high standards of living, produced more flourishing individuals than any other culture in history?

Since human beings are *essentially* and not just contingently encul-turated, any criterion of human flourishing will have to include a cultural dimension. A person will count as flourishing only if she is culturally as well as physically and materially well-off. She is cultur-ally well-off if she is richly fulfilled in her emotional, imaginative, artistic, intellectual and spiritual life. How many western commuters on the morning freeway would claim to be this?

The kind of culture that enables us to fulfil our conatus and hence to flourish as human beings is precisely the culture that understands and represents our interconnectedness with Nature. The reason for this is simply that, on the present view, *this is the way we are*. To represent us as anything less than this is in fact to *misrepresent* us to ourselves, and hence to interfere with our possibilities of self-realization. A central function of culture is, as we have seen, to provide a symbolic representation of the world. This representation may be more or less figurative, more or less universal, but if it is misleading or false in its presentation of the way things are, then neither society nor individual can flourish. Sooner or later they will stub their toe on reality, their predictions and expectations will be disappointed. The reason that we, unlike non-human animals, depend on a culture – an abstract representation of reality – to help us to negotiate the world, is that our actions are not narrowly programmed by instinct. This is not to say that the disposition to create a culture is not itself a programmed, naturally selected device. But it is one which is especially susceptible to error. If our world and our relation to it are not adequately represented in our culture, then our action will not be appropriate to the ontological facts. If the ontological facts are that we are cosmic beings, selves within wider selves, then our conatus can only be fulfilled – and we can only realize our true possibilities – if our culture represents this truth to us.

Non-human animals, being selves within wider selves, are cosmic beings in exactly the same sense that we are. They do not need to be aware of this metaphysical fact in order to act in ways appropriate to it however, because they do not depend on abstract representations of reality to guide their actions – their actions are more or less narrowly programmed. But that those actions do testify to the ontological facts is beyond doubt. Animals do not follow the so-called law of 'dog eat dog', in the manner of the human egoist, as was assumed above. They do indeed cherish their physical integrity and resist disintegration when they can – they would not qualify as selves if they did not. But this is consistent with their behaving in ways which benefit the species or the ecosystem more directly than they benefit their physical selves: they are unswerving if unwitting servants of the ecosystem. If there were thinking behind their behaviour, it would not be the thinking of the egoist, but it would rather be the kind of thinking that would affirm perfectly the view that their identity is simultaneously a unity yet a function of greater wholes. Egoism is the province of the free-rider, the one who takes, accumulates, consumes without returning, who abdicates roles of responsibility to family and society, and whose actions spring from the belief that his interests are defined in opposition to those of others and should prevail over them. If animals acted in accordance with this kind of 'thinking', they would not work indefatigably and tediously to nourish and defend their (totally 'un-grateful') young, they would not share food (as many do) but would try to accumulate it instead, they would bury their dead in an attempt to cheat the food chain, they would expand their territories and colonize, they would 'overgraze the commons', and engage in intraspecies conflict for reasons additional to those of territorial and sexual need. Animals generally act exactly as if the interests they serve are those of the self-in-environment; and the flourishing of the self-in-environment is self-perpetuating up through the levels of system.

For human beings to flourish then, on this view, requires that we be represented within our culture as selves-within-wider-selves, and that our actions be generated in the light of this awareness of our role in the scheme of things.

Each viable self does its best, within the terms of its own particular faculties, to further the interests both of itself and of the ecosystem through which it is defined. The faculties of human beings are not restricted to the physical and behavioural, but include the psychological. As self-conscious beings our conatus has psychological as well as physical and behavioural dimensions. We experience the conatus psychologically as self-love, as an intense emotional investment in everything that we see as falling within the circle of our being. When this self-love is expanded – by our awareness of our unity with Nature – to encompass the wider systems of Nature, then we experience the kind of joy in existence to which Spinoza was pointing.

Is this love, this will-to-exist, this ardent affirmation which takes the cosmos-as-a-whole as its object, merely a shadow cast in the mind, a kind of after-image of the physical impact of the conatus, an epiphenomenon of ecological dynamics, or does it also have an active function, contributing in its own way to the self-realization of the ecocosm? Let us put the question another way. Would it matter to Nature if, while acting in ecologically optimal ways, we did so from motives other than those of love – if we acted in the service of the ecocosm, yet without loyalty to it, without joy in it? It cannot be said that this is the way that animals act, because since they lack the faculty for such conscious affirmation they cannot be capable of withholding it either. Does the love itself then, the affirmation, help to keep the fabric of the world intact?

This is perhaps the hardest of all these hard questions to answer, and to say yes to it would be to go well beyond anything that even Spinoza attempted to say. Yet I think we must say it. For the conatus that animates the ecocosmic self is an emergent will, or 'spirit', which may be reinforced by us in 'spiritual' ways. But how is 'spiritual' to be understood here? Does it necessarily connote the self-conscious and the psychological? Is the ecocosmic will-to-exist transparent to itself, is it experienced, felt, as our will-to-exist is experienced, felt, as interest, expansiveness, energy, love? Or is this cosmic conatus unconscious of itself, animating physical reality but without an inner awareness of itself doing so? I do not think it is really necessary to decide whether or not the cosmic conatus is conscious of itself in order to resolve the question whether or not we can reinforce it through consciousness. The cosmic conatus is not *constituted* through our feelings of love of and joy in Nature, any more than it is constituted by our ecological actions; it is *expressed* through both feelings and actions. What is expressed is an impulse which in itself is neither purely physiological nor emotional nor behavioural, but is in us accompanied by sensations, feelings and actions. Perhaps the closest we can come to pinning down the quality of the conatus in itself is through the notion of unqualified affirmation. Such affirmation is not in itself emotional, although it may be accompanied by overwhelming feelings of joy and love. Nor is it in itself purely physiological, though it may be accompanied by overwhelming sensations of fullness, overflowing and bodily expansion. And it is not merely behavioural, though it will typically give rise to ecological actions. An act of affirmation, if it is not accompanied by any particular propositional content, is an expression of the 'inner' life of beings, an expression which is not essentially self-conscious, nor essentially unconscious, but may be expressed on conscious and unconscious levels. Perhaps this is what marks the quality of an assertion of the 'spirit'.

On this view then, the feeling that we call love is perhaps the faint psychological shadow in us of that inner spiritual impulse of which our universe is the external manifestation. The universe may be conceived as a gigantic act of self-affirmation. It is the inner affirmation which is the *sine qua non* of the outer reality.

Since our human conatus participates in the conatus of the ecocosm, our affirmation of our larger Self is a force for the *Self-realization* of the universe. Indeed this inner attitude of affirmation may ultimately be more important than the outer, ecologically beneficial actions which help to perpetuate selves up through the levels of system, precisely because it is this impulse to affirm which is, as I have said, the *sine qua non* of the external systems. This may be, if you like, the real work of conservation – cultivating in ourselves the unrestricted will-to-exist, the spirit of pure affirmation, the wellspring of 'love', that creates and perpetuates the ecocosm. In this lies the key to the third objection, which was left unanswered many pages ago. The objection was that the arisings and passings-away of particular life-forms are of no concern to the cosmic Self, since the cosmic Self persists perfectly unscathed through these comings and goings and is indeed the inexhaustible fountainhead of all beauties and wonders. This was a serious objection for anyone who takes identification with the cosmos (Naess' *Self-Realization*) to be a motive for the conservation of Nature. But if my identification with ever-wider self-systems right up to the ecocosm has this essentially affirmative character, then it follows that I cannot be indifferent to the particular life-forms that my world presents. To participate in their conatus, as the identification thesis requires, involves for me, as a human self, a sense of love for them. I cannot help, in light of this, wanting to prevent any harmful interference with them, and so the outer work of conservation is assured.

Meaningfulness, then, enters our life not merely through a passive, Spinoza-style contemplation of sublime Nature, and a joyful basking in our unity with it, nor even through our attempts to preserve its particular external manifestations – battling to save forests, ban bombs, to phase out the ever-proliferating forms of wanton exploitation. Meaningfulness is to be found in our *spiritual* capacity to keep the ecocosm on course, by teaching our hearts to practise affirmation, and by awakening our faculty of active, outreaching, world-directed love. Though a tendency to 'tread lightly' on the earth, and to take practical steps to safeguard the particular manifestations of Nature, will flow inevitably from such an attitude, the crucial contribution will be the attitude itself, a contribution of the heart and spirit.

This way of thinking may be deeply foreign – and objectionable – to the western intellect, but it has been central to the cosmologies of many primal peoples, who saw their vocation, executed in ceremony and ritual, as helping to sustain the order of things, helping to keep the fabric of the world well-knit. In his beautiful and profoundly informed book, *On the Gleaming Way*, John Collier, quoting anthropologist Laura Thomson, describes the Hopi worldview as follows:

> the message is simple, and its key ideas are reiterated again and again. Briefly they are: the unity and rhythm of nature; the correlating interdependence of nature and man; natural law as the basis for human law; the pervading power of prayer, ritual, art, and concentration on the 'good'.... Order and rhythm are in the nature of things. It behoves man to study them, and to bring his life and his society into harmony with them. Only so may he be free....

The Law (the Hopi believe) requires that, to be effective, man must participate not merely by performing certain rites at prescribed intervals in certain ways; but he must also participate with his emotions and thoughts, by prayer and willing....

Hopi traditional philosophy, therefore, ascribes to man a purposive, creative role in the development of his will. The universe is not conceived as a sort of machine at the mercy of the mechanical law. Nor is it viewed as a sum total of hostile, competitive forces struggling for existence. It is by nature a harmonious, integrated system operating rhythmically according to the principles of immanent justice, and in it the key role is played by man's will.

(pp. 101–2)[29]

Perhaps the last sentence goes beyond the argument of the present chapter in discovering *the* key to cosmic self-realization in 'man's will'. This smacks of anthropocentrism again, albeit in a different form from that to which we are accustomed in western culture. It has been no part of the thesis of this chapter that the human contribution to the self-realization of the cosmos is *uniquely* important, but rather that the peculiar contributions of all forms of self are vital to the viability of the cosmos. But perhaps this does place a special responsibility on us – and other enculturated denizens of the universe – to add our affirmation to the universal conatus in the unique modes of consciousness, to 'participate with our emotions and thoughts, by prayer and willing'. Collier reaffirms this active participation, commenting on the 'intense romanticism' of the religion of the Southwest Indians which teaches 'that the universe is a living being, and that the universe requires of man an inner concentration and a sustained action of desire and will, to the end that the universe itself may "carry on"' (p. 29). And the unquenchable will-to-survive that these embattled people to this day exhibit is only a means to an end: 'the end is spiritual survival ... and "spiritual" means that mystical fire which the universe, they believe, entrusted to them in a past time which must not die. The fire, they believe, even contains the inmost significance of the universe' (p. 40).

In other words, these people perceive their individual and tribal conatus as directly nourishing a universal conatus. The active identification of the lesser with the greater Self is the core of their cosmology and their spiritual calling. Collier explains how the Pueblo Indians meet at Blue Lake, to 'talk to their Great Spirit in their own language, and talk to Nature'. In describing the massive and transporting nocturnal dance ritual held at Blue Lake, Collier speaks of his sense of

> [f]orces or beings normally invisible, only half-personal . . . . The Indian's relationship to these forces or beings is not chiefly one of petition or adoration or dread, but of a seeking and sharing in joy. It is a partnership in an eternal effort whereby, from some remote place of finding and communion, the human and mechanical universes alike are sustained.   (p. 128)

It is perhaps the fact that we are implicated in the cosmic conatus that is the well-spring of spiritual feelings in cultures everywhere. For spiritual feeling involves, above all, faith – trust in the order of things, an affirmation and surrender of the ego to a wider reality. Such faith and affirmation necessarily lie beyond knowledge and reason, as spokespersons for religions invariably attest. If faith were merely a substitute for knowledge – an interim measure enabling us to lay claim to a belief while we wait for validation, or an abdication of our own reason in deference to the reason of higher authorities, higher intelligences, who *know* the laws that are beyond our knowing – then it would not be an authentic instance of spirituality. For when the knowledge for which faith was the substitute was, by whatever means, attained, the need for affirmation would vanish. Besides, I can be as indifferent to the 'facts' of karma and reincarnation, or whatever other esoteric matters, as I can to the facts of overpopulation and pollution. Knowledge of a reality can never logically compel an affirmation: we have not only to understand that reality, but to want it to exist. In the same way, knowledge of the facts of my own personal future – however rosy – could not compel my affirmation: I would have furthermore to *want* to experience them, to want myself to exist. Nor perhaps could a set of co-instantiable possibilities impart actuality to a merely abstract world. To exist, whether as an individual or as a world, requires a leap into existence that is in itself a declaration of trust, an act of affirmation, an instance of conatus. This leap, whether from knowledge or ignorance, into existence, is the locus of spirituality.

Happily, as self-realizing beings, this leap-inducing affirmativeness, which in its wider dimensions constitutes our spirituality, is innate to us. But although rational understanding of a reality cannot compel our allegiance or our readiness to affirm it, a misrepresentation of the world can rationally discourage us. When our culturally-endorsed cosmology represents the world as inert, blind, bereft of worth or purpose, indifferent to our attitudes towards it, then our natural urge to celebrate Nature may be thwarted. To yield to this natural urge may seem, in this case, to be succumbing to irrationality, and the impulse may be displaced or suppressed in favour of an altogether more constricted – egoistic – self-affirmation. It is therefore in the interests of both our greater and our lesser selves to remove such falsifying obstacles to our self-fulfilment.

Notes

Introductory Remarks

1 Stephen Toulmin, *The Return to Cosmology*, University of California Press, Berkeley, 1982, p. 274.

1 Atomism and its logical implications

1 J. Kepler, *Opera* 1, 423, quoted in J. H. Randall, *The Career of Philosophy*, vol. 1, Columbia University Press, New York, 1962, p. 321
2 ibid., p. 319.
3 Pierre Duhem, *Etudes sur Léonard da Vinci*, vol. III, v–vi. Cited in J. H. Randall, op. cit., p. 268.
4 S. Drake (ed.), *Discoveries and Opinions of Galileo*, Doubleday Anchor, New York, 1957, p. 274.
5 Lewis White Beck, *Early German Philosophy*, Harvard University Press, Cambridge, Mass., 1969, p. 164.
6 Randall, op. cit., p. 310
7 The theme of the ramifications of mind/body dualism throughout western thought has been explored in many recent works, such as Morris Berman, *The Re-enchantment of the World*, Cornell University Press, Ithaca, 1981; Stephen Toulmin, *The Return to Cosmology*, University of California Press, Berkeley, 1982; and perhaps most notably, Fritjof Capra, *The Turning Point*, Fontana Paperbacks, London, 1983.
8 For a thorough account of the Cartesian physics, see J. C. Graves, *The Conceptual Foundations of Contemporary Relativity Theory*, MIT Press, Cambridge, Mass., 1971.
9 I. Newton, *Opticks*, 2nd edition, London, 1718, p. 375.
10 E. A. Burtt, *The Metaphysical Foundations of Modern Science*, Routledge and Kegan Paul, London, 1950, p. 228.
11 Randall, op. cit., p. 571.
12 Thomas Hobbes, *Leviathan*, Collier Books, New York, 1962, ch. 46, p. 482.
13 G. Buchdahl, *The Image of Newton and Locke in the Age of Reason*, Sheed and Ward, London, 1961, p. 29.

14 M. C. Jacob, *The Newtonians and the English Revolution 1689–1720*, Harvester, Brighton, 1976, p. 29.
15 ibid., p. 146.
16 It is beyond the scope of the present chapter to detail the salient features of pre-Newtonian popular consciousness. This topic has been illuminated in Morris Berman, op. cit.
17 Newton, op. cit., 31st Query. Quoted in Jacob, op. cit., pp. 187–8.
18 Clarke states the argument as follows:

> that most universal principle of gravitation itself, the spring of almost all the great and regular inanimate motions in the world, answering . . . not at all to the surfaces of bodies (by which alone they can act upon one another), but entirely to their solid content, cannot possibly be the result of any motion originally impressed on matter, but must of necessity be caused . . . by something which penetrates the very solid substances of all bodies, and continually puts forth in them a force or power entirely different from that by which matter acts upon matter. Which is, by the way, an evident demonstration, not only of the world's being made originally by a supreme intelligent cause; but moreover that it depends every moment on some superior being for the preservation of its frame.

This argument gives us, Clarke thinks, 'a very noble idea of providence'. See Samuel Clarke, *A Collection of Theological Tracts*, ed. R. Watson, London, 1785. Quoted in Margaret Jacob, op. cit., pp. 191–2.
19 William Derham, *Physico-Theology: or, A Demonstration of the Being and Attributes of God, from His Works of Creation*, London, 1714. Quoted in Jacob, op. cit., p. 180.
20 Richard Bentley in A. Dyce (ed.), *The Works of Richard Bentley*, London, 1838, 3rd edition. Quoted in Jacob, op. cit., pp. 197–8.
21 Thomas Hobbes, op cit., p. 100.
22 J. Collins, *A History of Modern European Philosophy*, Bruce Publishing Co., Milwaukee, 1954, p. 121.
23 E. Barker (ed.), *Social Contract*, Oxford University Press, London, 1960, p. xxiii.
24 Carole Pateman, *The Sexual Contract*, Polity, Oxford, 1988.
25 Barker, op. cit, p. xxii.
26 Randall, op. cit., p. 564.
27 Quoted in ibid., p. 581.
28 Carolyn Merchant, *The Death of Nature*, Harper and Row, New York, 1980, p. 286. Morris Berman, too, writes fascinatingly of Newton's non-mechanism, his Hermeticism, op. cit., ch. 4.
29 See the works of Berman and Merchant already cited. Also William Leiss, *The Domination of Nature*, Braziller, New York, 1972; Rosemary Radford Ruether, *New Woman, New Earth*, Seabury Press, New York, 1975; Brian Easlea, *Liberation and the Aims of Science*, Chatto and Windus, London, 1973.
30 Easlea, op. cit., p. 255.
31 Francis Bacon, quoted in Easlea, op. cit., p. 257.
32 Francis Bacon, quoted in William Leiss, op. cit., p. 55, n.14.

33 The significance of the feminine personification of Nature, and of the link between the domination of women and the domination of Nature, is the theme of the whole new, burgeoning literature of ecofeminism. Works in this field include those of Merchant and Ruether, already cited; also Elizabeth Dodson Gray, *Green Paradise Lost*, Roundtable Press, Massachusetts, 1981; Susan Griffin, *Woman and Nature*, Harper Colophon Books, New York, 1980; L. Caldecott and S. Leland, *Reclaim the Earth*, The Women's Press, London, 1983; Evelyn Fox Keller, *Reflections on Gender and Science*, Yale University Press, New Haven, 1985; Andree Collard with Joyce Contrucci, *Rape of the Wild*, The Women's Press, London, 1988; Vandana Shiva, *Staying Alive*, Zed Books, London, 1988; Judith Plant, *Healing the Wounds*, New Society Publishers, Philadelphia, 1989.

It might be argued that the political legacy of Newtonianism, *viz.* the liberal idea of the equality of all individuals, in fact opened the way for female emancipation. Did not social contract theory, which rested on the idea of individual equality, overthrow the old patriarchal view of the foundations of political power (the view defended in the seventeenth century by Sir Robert Filmer)? While this inference certainly has some plausibility, I would refer those who are tempted to argue in this way to Carole Pateman's book, *The Sexual Contract*, already cited. Pateman showed that the overthrow of patriarchy (in the original sense, the 'rule of the fathers') was designed to secure fraternity (a 'rule of the brothers'), where the point of fraternity was that it afforded *all* men orderly sexual access to women. Under the old regime of patriarchy, access to women had been the monopoly of the fathers.

34 Easlea, op. cit., p. 256.

35 A. N. Whitehead, *Nature and Life*, Greenwood, New York, 1977, p. 9.

36 We could here appeal to the whole psychoanalytic literature of repression, from Freud to Reich. Capra has given an eloquent account of repression within a Cartesian framework in his already cited book, *The Turning Point*. Neo-Reichians, such as Alexander Lowen, (*The Betrayal of the Body*, Collier, New York, 1969, *The Language of the Body*, Collier, New York, 1958, and many other titles) have detailed the ways in which the repression of the body manifests itself in the context of our contemporary 'permissive' and hedonistic society.

37 Capra, again, has done an excellent job of tracing the implications of Cartesian dualism for the 'bio-medical model' of health and disease within our culture.

38 See, for example, Genevieve Lloyd, *The Man of Reason*, Methuen, London, 1984; more generally, Alison Jaggar, *Feminist Politics and Human Nature*, Rowman and Allanheld, New Jersey, 1983.

39 Burtt, op. cit., pp. 236–7.

40 The notion of social atomism, in the sense of individualism, is in currency across many theoretical fields, including social and political theory (see Steven Lukes, 'Methodological individualism reconsidered', *British Journal of Sociology*, XIX, 1968, for a brief review of the debate on methodological individualism in social theory), environmental philosophy and feminism. The impression that social atomism is part and parcel of a more

general atomistic metaphysic is certainly diffused through these various literatures, as the quotations from Randall and Barker attest. However, the logical relation between the two levels of atomism is rarely discussed in any detail. One environmental philosopher who has examined the social implications of methodological atomism is J. Baird Callicott, 'The metaphysical implications of ecology' in *Environmental Ethics*, vol. 8, no. 4 [reprinted in J. Baird Callicott, *In Defense of the Land Ethic*, SUNY Press, Albany, 1989].

Feminist authors and ecophilosophers have explored the notion of the atomistic self, as opposed to the relational self, but their inquiries have generally sprung from epistemological and psychoanalytic perspectives rather than from a metaphysical perspective. An illuminating synopsis of some of these views is present in Jim Cheney, 'Ecofeminism and deep ecology', *Environmental Ethics*, vol. 9, no. 2.

41 William Blake, *The Poetry and Prose of William Blake*, edited by David V. Erdman, Doubleday, New York, 1965.
42 Keith Thomas, *Man and the Natural World*, Penguin, Harmondsworth, 1984, pp. 267–8.
43 ibid., ch. VI.
44 Joseph Campbell, *Myths to Live by*, Viking Press, New York, 1972, pp. 214–15.
45 C. G. Jung was of course the pioneer in the study of the cultural and psychological significance of myth, and many works by psychoanalysts and social critics have been written under his influence. One recent work which penetratingly explores these themes in a contemporary context is Edward Whitmont, *Return of the Goddess*, Routledge and Kegan Paul, London, 1983.
46 Randall, op. cit., p. 565.

2 Geometrodynamics

1 Brian McCusker, *The Quest for Quarks*, Cambridge University Press, Cambridge, 1983, p. 150.
2 Fritjof Capra, *The Turning Point*, Fontana, London, 1983, p. 66. For popular accounts of the 'new physics', as elementary particle theory is called, see not only Capra's *The Turning Point*, but more especially *The Tao of Physics*, Fontana, London, 1976. Also, Gary Zukav, *The Dance of the Wu Li Masters*, Hutchinson, London, 1979; David Bohm, *Wholeness and the Implicate Order*, Ark Paperbacks, London, 1983; Stephen Weinberg, *The First Three Minutes*, Andre Deutsch, London, 1977; Paul Davies, *God and the New Physics*, Simon and Schuster, New York, 1983; Brian McCusker, op. cit; and many others.

For an elegant and simple technical introduction to quantum mechanics, see D. T. Gillespie, *A Quantum Mechanics Primer*, International Textbook Company, London, 1973.
3 Bernard d'Espagnat, *Conceptual Foundations of Quantum Mechanics*, Benjamin, California, 1971, p. 114.
4 Bohm, op. cit., pp. 69–70.

5 A. Einstein, N. Rosen, B. Podolsky, *Physical Review*, vol. 47, 1935, p. 777.

6 McCusker, op. cit., pp. 148–50. Excellent accounts of the Einstein, Rosen, Podolsky problem are to be found in Bohm, op. cit., and Capra, 1983, op cit.

7 The refutation of Einstein's interpretation of the paradox was delivered in a paper by John Bell, three decades later. For a discussion of Bell's theorem, see Capra, 1983, op cit. and Bohm, op. cit.

8 Capra, 1983, op. cit., p.77.

9 A thorough account of this interpretation is provided, 'from the horse's mouth', so to speak, by W. Heisenberg, in *Physics and Philosophy*, Unwin University Books, London, 1958.

10 Capra, 1983, op. cit., p. 77.

11 ibid., pp. 82–3.

12 A full account of the General Theory of Relativity and Geometrodynamics, from Wheeler's point of view, can be found in C. Misner, K. Thorne, J. A. Wheeler, *Gravitation*, Freeman and Co., San Francisco, 1970.

13 J. A. Wheeler, 'Curved empty space time as the building material of the physical world: an assessment', in E. Nagel, P. Suppes, A. Tarski (eds), *Logic, Methodology and Philosophy of Science*, Stanford University Press, Stanford, 1962.

14 An account of the background to the discovery of the Special Theory of Relativity, including the famous Michelson–Morley experiment, may be found in E. Taylor and J. A. Wheeler, *Spacetime Physics*, Freeman and Co., San Francisco, 1963.

15 ibid.

16 What is the difference between a flat and a curved spacetime? The properties of flat space were formalized in Euclidean geometry. They included such properties as that the sum of the angles of a triangle add up to two right angles, and that the shortest path between two points is a straight line. It was not until the nineteenth century that geometers 'discovered' curved space, that is, developed non-Euclidean geometries. Intuitively speaking, such curved spaces differ from flat space in the way that the surface of a sphere, or a puckered sheet of rubber, differ from a flat sheet. On the flat sheet, the angles of a triangle add up to 180°, just as Euclid dictates. But on the surface of a sphere the sum of the angles of a triangle exceeds 180°: the sides of the triangle 'bulge', and so do its angles. On a puckered sheet of rubber the angles may add up to more or less, depending on where the triangle is drawn, and accordingly on whether its sides curve in or out. Another difference in the properties of a flat and a curved space may be understood if we imagine ourselves as two-dimensional 'flatlanders', living in the two-dimensional spaces in question. A flatlander travelling along a straight path in a spherical two-space would eventually arrive back at its point of departure. A flatlander travelling along a straight path in a flat two-space would either continue travelling indefinitely, or would reach the boundary of the space in question. The properties of 'straight lines' then differ from geometry to geometry. (Straight lines in curved spaces are called 'geodesics'.) The differences between curved and flat two-spaces may be theoretically

generalized to any number of dimensions.

A good account of flat versus curved space occurs in William J. Kaufmann III, *Relativity and Cosmology*, Harper and Row, New York, 1977, ch.3.

17 A readable popular account of General Relativity, and of the Friedman models in particular, occurs in Paul Davies, *Space and Time in the Modern Universe*, Cambridge University Press, Cambridge, 1977.

18 ibid., p. 154.

19 See Hans Reichenbach, *The Philosophy of Space and Time*, Dover, London, 1957 and A. Grunbaum, *Philosophical Problems of Space and Time*, A. Knopf, New York, 1963.

20 A relationist theory of space, or spacetime, is one which denies that space or spacetime is an entity in its own right. In the words of a philosopher of space and time, Lawrence Sklar, the relationist holds that

> all spatial and temporal assertions should be seen not as attributing features to space or time or spacetime, but rather as attributing some spatial, temporal or spatiotemporal relations to material objects. To think of, say, space as an object is to think that because the relation of brotherhood can hold between male siblings, there must be in the world not only people and their relations but some mysterious entity, the brotherhoodness, as well.

L. Sklar, *Space, Time and Spacetime*, University of California Press, Berkeley, 1974, p. 167. In other words, what really *exist*, from a relationist point of view, are material objects, and it is a fact about them that they stand in certain relations to one another. Space and time are to be analysed in terms of these relations; space and time *per se* have no independent reality.

21 Graves, *The Conceptual Foundations of Contemporary Relativity Theory*, MIT Press, Cambridge, Mass., 1971, p. 152.

22 Graves gives a very satisfactory account of Mach's conjecture and discusses its influence on Einstein in ibid., pp. 198–202, 210–13.

23 W. K. Clifford, 'On the space theory of matter', *Proceedings Cambridge Philosophical Society*, 2, 157 (1876). Reprinted in C. W. Kilmister (ed.), *General Theory of Relativity*, Pergamon Press, Oxford, 1973, pp. 125–6.

24 B. Gal-Or, *Cosmology, Physics and Philosophy*, Springer-Verlag, New York, 1981, pp. 40–1.

25 Graves, op. cit., p. 314.

26 ibid., p. 315.

27 ibid., p. 296.

28 ibid., p. 316.

29 ibid., p. 317.

30 David Hume, *A Treatise of Human Nature*, ed. L. A. Selby-Bigge, Oxford University Press, Oxford, 1960, Bk 1, Part III, pp. 161–2.

31 David Hume, *Enquiry Concerning Human Understanding*, ed. L. A. Selby-Bigge, Oxford University Press, Oxford, 1960, ch. 25.

32 J. L. Mackie, *The Cement of the Universe*, Oxford University Press, Oxford, 1974, p. 224.

33 A thing is said to be divisible if it has parts which are logically independent of the thing as a whole, and hence capable of independently
preserving their identity. Does space have parts in this sense? Do the
imaginary boundaries drawn by us to demarcate different regions of space
represent any real edges or borders, or the potential of such? The remarks
of Clarke in his correspondence with Leibniz are pertinent in this respect.
In The Third Reply he writes:

> Nor is there any difficulty in what is here alleged about space having
> Parts. For infinite Space is One, absolutely and essentially indivisible.
> And to suppose it Parted is a Contradiction in Terms, because there
> must be Space in the Partition itself; which is to suppose it parted and
> yet not parted, at the same time.

Later, in the Fourth Reply, he adds, in the same vein:

> infinite space, though it may by us be partially apprehended, that is,
> may in our imagination be conceived as composed of Parts; yet those
> Parts (improperly so called) being essentially indiscernible and im-
> movable from each other, and not partable without an express Contra-
> diction in Terms, Space consequently is in itself essentially One, and
> absolutely indivisible.

H. G. Alexander, *Leibniz–Clarke Correspondence*, Manchester University
Press, Manchester, 1965.

Actually, the question whether space has parts, parts which can 'stand
alone', in the sense of constituting substances in their own right, is more
complicated than these remarks suggest. For it might be objected that
mathematically consistent, finite, bounded spaces may be physically
possible, that is may be capable of constituting possible worlds. If this
were allowed, such spaces would constitute true parts of our three-
dimensional, unbounded space, and this latter space would accordingly
no longer qualify as a plenum.

But could a finite, bounded, physical three-space exist independently?
Is not boundedness pathological in a physical space? What happens to
physics at the boundaries? What happens to the denizens of the space
when they reach its edges? Artificiality and ad hocness seem to infect
solutions to these questions.

Nevertheless, it can be demonstrated that a finite, bounded three-space
can be constructed in a manner that renders plausible the supposition
that it could exist independently. In the first place, take a finite, *un*-
bounded two-space, S2, embedded in a (finite or infinite) unbounded
three-space, S3: S2 exists as a laminate surface with respect to S3. An
example of S2 would be the surface of a sphere in (Reimannian or
Euclidean) three-space. Could S2 exist as a physical space, or world, in its
own right? Its unboundedness argues in its favour. So let's agree that it
could. Since S2 is embedded in S3, and our actual space is an instance of
S3, this is already tantamount to admitting that our actual space has
parts. But it might be objected that a two-dimensional space cannot count
as a true part of a three-dimensional space. In this case however, a
three-space which does count as a true part of S3 is not hard to construct,

given the ontological independence of S2. For allow S2, which we are taking to be a spherical shell, to stand alone, and add to it another concentric shell with a different radius, and another, until we arrive at an infinite number of concentric spherical surfaces of different radii. The set of these surfaces is a three-dimensional sphere – a finite, bounded three-space, which is capable of standing alone, and which thus constitutes a true part of S3.

However, this argument, applied to GMD, assumes that the curvature of one region or point of space is logically independent of that of the rest of space, and hence that the region or point exhibiting this curvature can be logically excised. But this is not the case. Any local curvature, within GMD, is logically influenced by global curvature, and cannot be logically isolated as the above argument requires. Graves makes a similar reply to the objection that space is not a single substance but a point-construct, where points are atomistically construed. See Graves, op. cit., p. 316.

34 Benedict de Spinoza, *Ethics*, translated by R. H. M. Elwes, Dover, New York, 1951, Part 1, Def. III, p. 45.

35 ibid., p. 45.

36 This interpretation of Spinoza's theory as yet enjoys little currency amongst Spinoza commentators. As far as I am aware, the only critic who anticipates it, though with major differences, is Jonathan Bennett in his book, *A Study of Spinoza's Ethics*, Cambridge University Press, Cambridge, 1984. Bennett's interpretation of Spinoza's theory of substance was adumbrated in two earlier papers, 'Spinoza's vacuum argument', *Midwest Studies in Philosophy*, vol. 1, ed. P. A. French, T. E. Euhling Jnr, University of Minnesota Press, 1976, and 'Spinoza's mind-body identity thesis', *Journal of Philosophy*, vol. LXXVIII, no. 10, Oct. 1981. My own geometro-dynamic interpretation of Spinoza's theory of substance was developed independently over a number of years, and advanced in papers delivered to AAP Conferences in 1979 and 1981; it appeared in a preprint series in 1983 in papers entitled 'Space and substance' and 'The shape of thoughts and the indexicality of actuality in Spinoza's theory of substance', Department of Philosophy, University of Melbourne Preprint Series, 1983. Elements of the interpretation presented in the text appear in my article, 'Some reflections on Spinoza's theory of substance', *Philosophia*, vol. 19, no. 1, May 1989.

Bennett distinguishes, as I do, between the essence of substance as it is perceived by the intellect (*viz.* the attributes) and the essence of substance as it is in itself. Bennett is also of the view that substance viewed under the attribute of extension is space. However he denies that the essence of substance as it is in itself, as opposed to how it is perceived by the intellect, is specifiable, whereas I argue not only that it is specifiable, but that Spinoza specifies it. It is this specification of the essence of substance which furnishes the explanation of why substance takes the form that it does.

37 Immanuel Kant, *Critique of Pure Reason*, 'Transcendental Aesthetic', Section 1 in *The Philosophy of Kant*, selected and translated by John Watson, Maclehose and Sons, Glasgow, 1901.

38 The assumption that only concrete entities may be actual is sometimes questioned, and it is proposed instead that a possible world may consist of abstract entities only, such as numbers. I reject this view, but it would take us too far afield to enter into this discussion here.
39 Spinoza, op. cit., p. 48.
40 ibid., p. 51.
41 ibid., p. 54.
42 ibid.
43 ibid., p. 89.
44 ibid., p. 45.
45 ibid., p. 83.
46 ibid., p. 93.
47 Spinoza states the Principle of Sufficient Reason as follows: 'Of everything whatsoever a cause or reason must be assigned, either for its existence, or for its nonexistence.'

   This certainly looks too strong. For intuitively PSR seems to presuppose either that existence is the 'natural' state, which calls for no explanation, or that non-existence is. If non-existence is taken to be the natural state, then the non-existence of a thing will not call for an explanation, while its existence will. If existence is taken to be the natural state, then it will be the failure of a thing to exist which will call for explanation. The requirement for an explanation both for existence and for non-existence is, apparently, redundant. However, when Spinoza claims that both the existence and the non-existence of things are demonstrable, he seems to have in mind the Euclidean analogy: from the axioms of Euclidean geometry it can be demonstrated either that a certain figure must exist, that is, its existence is entailed by the axioms, or that it cannot exist, that is, the attempt to derive its existence from the axioms leads to a contradiction. Spinoza seems to assume that this kind of completeness is attainable not only in geometry but in a theory of the world, or, as he puts it, in a theory of 'the order of universal nature in extension'. Thanks to Barry Taylor for illuminating suggestions in this connection.
48 op. cit., p. 46.

3 System and substance

1 Stafford Beer, *Cybernetics and Management*, John Wiley and Sons, New York, 1959.
2 J. C. Smuts, *Holism and Evolution*, Macmillan, New York, 1926, pp. 86–7.
3 Gregory Bateson, *Steps Towards an Ecology of Mind: Collected Essays in Anthropology, Psychiatry, Evolution and Epistemology*, Paladin, London, 1973, p. 472.
4 This very elementary example is adapted from Alan Roberts, coursenotes for Science and Systems Theory 1, Graduate School of Environmental Science, Monash University.
5 Ross Ashby, *Introduction to Cybernetics*, Chapman and Hall, London, 1956.
6 L. von Bertalanffy, 'The theory of open systems in physics and biology' in F. E. Emery (ed.), *Systems Thinking*, vol.1, Penguin, Harmondsworth, rev. edn., 1981, p. 89.

7 ibid., p. 83.
8 For an account of the mechanism of the Watt governor, see Beer, op. cit., p.29.
9 I developed the idea of self-realization as the criterion of living systems as a result of trying to understand the notion of conatus – which had long been ascribed to living things – in the light of the basic concepts of systems theory. It has since been drawn to my attention that my idea of self-realizability matches up, in essential respects, with Maturana's notion of autopoiesis. Autopoiesis is defined as follows:

> An autopoietic machine is a machine organized (defined as a unity) as a network of processes of production (transformation and destruction) of components that produces the components which:
>   (i) through their interactions and transformations continuously regenerate and realize the network of processes (relations) that produced them; and (ii) constitute it (the machine) as a concrete unity in the space in which they (the components) exist by specifying the topological domain of its realization as such a network.

See Humberto Maturana and Francisco Varela, *Autopoiesis and Cognition*, Reidel, Dordrecht, 1980.
   I must say that systems theory suggests the kind of analysis of telos that I outline in the text in a very immediate way, and I was surprised to learn that Maturana and Varela's presentation of the thesis was in fact the first in the literature of the biological sciences. My account – which is of course entirely innocent of any biological sophistication – differs from Maturana's in the following fundamental respect, however: where Maturana considers that autopoiesis dissolves the apparent telos of living systems, I see the capacity for self-realization, understood in systems-theoretical terms, as definitive of telos.
10 Jacques Monod, *Chance and Necessity*, Collins, London, 1972, ch. 1.
11 ibid., p. 24.
12 James Lovelock, *Gaia, A New Look at Life on Earth*, Oxford University Press, Oxford and New York, 1979.
13 Interestingly, I think this is the kind of idea for which Hobbes was reaching in the opening chapters of *The Leviathan* (see my discussion of Hobbes in Ch. 1). How he would have welcomed the conceptual resources of cybernetic theory in order to embellish his account of the 'human machine', which he characterized as a machine for self-preservation! A systems understanding of such a 'machine', however, would ironically have transformed the metaphysical framework within which Hobbes was deriving his social and political theories; such an understanding would have introduced into Hobbes' system notions and principles transcending the simple mechanism of his metaphysical premises. Foremost among these notions and principles would be, firstly, a recognition of the openness of self-realizing systems, and their consequent interconnectedness with and logical dependence on wider systems. This recognition would widen the scope of the interests which Hobbes ascribes to such systems. It would introduce an *ecological* perspective into his account of human identity. A systems-theoretic view would also enable Hobbes to see that

human beings are not the only 'machines' which are capable of preserving themselves. And, finally, such a view would reveal the holism of self-realizing systems, where this would overturn Hobbes' assumption that such systems can be constructed mechanistically – 'built' out of 'parts', so to speak.

I explain these and other implications of a systems understanding of 'machines-for-self-preservation' in the text.

14 The term 'intrinsic value' has quite a rich history in the recent literature of environmental philosophy. Environmental philosophers in the early 1970s took up the call of Aldo Leopold who, in his ecological classic, *A Sand County Almanac*, Oxford University Press, New York, 1949, had pointed to the need for a new biocentric ethic. A handful of philosopers began to argue, from the early 1970s onwards, that Nature, or particular aspects or elements of Nature, should be credited with value independently of their use-value for us – where 'use' was taken to encompass aesthetic, psychological and spiritual as well as material uses. This notion of value-detached-from-a-human-valuer was explicated in a variety of ways and denoted by a variety of terms and contrasted with a number of other closely related non-instrumental notions of value.

It would take me too far from the line of argument I am developing in this book to comment on this recent literature. I shall content myself with listing some of the seminal authors in this connection, and noting that the argument concerning intrinsic value which I present in the text is well within the mainstream of this literature, though the medieval notion of conatus, rather than this literature itself, was the original inspiration for my position.

One of the main protagonists in this philosophical development has been Arne Naess, who coined the name 'Deep Ecology' to refer to a view which we shall be examining in Chapter 4. Naess and some of the subsequent proponents of Deep Ecology accorded, in axiomatic fashion, intrinsic value to all natural entities – not only organisms but rocks, rivers, etc., as well. See Arne Naess, 'The shallow and the deep, long range ecology movement', *Inquiry*, 16, 1973, and Bill Devall and George Sessions, *Deep Ecology: Living as if Nature Mattered*, Peregrine Smith, Salt Lake City, 1985.

A number of authors have attempted to provide a theoretical foundation for the notion of intrinsic value. Again, different accounts have attached different labels to – and provided slightly different interpretations of – that concept which I am here denoting by the term 'intrinsic value'. These authors have included Richard and Val Routley: see for instance 'Human chauvinism and environmental ethics' in Don Mannison, Michael McRobbie and Richard Routley, *Environmental Philosophy*, Monograph Series, no. 2, Department of Philosophy, RSSS, Australian National University, 1980. They argue that the value of natural entities is not tied to the existence of any actual valuers, but only to that of possible, or counterfactual, valuers.

Theories which tie intrinsic value to the telos – or, in other formulations, the 'good' – of living organisms have been influential. The most sustained recent defence of such a view is probably that of Paul Taylor in his book *Respect for Nature*, Princeton University Press, Princeton, 1986. Taylor speaks of organisms as 'teleological centres of life'. To say that an organism is a teleological centre of life is, according to Taylor, to say that it strives to preserve itself and realize its good in its own unique way. It is to say that

> its internal functioning as well as its external activities are all goal-oriented, having the constant tendency to maintain the organism's existence through time and to enable it successfully to perform those biological operations whereby it reproduces its kind and continually adapts to changing environmental events and conditions. It is the coherence and unity of these functions of an organism, all directed toward the realization of its good, that make it one teleological centre of activity.   (pp. 121–2)

Taylor uses the term 'inherent worth' to denote the value possessed by such teleological centres of life. Although his account of inherent worth agrees in important respects with my account of intrinsic value, the difference between his overall position and mine resides in the scope that we each respectively assign to telos. For Taylor only individual organisms possess telos, or, in my terminology, qualify as selves. The position I develop in Chapters 3 and 4 extends selfhood to wider systems, up to the level of the cosmos as a whole.

Amongst the other authors who may roughly be said to be arguing from telos or specific good to 'intrinsic value' (variously named) are Kenneth Goodpaster, 'On being morally considerable', *Journal of Philosophy*, 75, 1978 and 'From egoism to environmentalism', in K. E. Goodpaster and K. M. Sayre (eds), *Ethics and Problems of the 21st Century*, University of Notre Dame Press, Notre Dame, Indiana, 1979; Robin Attfield, *The Ethics of Environmental Concern*, Basil Blackwell, Oxford, 1983; Tom Regan, 'Animal rights, human wrongs', *Environmental Ethics*, vol. 2, no. 2, 1980, and *The Case for Animal Rights*, University of California Press, 1983; Donald Scherer, 'Anthropocentrism, atomism and environmental ethics', *Environmental Ethics*, vol. 4, no. 2, 1982; and John Rodman, 'Four forms of ecological consciousness reconsidered' in Donald Scherer and Thomas Attig, *Ethics and the Environment*, Prentice-Hall, New Jersey, 1983.

Most of these authors disagree sharply on the kinds of natural entities to which telos or a good of one's own may be ascribed: Rodman and Goodpaster are generous, extending such telos or good to ecosystems as well as to organisms; Regan restricts it to animals; Scherer allows it to range over individual organisms, populations and species; Attfield, like Taylor, confines it to individual organisms. These differences in the perceived domain of telos lead to very different ethical conclusions; none of these positions is the same as that which I develop in Chapters 3 and 4.

Other seminal discussions of intrinsic value which do not tie the latter to telos or specific good include those of J. Baird Callicott, *In Defense of the Land Ethic*, SUNY Press, Albany, 1989, section III; and Holmes Rolston III, *Philosophy Gone Wild*, Prometheus Books, Buffalo, New York, 1986, section II, and *Environmental Ethics: Duties to and Values in the Natural World*, Temple University Press, Philadelphia, 1988.

See also Notes 1, 2, 16 to Chapter 4.

15 Bateson, op. cit.
16 Spinoza, *Ethics*, trans. R. H. M. Elwes, Dover, New York, 1951, Pt. III, Prop. VI, Proof.
17 ibid., Pt. III, Prop. VII.
18 D. Bidney, *The Psychology and Ethics of Spinoza*, Russell and Russell, New York, 1962, p. 94.
19 ibid., pp. 100–1.
20 ibid., p. 94.
21 ibid.
22 *Cogitata Metaphysica*, II, ch. vi, quoted in Bidney, op. cit., p. 97.
23 Bidney, op. cit., p. 96.
24 J. C. Graves, *The Conceptual Foundations of Contemporary Relativity Theory*, MIT Press, Cambridge, Mass., 1971, p. 316.
25 A. Angyal, 'A logic of systems', in F. E. Emery (ed.), *Systems Thinking*, vol. 1, Penguin Education, Harmondsworth, 1969.
26 Paul Davies, *God and the New Physics*, Simon and Schuster, New York, 1983, ch. 4.

Davies explains the issue of order out of disorder as follows. Can it be demonstrated, he asks,

> that cosmic complexity and order really have arisen spontaneously from the simple primeval state. At first sight this claim seems to be in flagrant contradiction with the second law of thermodynamics, which requires just the opposite – that order gives way to disorder, so that complex structures tend to decay to a final state of disorganized simplicity. Thus, E. W. Barnes wrote in the 1930s: 'In the beginning there must have been a maximum organization of energy . . . . In fact, there was a time when God wound up the clock (i.e. the cosmic mechanism) and a time will come when it will stop if He does not wind it up again.' We now know that this is wrong. The primeval state was not one of maximal organization but one of simplicity and equilibrium. The apparent conflict of this fact with the second law has only recently been resolved.
>
> The problem is that the second law strictly applies only to isolated systems. Now it is physically impossible to isolate anything from gravity . . . . In the expanding universe, the cosmic material comes under the influence of the cosmological gravitational field – the cumulative gravity of the rest of the universe. This coupling to gravity opens the way to the injection of order into the cosmic material by the gravitational field.

Davies proceeds to qualify this as follows.

> This cannot, however, be the whole story. The gravitational field, which is ultimately responsible for generating order via the cosmic expansion, presumably suffers some disordering tendency as a result. Thus we can explain the order of material things by shifting the responsibility onto gravity, but then we have to explain how the order

appeared in the gravitational field in the first place....

The issue turns on whether or not the second law of thermo-dynamics applies to gravity as well as to matter. Nobody really understands this. Recent work on black holes suggests that it does, but different physicists have drawn opposite conclusions.... Some, such as Roger Penrose, conclude that the large scale cosmic gravitational field is in a very low entropy ... state which therefore requires an input of order at the creation. Others, such as Stephen Hawking, claim that the cosmic gravity is highly disordered, and is the expected result of purely random and unstructured influences emerging from the initial singularity. Because no-one yet knows how to quantify the orderliness of a spacewarp (i.e. gravity) the issue remains undecided.(pp. 49–52)

27 It is fascinating to speculate on the analogy between the origin of the cosmic self (spacetime) and that of individual selves (organisms). The process of morphogenesis appears to parallel in significant respects the processes involved in geometrodynamic cosmogony. Spacetime 'grew' from a pointlike origin of infinitely high curvature, and its structure as it expanded was presumably a function either of initial information present in the singularity or of the geometrical and topological transformations involved in an expansion from a point of infinite curvature to a sphere of finite radius. An organism grows from a 'pointlike' zygote and owes its essential structure to information already present in that cell. The 'translation' of the information into structure is presumably effected at least partly by geometrical and topological means. The cell is a systemic whole which holistically influences its parts: the shape of the cell determines the shape and function of its components, as well as vice versa. Any deformation in the shape of the cell simultaneously, that is, geometrically rather than causally, effects changes in the structure and function of the parts of the cell. In these respects the 'expansion' and internal differentiation of the organism parallel that of space itself.

4 Value in nature and meaning in life

1 Environmental philosopher John Rodman puts this point as follows

one ought not to treat with disrespect or use as a mere means anything that has a *telos* or end of its own – anything that is autonomous in the basic sense of having a capacity for internal self direction and self-regulation. This principle is widely accepted but has been mistakenly thought (e.g. by Kant and others) to apply only to persons. Unless one engages in a high redefinition of terms, however, it more properly applies to (at least) all living natural entities and natural systems.

He goes on to say that the notion of natural entities and systems as having intrinsic value in the form of tele of their own is the basis for the attitude of respect toward Nature. See John Rodman, 'Four forms of ecological consciousness reconsidered', in Donald Scherer and Thomas Attig, *Ethics and the Environment*, Prentice-Hall, New Jersey, 1983.

Paul Taylor elaborates this Kantian position in ch. 2, Section 3 of *Respect for Nature*, Princeton University Press, Princeton, 1986. (Note:

Taylor refers to what I am calling 'intrinsic value' as 'inherent worth' –
though his concept of inherent worth is not in every respect the same as
my concept of intrinsic value.)

2 It is important to distinguish this sense of intrinsic value from a closely
related notion which those who are uncomfortable both with the idea of
'detached values', that is values detached from human valuers, and with
the idea that all value must be analysed in instrumental terms, sometimes
substitute for a truly objectivist notion of intrinsic value. Or, to put the
point less tendentiously, there is a distinction to be made between the
following two senses of value, which I shall call intrinsic value and
inherent value respectively:

  (i) intrinsic value is the value that beings have in themselves, regardless
of whether or not they are valued by external valuers;

  (ii) inherent value is the value that things have on account of being
valued for themselves – rather than for their utility – by external valuers.

Some authors affirm both these – non-instrumental – notions of value;
some, like Callicott in his article 'Intrinsic value, quantum theory and
environmental ethics', *Environmental Ethics*, vol. 7, no. 3, 1985 (reprinted in
In Defense of the Land Ethic, SUNY Press, Albany, 1989) see the notion of
inherent value as sufficing for the normative work that the notion of
intrinsic value is designed to do. In this way they avoid biting the
objectivist bullet, and make a subjectivist notion of value do the work of an
objectivist notion, in the process shedding the ontological commitments of
the latter.

In order to get the notion of inherent value to do the normative work of
the notion of intrinsic value, Callicott grounds his environmental ethic in
the Humean theory of moral sentiments. According to Hume – and,
Callicott adds, Darwin and latterday sociobiologists – human beings
naturally extend moral consideration to those they recognize as kin. The
trick, for environmental ethicists, then, is so to portray the rest of Nature
that human beings recognize it as constituting their wider community or
family. This is the project that Callicott thinks Leopold fulfilled so well in
A Sand County Almanac, Oxford University Press, New York, 1949.

Another writer who has attempted to walk the conceptual tightrope
between a hard objectivist notion of intrinsic value and outright instrumental value is Holmes Rolston III. In his article, 'Are values in
nature subjective or objective?', *Environmental Ethics*, vol. 4, no. 2, 1982, he
argues that the values we attribute to Nature are in general *grounded* in
Nature though they are simultaneously a function of our *interpretation* of
Nature. They are analogous to secondary qualities which are potentialities in Nature that are actualized through perception. For this reason
Rolston calls such values tertiary qualities. When we find the sunset
beautiful or an apple good we are in fact responding to a particular
constellation of conditions in the world which draws out our capacities for
value perception in the same sort of way that certain conditions in the
world draw out our capacities for colour perception. The value is no more
'in' those conditions than the colour is, yet it is just as much a potentiality
of certain conditions as colour is of others.

Rolston also develops a notion of value which is closer to the notion of intrinsic value which I present in the text, however, and which is thoroughly objective, in the sense that it is independent of perceivers. For his latest ideas on these topics, see his *Environmental Ethics: Duties to and Values in the Natural World*, Temple University Press, Philadelphia, 1988.

3 Practically every critic of utilitarianism has pointed out this objection to the theory. In order for utilitarianism to be usable at all, it requires supplementation with a principle of autonomy or (in a human context) a principle of respect for persons which usually has a Kantian flavour. See, for instance, Jonathan Glover, *Causing Death and Saving Lives*, Penguin, Harmondsworth, 1977.

4 Arne Naess, 'The shallow and the deep, long-range ecology movement', *Inquiry*, 16, 1973.

We might distinguish not only between shallow and deep forms of environmental ethics, but also, as J. Baird Callicott has put it, between Deep Ecology and deep ecology. Deep Ecology is a specific position, characterized by a 'platform' or set of tenets; deep ecology is an open-ended approach to environmental philosophy, which explores the meta-physical, epistemological and ethical implications of the principles of ecology. I shall mainly be concerned with Deep Ecology in this chapter.

5 B. Devall and G. Sessions, *Deep Ecology: Living as if Nature Mattered*, Peregrine Smith, Salt Lake City, 1985, p. 70.

6 The objects of moral concern are not *necessarily* restricted to human beings, of course, from a utilitarian point of view. They can in principle include all sentient beings, that is non-human as well as human animals. The chief contemporary exponent of this version of utilitarianism is Peter Singer.

7 This raises the question of the status of species. Do species themselves possess intrinsic value, or do only the organisms which instantiate them do so? This again is a question which has been widely debated in the literature of environmental philosophy.

If species are to have independent moral status, on the present view, then they must possess an intrinsic value grounded in telos. They must qualify as selves, systems devoted to their own self-realization. On the face of it, it seems nonsensical to suggest that species *per se* could be considered selves. Species are, at least prima facie, classes rather than systems. Nor are they analysable in terms of concrete populations, since they include all possible as well as all actual instances of the relevant universal. Species are thus, apparently, abstract entities, and abstract entities cannot seek to maintain their own existence because, *qua* abstract entities, they do not exist (in a concrete sense) in the first place. Only concrete entities could conceivably possess conatus, and hence qualify as selves. The instances of a given species are concrete entities, but the species itself is not.

Holmes Rolston III has argued persuasively against this view of species. In 'Duties to endangered species', *Philosophy Gone Wild*, Prometheus Books, Buffalo, New York, 1986, he portrays species as evolutionary entities in their own right; a species, he says, 'is a coherent, ongoing form of life expressed in organisms, encoded in gene flow, and shaped by the environment' (p. 210). Indeed, he claims that species possess their own telos: there is a 'specific groping for a valued *ought*-to-be beyond what now *is* in any individual' (p. 212). Moreover the telos of the individual is subordinate to that of the species – the individual is the species' means for achieving its own telos.

In spite of Rolston's illuminating arguments I remain uncomfortable with his characterization of species as concrete entities, capable of sustaining an interest in self-perpetuation, of possessing telos. I can accept that species are not to be conceived in the manner of Platonic Forms, but should rather be seen in four-dimensional terms, as Minkowski world-lines, or evolutionary processes. To this extent I can concede their concreteness. But it does not seem plausible to me to suggest that these evolutionary processes are in any sense striving to preserve continuity of form. Their continuity of form is the *outcome* of the strivings of individual organisms and ecosystems: there is no 'ought-to-be' at which the species itself is aiming. Rolston says himself, a 'species has no self' (though of course he does not mean 'self' in the special sense that I do). A species is not organized around the goal of self-maintenance: it does not matter to it if it ceases to be perpetuated.

Why then do we consider species preservation important? I think there are two reasons for this:

(i) From the point of view of a member of the species, the preservation of the species is important because the perpetuation of its own kind is one of the strategies of self-realization employed by individual organisms.

(ii) It is vitally important to the self-realization of ecosystems that species diversity, or the right mix of species, is maintained. Since, as we shall see in Section III, ecosystems qualify as selves on the present view, the value that attaches to species is not intrinsic value, but is derived from the intrinsic value of ecosystems. It is not the case that every species is vital to the integrity of some ecosystem, but it is generally beyond our powers of prediction to tell which species do and which do not constitute vital pieces of information from an ecosystemic point of view. The value of species is thus related to that of diversity (which I discuss in the text), and the value of diversity supervenes on the intrinsic value of ecosystems and of the biosphere as a whole.

Arguments against either the intrinsic value or the concrete reality of species may be found in Robert Elliot, 'Why preserve species?' in Don Mannison, Michael McRobbie, Richard Routley (eds), *Environmental Philosophy*, Monograph Series, no. 2, RSSS, Australian National University, 1980; B. H. Burma, 'Reality, existence and classification: a discussion of the species problem', in C. N. Slobodchikoff (ed.), *Concepts of Species*, Dowden, Hutchinson and Ross, Pennsylvania, 1976; incidental discussions concerning the moral status of species also occur in many of the works on environmental philosophy already cited.

8 Devall and Sessions, op. cit., p. 67.
9 Paul Taylor, for instance, although no Deep Ecologist, does subscribe to the principle of biocentric egalitarianism. The defence of biocentric egalitarianism that he offers, however, involves an attempted refutation of the principal traditional grounds for the posture of human supremacism. It is thus a very different kind of defence from the one I offer here.

10 Naess, op. cit., p. 95.
11 Deep Ecologists are not the only philosophers who affirm the value of diversity. For ethical holists such as Aldo Leopold, and his contemporary champions, for example J. Baird Callicott, diversity is, along with complexity, stability, beauty and integrity, one of the fundamental attributes of 'the land', or ecosystems, which an environmental ethic is designed to protect. See Aldo Leopold, *A Sand County Almanac*, Oxford University Press, New York, 1949 and J. Baird Callicott, *In Defense of the Land Ethic*.

Rodman draws this implication out of the land ethic (see 'Four forms of ecological consciousness reconsidered', in Scherer and Attig, op. cit., pp. 90–1) but sees such ecological characteristics as deriving their value independently of telos, even though he presents telos too as a basis for intrinsic value. For comments on the relation of the value of diversity to that of species, see note 7.
12 Natural selection can operate only for as long as the rate of speciation outpaces the rate of extinction. When the number of species on the earth drops below a certain threshold, evolution may lack the genetic base to proceed.

> If large scale habitat disruption and destruction continue to accelerate, we run a real risk that the diminished stock of species will not represent an adequate resource base on which natural selection can work to rebuild the rich panoply of life. So far as we can discern from the fossil record, the 'bounce-back' period could well extend over several million years. The process of species formation will clearly continue ... but it will be outrun by extinction. We should be worried about the loss of diversity for its own sake .... But the implications of the headlong destruction of species for the future course of evolution are more worrying still.

Norman Myers (ed.), *The Gaia Atlas of Planet Management*, Pan Books, London, 1985, p. 154.
13 See, for instance, Devall and Sessions, op. cit., Ch. 5.
14 Naess concurs with this kind of qualified species loyalty, arguing that while the right to live is the same for all species, the vital interests of our nearest have priority of defence. He writes,

> Under symbiotic conditions, there are rules which manifest two important factors operating when interests are conflicting: vitalness and nearness. The more vital interest has priority over the less vital. The nearer has priority over the more remote – in space, time, culture, species. Nearness derives its priority from our special responsibilities, obligations and insights ....
>
> It may be of vital interest to a family of poisonous snakes to remain in a small area where small children play, but it is also of vital interest to children and parents that there are no accidents. The priority rule of nearness makes it justifiable for the parents to remove the snakes. But the priority of vital interest of snakes is important when deciding where to establish the playgrounds.

From 'Identification as a source of deep ecological attitudes', in Michael Tobias (ed.), *Deep Ecology*, Avant Books, San Diego, 1985.

15 Devall and Sessions, op. cit., p. 71.

16 Among those authors who ground intrinsic value in the telos of living things there is, as I have already noted (see chapter 3, note 14), sharp disagreement as to which entities may be credited with telos. Some authors restrict the scope of telos to human beings, some to sentient beings, some to individual organisms; other authors extend it to eco-systems and to the biosphere as a whole, others again to species, popu-lations, communities. Some authors attribute intrinsic value to all natural entities, whether alive or not. I do not propose to comment on all these positions, but merely to present the position which I regard as flowing most naturally from my metaphysical premises.

17 E. P. Odum, *Basic Ecology*, Saunders College Publishing, New York, 1983.

18 Rachel Carson, *Silent Spring*, Houghton Mifflin, Boston, 1962.

19 James Lovelock, *Gaia, A New Look at Life on Earth*, Oxford University Press, Oxford, 1979.

20 Mary Midgley, *Beast and Man: The Roots of Human Nature*, Methuen, London, 1978, pp. 52–3.

21 Konrad Lorentz, *On Aggression*, Methuen, London, 1966, pp. 264–5, quoted in Midgley, op. cit. p. 297.

22 'The pattern that connects' is a key expression in Gregory Bateson, *Mind and Nature*, Wildwood House, London, 1979.

23 For Naess the notion of self-realization is certainly central to Deep Ecol-ogy. Of the avowed exponents of Deep Ecology, Warwick Fox is probably the one who places the greatest emphasis on self-realization. For instance, in his 'Post-Skolimowski reflections on deep ecology', *The Trumpeter*, vol. 4, no. 4, Fall, 1987, he writes that the 'philosophically distinctive aspect of deep ecology lies in the fact that, instead of arguing for the intrinsic value of the non-human world, deep ecology thinkers argue for a state of being that sustains the widest possible identification'.

Fox develops his theory of self-realization at length in his dissertation, *Toward a Transpersonal Ecology: the Context, Influence, Meaning and Distinctive-ness of the Deep Ecology Approach to Ecophilosophy*, forthcoming, 1990, in book form from Shambhala Press.

24 Arne Naess, 'Identification as a source of deep ecological attitudes', in Tobias (ed.), op. cit., p. 260.

25 ibid., p. 363.

26 Naess, of course, in his article 'The shallow and the deep, long-range ecology movement' adumbrates a field-theoretical metaphysic of inter-connectedness. Warwick Fox reveals the parallels between Deep Ecology and the new physics in 'Deep ecology: a new philosophy of our time?', *The Ecologist*, 14, 1984. J. Baird Callicott has explored the metaphysical implications of ecology in 'The metaphysical implications of ecology', *Environmental Ethics*, vol. 8, no. 4, 1986, reprinted in *In Defense of the Land Ethic*.

27 The care perspective in ethics, resting on moral sentiment, has been contrasted by feminist authors with the justice perspective, based on

reason. The seminal work in this connection is Carol Gilligan, *In a Different Voice*, Harvard University Press, Cambridge, Mass., 1982.

28 For a careful account of how Spinoza helps himself to teleology in his account of the conatus, despite his protestations against teleology, see Jonathon Bennett, *A Study of Spinoza's Ethics*, Cambridge University Press, Cambridge, 1984.

29 John Collier, *On the Gleaming Way: Navajos, Eastern Pueblos, Zunis, Hopis, Apaches, and Their Land; and Their Meanings to the World*, Sage Books, Denver, 1949.

Bibliography

Alexander, H. G. (1965), *Leibniz–Clarke Correspondence*, Manchester University Press, Manchester

Angyal, A. (1969), 'A logic of systems', in Emery (1969)

Ashby, R. (1956) *Introduction to Cybernetics*, Chapman and Hall, London

Attfield, R. (1983), *The Ethics of Environmental Concern*, Basil Blackwell, Oxford

Barker, E. (1947), *Social Contract*, Oxford University Press, London

Bateson, G. (1973), *Steps Towards an Ecology of Mind: Collected Essays in Anthropology, Psychiatry, Evolution and Epistemology*, Paladin, London

——(1979), *Mind and Nature*, Wildwood House, London

Beck, L. White (1969), *Early German Philosophy*, Harvard University Press, Cambridge, Mass.

Beer, S. (1959), *Cybernetics and Management*, John Wiley and Sons, New York.

Bennett, J. (1976), 'Spinoza's vacuum argument', in French and Euhling (1976).

——(1981), 'Spinoza's mind-body identity thesis', *Journal of Philosophy*, vol. LXXVIII, no. 10, October 1981

——(1984), *A Study of Spinoza's Ethics*, Cambridge University Press, Cambridge

Berman, M. (1981), *The Re-enchantment of the World*, Cornell University Press, Ithaca

Bidney, D. (1962), *The Psychology and Ethics of Spinoza*, Russell and Russell, New York

Blake, W. (1965), *The Poetry and Prose of William Blake*, edited by D. V. Erdman, Doubleday, New York

Bohm, D. (1983), *Wholeness and the Implicate Order*, Ark Paperbacks, London

Buchdahl, G. (1961), *The Image of Newton and Locke in the Age of Reason*, Sheed and Ward, London

Burma, B. H. (1976), 'Reality, existence and classification: a discussion of the species problem', in Slobodchikoff (1976)

Burtt, E. A. (1950), *The Metaphysical Foundations of Modern Science*, Routledge and Kegan Paul, London

Caldecott, L. and Leland, J. (eds) (1983), *Reclaim the Earth*, The Women's Press, London

Callicott, J. B. (1985), 'Intrinsic value, quantum theory and environmental ethics', *Environmental Ethics*, vol. 7, no. 3, reprinted in *The Defense of the Land Ethic*.

——(1986), 'The metaphysical implications of ecology', *Environmental Ethics*, vol. 8, no. 4, reprinted in *In Defense of the Land Ethic*.

——(1989), *In Defense of the Land Ethic*, SUNY Press, Albany

Campbell, J. (1972), *Myths to Live by*, Viking Press, New York

Capra, F. (1976), *Tao of Physics*, Fontana, London

——(1983), *The Turning Point*, Fontana, London

Carson, R. (1962), *Silent Spring*, Houghton Mifflin, Boston

Cheney, J. (1987), 'Ecofeminism and deep ecology', *Environmental Ethics*, vol. 9, no. 2.

Clifford, W. K. (1876), 'On the space theory of matter', *Proceedings Cambridge Philosophical Society*, 2, 157

Collard, A. with Contrucci, J. (1988), *Rape of the Wild*, The Women's Press, London

Collier, J. (1949) *On the Gleaming Way: Navajos, Eastern Pueblos, Zunis, Hopis, Apaches, and Their Land; and Their Meanings to the World*, Sage Books, Denver

Collins, J. (1954), *A History of Modern European Philosophy*, Bruce Publishing Co., Milwaukee

Davies, P. (1977), *Space and Time in the Modern Universe*, Cambridge University Press, Cambridge

——(1983), *God and the New Physics*, Simon and Schuster, New York

d'Espagnat, B. (1971), *Conceptual Foundations of Quantum Mechanics*, Benjamin, California

Devall, B. and Sessions, G. (1985), *Deep Ecology: Living as if Nature Mattered*, Peregrine Smith, Salt Lake City.

Drake, S. (ed.) (1957), *Discoveries and Opinions of Galileo*, Doubleday Anchor, New York

Easlea, B. (1973), *Liberation and the Aims of Science*, Chatto and Windus, London

Einstein, A., Rosen, N., Podolsky, B. (1935), 'Can quantum-mechanical description of physical reality be considered complete?' in *Physical Review*, vol. 47

Elliott, R. (1980), 'Why preserve species?' in Mannison *et al.* (1980)

Emery, F. E. (ed.) (1969, rev. edn 1981), *Systems Thinking*, vol. 1, Penguin Education, Harmondsworth

Fox, W. (1984), 'Deep ecology: a new philosophy of our time?' *The Ecologist*, 14

——(1987), 'Post-Skolimowski reflections on deep ecology', in *The Trumpeter*, vol. 4, no. 4.

——(1989), *Toward a Transpersonal Ecology: The Context, Influence, Meaning and Distinctiveness of the Deep Ecology Approach to Ecophilosophy*, PhD dissertation, Murdoch University; forthcoming 1990 in book form from Shambhala Press, Boston

French, P. A., Euhling Jnr, T. E. (eds) (1976), *Midwest Studies in Philosophy*, vol. 1, University of Minnesota Press, Morris

Gal-Or, B. (1981), *Cosmology, Physics and Philosophy*, Springer-Verlag, New York

Gillespie, D. T. (1973), *A Quantum Mechanics Primer*, International Textbook Company, London

Gilligan, C. (1982), *In a Different Voice*, Harvard University Press, Cambridge, Mass.

Glover, J. (1977), *Causing Death and Saving Lives*, Penguin, Harmondsworth

Goodpaster, K. E. (1978), 'On being morally considerable', *Journal of Philosophy*, 75

——(1979), 'From egoism to environmentalism', in Goodpaster and Sayre (1979)

——and Sayre, K. M. (eds) (1979), *Ethics and Problems of the 21st Century*, University of Notre Dame Press, Notre Dame, Indiana

Graves, J. C. (1971), *The Conceptual Foundations of Contemporary Relativity Theory*, MIT Press, Cambridge, Mass.

Gray, E. D. (1981), *Green Paradise Lost*, Roundtable Press, Massachusetts

Griffin, S. (1980), *Woman and Nature*, Harper Colophon Books, New York

Grunbaum, A. (1963), *Philosophical Problems of Space and Time*, A. Knopf, New York

Heisenberg, W. (1958), *Physics and Philosophy*, Unwin University Books, London

Hobbes, T. (1651), *Leviathan*, reprinted in Collier Books, New York, 1962

Hume, D. (1960), *A Treatise of Human Nature*, edited by L. A. Selby-Bigge, Oxford University Press, Oxford

——(1960), *Enquiry Concerning Human Understanding*, edited by L. A. Selby-Bigge, Oxford University Press, Oxford

Jacob, M. C. (1976), *The Newtonians and the English Revolution 1689–1720*, Harvester, Brighton

Jaggar, A. (1983), *Feminist Politics and Human Nature*, Rowman and Allanheld, New Jersey

Kant, I. (1901), *Critique of Pure Reason*, reproduced in part in J. Watson, *The Philosophy of Kant*, Maclehose and Sons, Glasgow

Kaufmann III, William J. (1977), *Relativity and Cosmology*, Harper and Row, New York

Keller, E. F. (1985), *Reflections on Gender and Science*, Yale University Press, New Haven

Kilmister, C. W. (ed.) (1973), *General Theory of Relativity*, Pergamon Press, Oxford

Leiss, W. (1972), *The Domination of Nature*, Braziller, New York

Leopold, A. (1949), *A Sand County Almanac*, Oxford University Press, New York

Lloyd, G. (1984), *The Man of Reason*, Methuen, London

Lorentz, K. (1966), *On Aggression*, Methuen, London

Lovelock, J. (1979), *Gaia, A New Look at Life on Earth*, Oxford University Press, Oxford and New York

Lowen, A. (1958), *The Language of the Body*, Collier, New York

——(1969), *The Betrayal of the Body*, Collier, New York

Lukes, S. (1968), 'Methodological individualism reconsidered', *British Journal of Sociology*, XIX

Mackie, J. L. (1974), *The Cement of the Universe*, Oxford University Press, Oxford

Mannison, D., McRobbie, M., Routley, R. (eds) (1980), *Environmental Philosophy*, Monograph Series, no. 2, RSSS, Australian National University

Mathews, F. (1983), 'Space and substance' and 'The shape of thoughts and the indexicality of actuality in Spinoza's theory of substance', Department of Philosophy, University of Melbourne Preprint series
——(1989), 'Some reflections on Spinoza's theory of substance', *Philosophia*, vol. 19, no. 1, May
Maturana, H. and Varela, F. (1980), *Autopoiesis and Cognition*, Reidel, Dordrecht.
McCusker, B. (1983), *The Quest for Quarks*, Cambridge University Press, Cambridge
Merchant, C. (1980), *The Death of Nature*, Harper and Row, New York
Midgley, M. (1978), *Beast and Man: The Roots of Human Nature*, Methuen, London
Misner, C., Thorne, K., Wheeler, J. A. (1970), *Gravitation*, Freeman and Co., San Francisco
Monod, J. (1972), *Chance and Necessity*, Collins, London
Myers, N. (ed.) (1985), *The Gaia Atlas of Planet Management*, Pan Books, London
Naess, A. (1973), 'The shallow and the deep, long-range ecology movement', *Inquiry*, 16
——(1985), 'Identification as a source of deep ecological attitudes', in Tobias (1985)
Nagel, E., Suppes, P. Tarski, A. (eds) (1962), *Logic, Methodology and Philosophy of Science*, Stanford University Press, Stanford
Newton, I. (1718), *Opticks*, 2nd edition, London
Odum, E. P. (1983), *Basic Ecology*, Saunders College Publishing, New York
Pateman, C. (1988), *The Sexual Contract*, Polity, Oxford
Plant, J. (1989), *Healing the Wounds*, New Society Publishers, Philadelphia
Randall, J. H. (1962), *The Career of Philosophy*, vol. 1, Columbia University Press, New York
Regan, T. (1980), 'Animal rights, human wrongs', *Environmental Ethics*, Vol. 2, No. 2
——(1983), *The Case for Animal Rights*, University of California Press, Berkeley
Reichenbach, H. (1957), *The Philosophy of Space and Time*, Dover, London
Rodman, J. (1983), 'Four forms of ecological consciousness reconsidered', in Scherer and Attig (1983)
Rolston, H. (1982), 'Are values in nature subjective or objective?, *Environmental Ethics*, vol. 4, no. 2
——(1986), *Philosophy Gone Wild*, Prometheus Books, Buffalo, New York
——(1988), *Environmental Ethics: Duties to and Values in the Natural World*, Temple University Press, Philadelphia
Routley, V. and R. (1980), 'Human chauvinism and environmental ethics', in Mannison *et al.* (1980)
Ruether, R. R. (1975), *New Woman, New Earth*, Seabury Press, New York
Scherer, D. (1982), 'Anthropocentrism, atomism and environmental ethics', *Environmental Ethics*, vol. 4, no. 2
——and Attig, T. (1983), *Ethics and the Environment*, Prentice-Hall, New Jersey
Shiva, V. (1988), *Staying Alive*, Zed Books, London

Sklar, L. (1974), *Space, Time and Spacetime*, University of California Press, Berkeley

Slobodchikoff, C. N. (ed.) (1976), *Concepts of Species*, Dowden, Hutchinson and Ross, Pennsylvania

Smuts, J. C. (1926), *Holism and Evolution*, Macmillan, New York

Spinoza, B. (1951), *Ethics*, translated by R. H. M. Elwes, Dover, New York

Taylor, E. and Wheeler, J. A. (1963), *Spacetime Physics*, Freeman and Co., San Francisco

Taylor, P. (1986), *Respect for Nature*, Princeton University Press, Princeton

Thomas, K. (1984), *Man and the Natural World*, Penguin, Harmondsworth

Tobias, M. (ed.) (1985), *Deep Ecology*, Avant Books, San Diego

Toulmin, S. (1982), *The Return to Cosmology: Postmodern Science and the Theology of Nature*, University of California Press, Berkeley

Von Bertalanffy, L. (1981), 'The theory of open systems in physics and biology', in Emery (1981)

Weinberg, S. (1977), *The First Three Minutes*, André Deutsch, London

Wheeler, J. A. (1962), 'Curved empty spacetime as the building material of the physical world', in Nagel *et al.* (1962)

Whitehead, A. N. (1977), *Nature and Life*, Greenwood, New York

Whitmont, E. (1983), *Return of the Goddess*, Routledge and Kegan Paul, London

Zukav, G. (1979), *The Dance of the Wu Li Masters*, Hutchinson, London

Index